Praise for Be\

"*Benita: prey for him* is a unique, harrowing account of vicious betrayal by a Church that had pledged itself to protect its most vulnerable. The abuse Benita suffered took place decades ago, but the fear, pain, trauma and shame followed her through the years. She triumphed over these deadly effects to become an effective advocate for others and a persistent, courageous voice for justice."

—Tom Doyle

"Benita Kane Kirschbaum's story, her life and this work are timely and important . . .a testament not only to her courage for sharing her journey in vivid and painful detail, but also to the difference she and others like her are making by lifting the veil shrouding clergy sexual abuse. By confronting the secrecy imposed and power abused, we all draw lessons and awareness."

—Jeff Anderson

"The quiet farm fields and gentle rolling hills of Iowa hold dark secrets that are laid bare in this compelling, sincere and powerful story. It will be difficult to set down once you start reading it. Benita's story reveals her tragic seduction from childhood into a long, catastrophic involvement with a priest. Everyone needs to understand what she endured so no child is ever abused like this again."

—Barbara Blaine

"With fine brushstrokes, Virginia Tranel tells the story of a young girl and the challenges of growing up in a Catholic-dominated Midwestern town. What is unique about this book is that one relives what young Benita went through and thereby begins to understand how complicated exploitation is. A 'must-read' for anyone seeking to truly understand how a sexually abusive relationship evolves between a priest and a young woman."

—Gary Schoener

"For those who don't understand how, or even if this can happen, read this book. It clearly demonstrates the dynamics of clergy sexual abuse: the combination of loveable, vulnerable victim, cunning perpetrator and an institutional church that imposes silence to prevent scandal. As a psychologist working in the field of abuse recovery, I encourage you to read this fascinating story, and as you do so, to appreciate the courage required for Benita to share it with us."

—Laura Helling-Christy

". . .a haunting story. Knowing Benita's story and knowing her in her recovery and healing have been an honor and privilege for me as a spiritual counselor. While stories like hers involve great pain and suffering, seeing Benita survive betrayal and strive to regain her wholeness gives hope."

—Nancy A. Lindgren

"*Benita: prey for him* is a very powerful story. . .I commend Benita for telling it. Her courage and strength will comfort others as they begin their healing journey from clergy sexual abuse."

—Karen Dunkel Nurre

BENITA

PREY FOR HIM

ALSO BY VIRGINIA TRANEL:

Ten Circles Upon the Pond
Reflections of a Prodigal Mother

BENITA

PREY FOR HIM

VIRGINIA TRANEL

1st WORLD
PUBLISHING

© Virginia Tranel 2010

Published by 1stWorld Publishing
P.O. Box 2211, Fairfield, Iowa 52556
tel: 641-209-5000 • fax: 866-440-5234
web: www.1stworldpublishing.com

First Edition

LCCN: 2010927031
SoftCover ISBN: 978-1-4218-9152-1
HardCover ISBN: 978-1-4218-9153-8
eBook ISBN: 978-1-4218-9154-5

Grateful acknowledgment is made to the following for permission to reprint previously published material:

By permission of Oxford University Press on behalf of The British Provence of the Society of Jesus. Excerpt from the poem, "Carrion Comfort" from *The Poems of Gerard Manley Hopkins* 4/e by Hopkins, Gerard Manley edited by Gardner, W.H. & MacKenzie, N.H. (1967)

Lyric excerpt from 'On Eagle's Wings' copyright 1979 by Jan Michael Joncas, published by OCP, 5536 NE Hassalo, Portland, Or 97213.

For Benita

In memory of the girl who might have been

With respect for the woman who IS

AUTHOR'S NOTE

This is a work of nonfiction. Material in this book not based on my own observation and experience is either taken from letters and documents or from interviews with people directly concerned, including numerous interviews with Benita, her brother, Walter, (now deceased) and her sister, Carol. Additional information was provided by interviews with grade, high school and college classmates. Many of the situations and conversations described occurred in my presence; others were recounted to me by people directly involved. Reconstructed scenes that occurred decades ago were designed to capture the spirit of those events. The thoughts and dialogue I have attributed to some people were plausibly described to me. Some names have been changed. I am deeply indebted to Benita for summoning the courage to return to these tragic decades of her life.

The church says the earth is flat. But I know that it is round. For I have seen the shadow on the moon. And I have more faith in a shadow than in the church.

—Ferdinand Magellan

BENITA

prey for him

PROLOGUE

The handsome young priest arrived at our parish in August of 1945, just as the United States dropped a horrifying new weapon on Hiroshima and Nagasaki. The long awful Second World War was over. He came like a harbinger of hope, his dignity higher than any earthly dignity because he could convert bread and wine into the Body and Blood of Christ; he could say 'I absolve thee' and save a sinner's soul from hell. And he could ravage a young girl's life. I know, because I was one of Benita Kane's closest friends.

The setting was hilly, Democratic, Catholic Dubuque, a town that rises up from the Mississippi river flats over seven hills, a lofty vantage point that enabled us to look down on our surroundings: east to the bridge spanning the mile-wide muddy river to Illinois and Wisconsin; west to the flat, Republican, Protestant cornfields that made up the rest of Iowa. The seven hills and the religious structures on top of them earned our town the nickname 'Little Rome' even though that fertile farmland was settled, not by Italians, but by Catholics from Ireland and Germany and Luxembourg. They were the uneducated, trusting immigrants who built the churches and flocked to them and seldom left the state of Dubuque.

Nor do all roads lead there, not even an interstate in the year 2007. Still, it's common to encounter people who recall crossing the Mississippi at Dubuque. They marvel at the tree-covered bluffs, greener than Ireland in the summer, and in the fall ablaze with oaks and maples. They ask about the multitude of church steeples jutting above buildings and trees: 'All Catholic?' They know someone who went to Clarke or Loras, the two Catholic colleges there; or a priest who studied at the Dominican seminary. They've heard of 'the little old lady in Dubuque'—a phrase coined by Harold Ross, the founding editor of the *New Yorker*—and connect her, correctly, to Midwestern provincialism. Today's population of fifty-eight thousand is still overwhelmingly Catholic and white. In the forties and fifties, it was the kind of town where Catholic kids scurried past Protestant churches with eyes straight ahead, like mythological sailors warned that the slightest glance would shipwreck them on the shoals of heresy.

Benita and I were seven-year-old second-graders at St. Columbkille's when we met. We were twenty-one-year-old graduates of Clarke college in 1955 when our paths diverged. We lived the years between inside an invisible circle with the church at its center. Everything outside was dangerous, irrelevant, or part of another parish. Nativity. Saint Patrick's. Sacred Heart. Saint Mary's. Our family lived on the circle's perimeter at 1445 South Grandview Avenue, a street originating at Mount Carmel, the motherhouse of the Sisters of the Blessed Virgin Mary. From that wooded bluff, the avenue trailed westward opening into a boulevard beneath a leafy arch of elm trees, gathering up side streets, establishing boundaries that told inhabitants they belonged to St. Columbkille's parish.

Benita's house at 1125 Cleveland Avenue was smaller than ours and without hot running water, but strategically located two blocks from the church. For many Catholics, proximity to the parish was the deciding factor for a home, to be within walking distance of everything that mattered. They could drop into church for a visit, stop by for a hasty morning Mass on the way to work, participate in the Holy Name Society, the Legion of Mary, make the Way of the Cross, serve on committees, enjoy chance encounters with Father, no mean thing, since he was the church and the church was their rock. Decades later, the dark side of geographic accessibility would be unearthed.

Eight hours after my marriage at St. Columbkille's in January of 1957, I left my hometown for the West of my husband's dreams. I returned every summer during my parents' lifetime, but all I heard of Benita during those years were occasional fragments: she had moved to Minneapolis; she had married, but not until her early 30's, a decade later than most of us; she hadn't had children, another intriguing discrepancy in a generation of Catholics inclined to increase and multiply. The ghost of Father Henry Dunkel always haunted news of her.

Early in 2004, my sister in Dubuque told me in a phone conversation that she'd seen Benita Kane's name in a recent article in the *Telegraph Herald*. 'She said she was raped in a confessional by a priest at St. Columbkille's when she was fifteen years old.' The ghost now loomed large. Father Dunkel's name wasn't mentioned, said my sister. But—a confessional? The two confessionals I remembered were located in the most remote corners of the church. Behind each ornately carved wooden door was a dark, stuffy box just big enough for one kneeling penitent. There was a third confessional, my sister said. A small room sequestered between the center and left vestibules. It was a place I never knew existed.

I decided it was time to reconnect with Benita, friend of my youth, whose life I had watched and shared and sometimes envied, but clearly failed to understand. A few phone calls later, I found her.

She was eager to talk. After decades of shame and secrecy, she was impatient to shed light on her life. We talked on the phone;

we exchanged e-mails; she sent me letters and documents and notes and photographs. She referred me to her sister, Carol; her brother, Walter; to mutual friends; to our grade and high school classmates at St. Columbkille's. I learned the story of a life that started out rich with promise and slowly, relentlessly, went wrong.

PART ONE

Childhood's joyland

CHAPTER ONE

Of the forty second-grade children at the parish school, I notice her first. Pretty, curly-haired, blonde, blue-eyed Benita. *Benita*. A name I've never heard in any saintly litany. A musical name that rolls off the tongue, while mine—Virginia—is a collision of harsh consonants, a name tarnished by two years in the public school, where as a Catholic born two days after the Feast of the Immaculate Conception, baptized on Christmas Eve and named for the Blessed Virgin Mary, I had no right to be. My mother knew perfectly well that she was going against the orders of the priest when she sent me at age four to Bryant School. Sunday after Sunday, I'd sat next to her watching Monsignor's face go red above his collar as he pounded the pulpit and said, you parents, unless you want to risk your eternal soul, you must send your children to the parish school. There's more to learning than reading and writing and arithmetic. There's religion, too, and preparation for the Sacraments and the next world to think about and the salvation of your child's soul and your own, too. At the end of his warnings, he would calm down long enough to say that if there was some reason parents couldn't follow this rule, they had to ask the archbishop to excuse them.

My mother excused herself and gave her reason to my dad in the kitchen: how is any child going to learn anything in a classroom crowded with forty or fifty kids? With only poor Sister up in front trying to corral them. And on the playground, those big high school boys teasing the kindergartners, making them cry. Nuns or no nuns, that's a rowdy situation. I'm not sending my baby there. Not after what John and Anne Marie went through. I was her baby. John and Anne Marie were my older siblings.

Cheery Miss Yates, dressed in the amiable fashion of an ordinary woman, her dark, abundant hair waved and stylish and showing, welcomed me to kindergarten with a worldly, lipsticked smile. She pointed out the small chair with my name on it and the bin in which to stow my naptime rug. At midmorning, I lay down contentedly in the midst of twenty little Protestants.

In the three-story red brick building a block away, the Catholic kindergarteners were napping, too. On the wall above them hung the crucified Jesus to whom they had already offered 'all they would think or do or say' that day. One little girl, just-turned-five and still shaken at the sudden wrench from home, fisted away her tears and curled up quietly on the small rug she'd brought to school. She covered her eyes with her hands and in the light that squeezed between her fingers, imagined her mother's face. A rough tug roused her. Nearby, a boy hooted and yanked on her rug. 'Sister,' she called to the wimpled woman brushing by in her floor-length black skirt. 'Joe Barth pulled on my rug and woke me up.' The wooden rosary beads attached to Sister's waist clacked as she leaned over the little girl and shook a warning finger. 'Benita Kane, don't you be a tattle tale.' Benita's eyes rounded. She looked from Sister to Joe, back to Sister again, then closed her parted lips and lowered her gaze to the floor.

My mother's Protestant revolt was brief. Second-grade was the year the nuns prepared children to receive First Confession and First Communion. Seven-year-old children had reached the age of reason. They could learn right from wrong. They could memorize the Ten Commandments, the Seven Deadly Sins, the Seven Sacraments, the Seven Virtues, as well as the Hail Mary, Our Father, Apostle's Creed and Act of Contrition. My mother's worries over the crowded, rowdy Catholic situation had to give way to my need for sacramental preparation. She yielded to her conscience and reluctantly turned me over to the Catholic enterprise.

Now, children. Put your palms together like this, says Sister Mary Carol, a young nun with a pretty face. The rest of her is a shapeless black wool bundle. Her starched white wimple, stiff headdress, and flowing black veil tell us she's working for God. *Point your fingertips up. Up, Benita! Toward heaven. That's right.*

The second grade class is lining up to practice walking the fifty steps from school to church. There we will practice kneeling at the Communion rail and sticking out our tongues. In a week, we will receive First Communion, the thin wafer changed by the priest into the body and blood of Christ. *Remember, children. Never, never chew the host. Let it melt on your tongue. Then swallow it carefully. And be sure to keep your hands folded and your eyes down as you return to your pew. Roger, stop that silliness this minute.*

Roger is gazing cross-eyed at his friend Elmer who is rolling his head toward Donny, who is lolling his tongue to receive God. They made their First Communion last year when they were second-graders for the first time. They're the 'dumb kids' who practice mischief from the back of the classroom where Sister put them with the hope that out of sight would mean out of mind.

Monsignor Halpen pays daily surprise visits to the second grade classroom to check up on Sister Carol and us. *Are we ready for First Communion?* he wants to know. His pink scalp shows through a drift of snowy hair. When he smiles, his eyes crinkle into bright blue crescents. *What is a sacrament, children? Who can tell me?* The class goes mute. We corner our eyes at each other while Sister clears her throat and glares smilingly at us, one face at a time, until a girl puts up her hand. A girl always gives in first.

'A sacrament is an outward sign instituted by Christ to give grace,' trills Katie or Mary Jane or Sally or Benita.

'Very good. And how many sacraments are there?'

Sister's eyes wave like a baton before a chorus until Katie or Sally or Mary Jane sings out the list. Baptism. Penance. Holy Eucharist. Confirmation. Extreme Unction. Holy Orders. Matrimony. Sister doesn't seem to notice, or mind, that her job as Bride of Christ isn't on it, that she's like the Little Red Hen in the story book, the one who plants, tends, harvests and makes the wheat into bread that somebody else declares his.

The afternoon before our First Communion, we make our First Confession, carefully following the formula Sister taught us. First, examine your conscience, which means dredging up the bad things we've done recently. Second, feel sorry for offending God by doing those things. Third, promise never, ever to do them again. After that, we're ready to confess our sins to the priest and do the penance he assigns. Mortal sins have to be confessed because they make you an enemy of God and if you die with even one on your soul, you'll go straight to hell. A mortal sin is something you know is very bad and do anyway. A venial sin is something you do on the spur of the moment, like knocking over the Lincoln Log cabin your brother just built, or something that's only slightly wrong, like grumbling when your mother asks you to set the table. Even if you do something that's very bad, like stealing an expensive bicycle, it's still only a venial sin if you thought the bike wasn't worth very much. Venial sins don't have to be confessed, but as seven-year-old children, they're all we have.

On that First Confession Saturday, I'm waiting in line outside the confessional, rehearsing my list and trying to feel bad about what I've done, when Benita comes down the aisle, head bowed, eyes lowered, hands folded at her waist. She looks as holy as the plaster statues that flank the altar, Saint Columbkille on the right, and on the left, the Blessed Virgin, who looks surprisingly calm for someone with a snake coiled under her foot. Benita's angelic expression implies that she has nothing to tell, that she does not consider sinful the scandal she caused yesterday in reading class by announcing in the middle of a sentence that angels are women and so is God.

"Now where on earth did you get an idea like that?' Sister had asked with a twitchy smile.

'Their pictures are right here in our book. Gabriel is wearing a white dress. So is Luke. And Jesus is, too. And he has hair like a woman.' She pointed to the pliant, long-haired person in a graceful pastel dress.

'Angels are spirits without bodies, Benita. That picture is just trying to help you imagine. Jesus' long garment is what all the men wore then.'

'You told us Jesus was God. And he's wearing a dress. So God must be a woman.'

Annoyance played at the corners of Sister's smile. She told Benita to pray for faith because life was full of mysteries that not even pictures could help us understand.

'Well, if he's not a woman and he's not a man, then what is he?'

'He's God, Benita.' Sister sounded worn out first and then cross. 'And that will be enough from you right now.'

Benita chewed on her lower lip and kept looking at the picture.

When it's my turn, I stumble into the stuffy pitch-black of the confessional, kneel down and wait with a chest tight with dread. The slide slams back and throws a rectangle of dim light into the box along with a grim profile and the sweet-sour odor of shaving lotion and onions.

Bless me, Father, for I have sinned, this is my first confession, I rattle off into the unseen ear inches from my lips and then launch into what would become my usual childhood list: 'I fought with my sister six times.' (This means I kicked and butted her when she rolled into the hollow in the center of our double bed, details I skip because Sister said we shouldn't waste the priest's time with chatter.) 'I hit my brother twice. I talked back to my mother four times.' I take a breath and blurt, 'I was jealous every other day.' Sister said jealousy is a sin against the tenth commandment, *Thou shalt not covet thy neighbor's goods*. She said jealousy means wishing you had something *like* someone else has, something you admire. But envy means you would like to take that something away from the other person and have it for your self. Sister said that's what it means to 'covet.' She said to covet is a bigger sin than jealousy. My admiration for Benita makes this distinction critical. Sometimes I long for wide blue eyes and soft curls *like* Benita's instead of my greenish eyes and defiant waves. Or wish for an A+ in arithmetic *like* she has on her report card, instead of the plain A on mine. Or that my dad will give me a nickel if I get all A's on my report card, *like* her dad does. I wish I had a sweet expression *like* hers instead of a sassy face nuns instinctively mistrust. After unburdening myself of the thoughts, words and deeds I regret, I exit the ponderous secrecy of the box. As I go out into the light with my penance, three Our Fathers and three Hail Marys, Benita enters.

After everyone has made their First Confession, Sister reminds us to say our penance and spend the rest of the day quietly. 'Go home and prepare your minds and hearts to receive the body of Christ tomorrow.' We have a different plan in place, one that involves playing, not praying. We walk home by way of Benita's house where we keep the letter, if not the spirit, of Sister's law by offering up our play to God.

For awhile, we squat on a worn patch near the backdoor of Benita's house and play marbles, propelling the brilliant glass balls with deft thumbs and earnest aspirations.

'Jesus!' yelps Mary Jane and lowers her voice. 'Mary and Joseph.'

'Is that swearing I hear over there and not an hour since your First Confession?' pipes up Benita's dad from the vegetable garden where he is hoeing. He's obliged to correct us, both as a member of the Holy Name Society, a men's group out to stop the evil of cursing and swearing, and as a neighbor to Bud and Hilda Saul whose daughter, Mary Jane, is Benita's friend and pretty brunette complement.

We go inside, out of his earshot, and race to the top of the stairs where we invent a game of going back down, one step at a time, progress dependent upon guessing correctly in which hand the leader holds the penny. Whoever arrives first at the bottom wins, although there's nothing tangible to win. We chorus a sign of the cross on the top step, 'In the name of the Father, the Son and the Holy Ghost' and proceed downward, reciting on each step the age-old verse, 'Eeenie, meenie, miney, mo, Catch a nigger by the toe, if he hollers make him pay, sixty dollars every day. My mother says *You're It*.' At that point we make our guess.

'You kids think of something else to catch,' calls Benita's dad when our descent is barely underway. He has relocated inside, too, and is crouching amidst a clutter of tools beneath the dining room table, humming along to the piano her mother is playing in the living room. She breaks into the middle of a measure with more advice. "And don't let me hear you say the word 'nigger' *ever* again.'

'*Say badger*,' orders Benita with the easy authority of a child who possesses both good grades and good looks.

'Don't you be forgetting to do your Saturday work, young lady,' says her dad. His strict tone contradicts the permanently turned-up corners of his mouth and the constant smile in his eyes; he seems to be watching for something to justify an all-out laugh. Benita's Saturday work is cleaning the house. 'I'll be checking up on you in the morning when I get home,' he promises.

Her dad is a nuisance. He's also a policeman. Early every evening, just after supper, he puts on his navy blue uniform, fastens a row of gleaming brass buttons over his tidy paunch and boards the seven p.m. city bus for the trip downtown where he walks a night beat. Whenever he meets a fellow parishioner, his round face breaks into a ruddy Irish smile and his limpid blue eyes twinkle beneath the visor of his cap. If he spots a staggering priest, he calls a squad car to haul him back to the rectory, the respectful gesture of a faithful Catholic. My mother says Eldon Kane is a 'good man,' which means he takes care of his family, goes to church on Sunday, and doesn't 'carouse around.' This is the flaw she decries in her twin, Tom, and her younger brother, Joe. Carousing around is not a trait she admires in a married man. My father, who calls cigarette smoking a vile habit akin to sin, is either unaware of, or more tolerant toward the cigars Eldon Kane occasionally smokes, because he, too, considers him a man of exemplary character. If he knew that Eldon Kane gave up cigarette smoking because of the cost, he might admire him even more.

Benita invites us to help with her Saturday work, which we would do happily, but her mother intervenes, suggesting that our mothers are probably worried sick and besides, don't we have our own work to do at home? We do, and more. We now have the burden of a conscience. Obediently, we go home.

Benita's mother is a devout woman with short, taffy-colored hair, large, wistful eyes and a ready, slightly apologetic smile, as if she's happy but not sure she ought to be. Every morning, she hurries off to six o'clock Mass and Communion at St. Columbkille's church. But that spring, she walks down the steep streets to Bluff Street and attends Sunday Mass at the Cathedral where she won't be recognized and humiliated by her swollen belly. Her fifth child is due in two months, shortly before Benita's eighth birthday on August 4. Her other children include two sons, Richard, seventeen and Walter, fifteen, and thirteen-year-old, Irene.

'A tag-a-long. An after-thought. A big surprise,' says my mother of that birth arrangement. Couples without children or who have long lapses between them are highly suspect. My mother was thirty-seven years old when she married my dad, or she'd have some explaining to do for her own paltry three-child harvest.

On this Saturday before our First Communion, Benita and I are beset by the same concern. Will our mothers come to church tomorrow to see us receive Communion? Will hers go down the hill to the Cathedral where no one knows her? Will mine be confined to her bed?

My mother's trouble isn't caused by a baby—she's almost fifty—but something in that vicinity has gone wrong. The doctor called it 'the change' and told her she must stay in bed until the bleeding stops. When I return home from Benita's house that afternoon, I go straight upstairs to her room. She strokes a few wayward strands of hair from my forehead and tells me she won't be able to come to my First Communion tomorrow.

That night, I pull up my knees, place the soles of both feet against my sister's back and shove her out of the middle of the bed, then lie in the dark and watch the street light make animal shadows on the neighbor's green-shuttered house, like sin prowling across my soul. I try to think about receiving Christ's body but my mind keeps traveling to my mother who won't be there. I turn my face into the pillow and smother my tears so my irksome sister won't ask questions. I think I hear my mother crying, too, on the other side of the bedroom wall.

Sunday morning, at my mother's bedside, I preen in my sister's elaborate hand-me-down Communion dress and frothy veil, fancying myself a bridesmaid of Christ, but never a Bride, unimpressed as I am by the benefits of that work. My dad starts the 1936 Chevrolet that only he can drive, and slowly, proudly backs it out of the garage. We arrive at church just as Benita's mother, on her dad's arm, crosses the street and steps onto the curb. It isn't envy I feel, I know that. I simply wish that my mother could be there in church with me, like Benita's.

School is out. My mother is up again tending the geraniums she planted in the loamy soil along the east side of the garage. Now Benita's mother is in bed. Her arms and legs have swollen up until the skin looks varnished. Her thin, pale face is moon-shaped. The doctor said she has to stay in bed until her baby is born. In the morning, Benita helps with housework. In the afternoon, she rides her big tricycle up and down the sidewalk, up and down by herself. She doesn't want to play. Sometimes she rides to the neighbor's and hides inside their garage where she can sit and contemplate her options if her mother dies and her grandmother takes over her upbringing. She's a pious, stubborn woman with merciless blue eyes and a monk's fetish for silence.

Benita has acquired a new talent—whistling—and goes about the house showing it off. But merely pursing her lips within earshot of her grandmother brings a cranky shush. 'A whistling woman and a cackling hen are sure to come to no good end.' The peevish prophecy bewilders Benita, who is not yet a woman and will never be a hen. Sharing a bed with the cantankerous old woman is an unbearable, but likely prospect. The three upstairs bedrooms are fully occupied. Country cousins attending high school in town pay board and room for space with Benita's brothers and sister. She sleeps on a daybed in her parent's room. The thought of being squeezed against her grandmother all night makes her want to run away.

I feel sorry for her. I've never had a grandmother, but I remember how strange the kitchen felt when my mother wasn't in it, how we talked in whispers at the table, like people at a funeral viewing, how sometimes I cried in bed at night. Benita doesn't cry. Instead, she makes a deal with God. If he will let her mother live, she'll put every cent of the two dollars she received for her First Communion into the collection box at school. Sister sends that money across the ocean to 'save the pagan babies.' This project excites our imaginations and the motherly feelings awakening in our female hearts.

On July 22, Benita's sister, Carol, is born. A few weeks later, Benita and I chalk squares on the sidewalk in front of her house. August heat sticks our shirts to our backs and frizzes our hair as we hop from square to square to pick up the tossed stone. Mary Jane comes along, as she always does, and we switch to jump rope. *M-i-crooked letter, crooked letter, i,* we chant in rhythm with our feet. *Crooked letter, crooked letter, i, humpback, humpback, i.* We skip on the simmering sidewalk, the jump rope swinging over and under, connecting to hot concrete in nervous clicks. When it's Benita's turn, she leaps with the rhythm of the rope, landing on two feet for the *M*, one for the *i* and on every *s* crossing her ankles and executing a nimble landing. But she doesn't bend over like a humpback for the *p*.

'You're supposed to be a humpback when you say *p*,' I tell her.

'What if I don't *want* to be a humpback?' For someone whose fortune is on its way to a pagan land, she is being very uncooperative.

'It's a rule. You have to hump your back to make *P*.' The joke hits Mary Jane and me simultaneously and doubles us over in giggles but Benita's straight-faced attention is on the front door and her dad, who has just come out.

'You'd better not let your mother hear that talk,' he warns Benita in his smiley voice. Her mother's word for pee is 'make a river.' In his dignified policeman's uniform, Eldon Kane looks noble and heroic, not at all like the pest crouched under the dining room table interfering with our games. Being a policeman was not his first choice. Like many other people in the neighborhood, at heart he was a country boy who had begun married life on a farm south of Dubuque. Like many others during the depression, he'd unmysteriously 'lost' the farm, thereby relocating them, reluctantly and unsatisfactorily, in town.

'I have to go in and help now,' says Benita. 'Daddy's going to work.'

'How come you always have to help? Doesn't your big sister ever do anything?' asks Mary Jane, disgustedly.

'She helps with meals. I help with cleaning.'

'Yuk,' I say. 'I hate cleaning.'

'I'm good at it. Daddy said so.' Benita goes inside.

At last, an aptitude in her that I have no wish to own or imitate.

We roam the summer with abandon, roller skating, playing hide and seek, climbing trees, swinging in the park, secure within the invisible boundaries of neighborhood and parish. Eyes watch us all summer long, neighbors from a kitchen window or porch swing, their hands fanning back and forth in slow complaint, 'It's not the heat, it's the humidity.' People tell us stories about women of earlier generations disciplining neighborhood children on the spot, washing out the mouth of any child who needed it, related or not, because everybody knows that the only way to raise good children is to punish bad behavior promptly.

No one washes out my dad's mouth for his remarks. 'A nigger must have walked past the power house' he says when the lights suddenly go out. 'There must be a nigger in the woodpile somewhere,' means there's something going on that he doesn't trust. Plenty of people brag about a financial deal in which they've 'Jewed down' the seller, or just the opposite, they've been 'Jewed down.' Maybe that's why Mr. Belsky, who owns a car dealership, changed his name to Mr. Belle when he married a Catholic. 'Banana peddlers' is what my dad calls the Italian couple who run a fruit store downtown.

No one seems offended by his racial slurs. Who is there to

offend? Not the hard-working Germans who settled the fertile land on the north side of town. Nor the wistful Irish who made do on the thinner soil to the south. They till ethnic turf but they're citizens of a common Catholic world. The real aliens are the Lutherans and Presbyterians and the occasional Episcopalian scattered among us, strangers we dismiss with the term, 'non-Catholic.' The two Greek Orthodox families who have moved onto our block are more puzzling. We can accept their black hair, heavy eyebrows and downtown restaurants, but their religion, with its archbishops and saints and feast days, makes us wonder if they're trying to imitate us.

Summer evenings we sit on the front porch, slapping mosquitoes and discussing the lawns and houses and habits of the people who live there. Every night at nine-thirty, a tiny point of light moves down the sidewalk toward us, closer and closer, until Cy Vogler strolls by, coughing and smoking his day's last cigarette. 'There goes another nail in his coffin,' mutters my dad, not quite under his breath, when Cy is not quite past. One morning as my dad is driving me to school, a woman comes down the steps of her home carrying a shiny-eyed Yorkshire terrier in her arms. 'Look at that,' he sneers. 'She should be carrying a baby."

'What if she doesn't have one to carry, Dad?'

'Well, she ought to. Unless she's doing something she shouldn't be doing.'

Priests are excused from the rules that apply to us. A priest represents Christ and even if he doesn't act like Christ, we're supposed to greet him respectfully. 'To calumniate a priest is a sacrilege,' Sister told us in school. That means it's a sin to say anything bad about a priest, even if it's true. Gossiping or poking fun at a man of God is an egregious sin. Sister told us that, too. Egregious sounds even worse than mortal, but we're tempted to commit it whenever we're in the presence of a certain monsignor. His hennaed, parted-in-the-middle toupee wiggles around like it's alive. While he chastises the congregation for being anxious and tells them to 'look at the birds of the air, they do not sow or reap or gather into barns,' we watch his wandering hair and hope for the worst.

Socializing with priests makes people important. Rich people take Father to expensive restaurants. Regular families invite him to supper at their house. Widows tell priests their troubles. Women like to talk to priests because they nod and say, 'Yes, yes, I understand' instead of 'Can you save it for another time when I'm not ready to drop?' Even though my mother is related to a bishop who died a long time ago, she never invites priests to our house. Not to talk or eat supper or anything. She worries about the worn-out furniture in the living room and about my dad's grammar—he says 'ain't,' and 'we was.' But I think the real reason has to do with her brother, Joe. He blames a priest for taking away his wife, Nell, the mother of his five children. 'The son-of-a-bitch wrecked my marriage,' were the words he said to my mother in the kitchen. I wanted to ask her what he meant, but I wasn't supposed to be listening. It had something to do with Father F squiring Nell about town, out to dinner, and for drives in the countryside. Now and then after that, I would look at a priest and wonder if he was a son-of-a-bitch.

When my dad says 'ain't' or talks about banana peddlers and niggers, it's not because he's mean. I know that. It's because he quit school at age ten and went to work in a foundry and never traveled outside Iowa. He's like the other dads in our parish, who are working hard to make ends meet and trying to raise their children to know love and serve God and follow the rules of the church. Anytime there's a question about those rules, they go to Father for the answer. 'Father, my wife's aunt married a divorced man out of the church. Will it give scandal to my children if they come for Easter dinner?' 'Father, is it okay to plow my field on Sunday if that's the first dry day all week?' 'Father, my wife and I. . .we can barely feed the six kids we have now. . .what are we supposed to do?' Father tells these grown-ups what they're supposed to do, but they go away as bewildered as four-year-old children.

Bewildered is how Eldon Kane feels in late August of 1941 as he boards the city bus that will take him downtown to walk his beat. He's the father of five children. Good children, all of them, he muses, and with sunny dispositions. Bright, like their mother, a high school graduate who taught school before their marriage. He's done well enough himself, too, for a boy half-orphaned at age ten, and blown about by life for the next ten years. It was meeting Marcella that had settled him down. They had plans to buy a farm of their own, but there was a baby right away and the depression and they had to abandon their notions and move to a job in town.

Richard will be eighteen in a few months, a self-reliant boy who chose to work and pay his own tuition to Loras Academy rather than endure the harsh discipline of Father Craney at St. Columbkille's. Now, with the draft on and a war heating up, the Army will claim Richard the minute he graduates in the spring. Eldon is trying to hide his worry from Marcella who has enough on her mind with the new baby.

Walter is fifteen, a sophomore at the parish school, a hard-worker, kind to his sisters, and scheming to buy himself a car next year, a luxury Eldon gave up years ago. Happy-go-lucky Irene, thirteen, has the coloring of an Irish colleen and a heart set on being a nurse, if only he can put aside enough money for her training.

And Benita—ah, his plucky, pretty, eight-year-old daughter—a mind of her own, that one, no telling what she'll become. A *star* ballet dancer, she says one day, and the next, a *star* ice skater like Sonja Henie, but always it's a star, never anything down to earth. She's been begging to take piano lessons from Sister at school. *Please, Daddy, please, I'll practice every single day.* So you want to be a star piano player now, is that it, he teased, and out-shine your mother? *Uh-huh, and then you could sing for me like you do for her.* But in spite of those coaxing blue eyes, he had to say no, not this year. Every cent he earns will have to go toward the hospital bill, an expense they didn't have with the other four babies, all born at home.

Eldon greets the bus driver and takes a seat near the front. Seeing a cop makes people feel safe, although there's nothing much to fear in a town where nearly everybody goes to Confession on Saturday. He and Joe Strub, the Chief of Police, joined the department together and are now good friends. Making friends comes easy for Eldon. 'How are you today, Mrs. Kennedy,' he smiles to the pleasant, heavy-limbed woman who hoists herself onto the bus at the next stop. Mrs. Kennedy is an English Protestant who is keeping the promise she made when she married Catholic Mr. Kennedy: to raise their children—three daughters—in the Faith. Eldon makes an effort to be friendly toward the non-Catholics on their block, especially those laboring behind an Irish name.

She asks about the new baby.

We've named her *Carol*, he tells her, after Sister Carol. Marcella admires the gentle, young nun who prepared Benita for her First Holy Communion.

Did they want this child is the question barely contained in Mrs. Kennedy's protruding Episcopalian eyes. She knows that the church's teaching, if not on the tip of every Catholic tongue, is buried deep in every Catholic soul: *the primary purpose of marriage is the begetting and rearing of children in the fear and love of God, in order that they may join Him in heaven some day.* It bothers her that Catholic couples don't think in terms of wanting or planning. They obey church laws about the marriage act with no thought of challenging the right of celibate priests to impose them. She doesn't mind the Baptism part, or even the rule about Catholic school, but she let Mr. Kennedy know straight off what she thought about leaving everything to Divine Providence.

What a man wants and what God sends him aren't always the same thing, Eldon would like to explain. God gives you a child you didn't know you wanted, and then you love that baby so fiercely, you decide God's ideas might be better than your own.

If Eldon could see into the future, into the lives of his own children and grandchildren, he would be astonished by their ways, couples married for years still trying to decide whether or not to have a child, discussing would it be convenient and can they afford it. And then watching over the whole process from start to finish with machines, listening to the heartbeat, peeking in at the baby's private parts, using their curiosity like a crowbar to pry the mystery from every nook and cranny in life. 'Ah, well, we have a good life,' he would sigh and turn to tell his wife, as he does every night, 'You are so beautiful. And I am a lucky man.' He means it. Marcella has put a center into his life. Sure, he floundered during those hard, first years, from farm to town and job to job, but she was there, encouraging him. She was the one who insisted that he take the Policeman's Examination and who showed no surprise when he passed third highest.

And Marcella? How is she? Mrs. Kennedy wants to know now.

Eldon smiles through a throb of guilt. 'Doin' better, he tells her, much better, thank you, Mrs. Kennedy. I'll tell her you were askin.' He thanks God Marcella has made it through this pregnancy. He thinks of the nights he spent lying awake beside her, especially those last weeks before the child was born, listening to her restless breathing, watching her struggle to turn over, to find a position comfortable for her swollen body. He worried about her, about the child, about his own responsibility. Then the memories would start and with them, the fears. His own mother, Mary, was only thirty-six years old when she died and left behind the five of them—Marie, the oldest at thirteen; himself next, ten years old, then Larry and Genevieve and little Wilfred, barely two. What a scramble it was, a bunch of kids trying to grow up without a mother. Their father sent Wilfred off to live with relatives in Dubuque; the rest of them were the "Kane brats" farmed out every summer. As teenagers, he and Larry followed their dad around from job to job, from Virginia to Canada to Chicago to Alabama. Eldon enlisted in the army and did a stint at the end of World War I, then returned to Iowa and went to work on a farm with a dream of buying his own. Faith in God's goodness, that things would get better, that's what kept them going through those years.

More faith is what he needs now. He and Marcella are running out of resources—out of bedrooms in their house, out of money, out of time and energy and patience and health. Their faith tells them to trust. It tells them that life is a greater thing than food and the body than the clothing.

Consider how the lilies of the field grow; they neither toil nor spin yet I say to you that not even Solomon in all his glory was arrayed like one of these. . . Therefore do not be anxious saying, what shall we eat? or what shall we drink? or what are we to put on? Seek first the kingdom of God and his justice and all these things shall be given you besides.

The church declares that marital relations must be 'open to life.' No drugs, medications, instruments, devices, cleansings, nothing can be used to frustrate the natural purpose of the act, conception and birth. To do so is morally wrong, a violation of the natural law, although those Protestant families with two kids living in their fine houses along Grandview Avenue don't seem to know or care that the pope's rule applies to them.

The doctor has advised Marcella that another pregnancy could be dangerous, even life-threatening. Perhaps she should consider surgery, said the doctor, who strangely enough, is not a Catholic, but a Jew sympathetic to the predicament of Catholic couples. He tells them there are medical reasons to justify the solution of last resort: a Catholic hysterectomy.

What are they going to do, Eldon wonders. Marcella says she will talk to Father when she goes to confession, but Eldon knows what the answer will be. He's talked to Father himself. 'God does not ask you to have another child in your situation, my son, but He does expect you to abide by the natural law. Abstinence from your marital rights is the only morally acceptable solution.' A fancy way to put it, thinks Eldon, although sometimes the priest says straight out, 'You must live like brother and sister.' Easy for him to say, a man who doesn't lie night after night by the woman he loves, or put his arm around her and feel the warmth of her body beneath her nightgown, or slide his palm along the slope of her hip and sense the longing that begins within his own body. . . ah, what's the use, stop the longing. . .turn away, move to the edge of the bed and go to sleep. Night after night. Unless it's the 'safe period,' says Father. And how many children are conceived during the safe period?

From the day of their marriage, eighteen years ago last April sixteenth, they have been open to children, the first born nine months and three days after their wedding day (it was the three days that saved them from the neighbors' tongues). Eldon turned forty-five on the first of August; Marcella is thirty-nine. In a few more years, this dilemma will be in the past. Meanwhile, what do they do? Wait to get old? It's enough to drive a man to drink, if he didn't know better. He's seen too many Irishmen staggering the streets of his beat with their slobbering excuses. He won't be one of them.

Instead, he tries to count his blessings: a job in a sluggish economy, Marcella for his wife, healthy children, a roof over their heads, (even if the rooms under that roof are crowded), food on the table, enough to share with the hungry vagrant who knocks on the screen door and tells Marcella he'll work for an hour in exchange for a meal. It was an opportunity to practice the Corporal Works of Mercy, she tells Eldon afterward. He knows the passage from Matthew's gospel, too: 'For I was hungry and you gave me food, I was thirsty and you gave me drink. I was a stranger and you welcomed me, I was naked and you clothed me, I was sick and you visited me, I was in prison and you came to me. . .'

Now Eldon has an ongoing opportunity to practice the corporal works, as corporal and as difficult as any work a man can do: abstain from marital relations with his wife. But there is no mercy in it, no mercy at all.

When the bus stops in front of Renier's Music Store at Sixth and Main, Eldon steps off into the quiet early evening streets. The offices and stores have been closed since five; the troublemakers aren't out yet. A dim light glows at the back of the music store where Mr. Renier can be seen working over his books. He looks up, signals, comes to the front door, and unlocks it. 'Evening, Eldon. Is the missus enjoying the recording machine?' He sent the machine home with Eldon a month ago to try out. Whenever Eldon mentions returning it, the answer is 'no hurry, keep it awhile longer and tell me how your kids like it.' Eldon says the kids like it and so do the neighbor kids. He thanks Mr. Renier and tells him how it lifted his spirits to take that little bit of luxury home to his family. He thinks Mr. Renier might be practicing the works of mercy on him.

CHAPTER TWO

*A*h, yes, *I've got good news tonight!* comes the breezy greeting from Station KDTH every evening precisely at six-thirty. While my mother clatters in the kitchen, my dad hunches in front of the console radio in the corner of our living room and listens to Gabriel Heatter break his cheery promise with a staccato report of harsh facts. The European war hangs like a dark cloud over the world. Germany has attacked Yugoslavia and Greece and is sweeping across Russia toward Moscow. Roosevelt has taken to the airwaves, too, trying with his Fireside Chats to rally Americans to fight the depression and to lend war supplies to countries fighting the Nazis. My dad shakes his head and mutters disgruntled remarks about Roosevelt 'selling us down the river.' As a blue-collar worker and a fervent Catholic, Charlie Holmberg is a Democrat, but FDR is not the pope and his politics are not infallible and my dad argues with them vociferously from his ringside seat in the living room.

Adults rely on geographic isolation and optimism to keep the war at bay. As third-graders, we linger within the sunny security of our parochial childhood, the sort of place Victor Herbert may have envisioned when he wrote the lyrics to his turn-of-the-century musical, *Toyland.* Once a child escaped those borders there was no returning.

We spend these fallow years before the storm of puberty putting away the things of a child and learning to work. At home, we set and clear the table, dry dishes, take out the garbage, dust and sweep because that's our job as members of a family. At school, we do our reading, writing, arithmetic and catechism because that's our job as students. Without knowing it, we're learning skills that will help us thrive beyond our sheltered world. Patrolling the borders of that world are policemen in smart brass-buttoned suits, like Benita's dad; priests in black cassocks and Roman collars; nuns in flowing black habits; the Knights of Columbus en masse at Mass with their plumed hats and swords; nurses in starched white uniforms and jaunty caps; businessmen in double-breasted suits; bus drivers and mailmen; homemakers corseted in practical, cotton housedresses. The uniforms of these devoted men and women announce their authority and promise our well-being.

At night, Eldon Kane walks a beat; by day, he hangs around in the casual dress of dad, guardian of home, family and the neighborhood children who collect in the large yard surrounding their small house. Their two-lot site invites games of kick-the-can, baseball, pick-up basketball and the horseshoe matches Benita's mother routinely wins.

'C'mon in here,' Eldon Kane calls and gestures three or four of us from the yard into the house. There, on a table in the living room is the brand new recorder and microphone on loan from Renier's Music Store. One at a time, he summons us to the center of the room to conduct an interview befitting a visiting dignitary.

Welcome to the Kane household.

What is your name, please?

And where do you live?

What is your favorite subject in school? Why?

What do you plan to be when you grow up?

Have you ever considered becoming an astronomer?

The last question is designed for Benita, whose desire to be a star has evolved into a fascination with the celestial bodies suspended in the dark over her backyard. Like a whimsical Socrates, Benita's dad dignifies us by giving us his time and attention and teaching us what he knows. Eldon wishes he knew more about the stars so he could instruct Benita.

The closing number for these interview sessions is a piece played on the piano by Marcella with Eldon singing along in the tenor brogue he adopts for song. *When Irish Eyes Are Smiling. I'll Take You Home Again, Kathleen.* When he takes requests, Benita asks for *The Ghost of Anne Boleyn* or *Nine Little Pigs,* tunes I'd never heard of before. Afterward, Eldon sets an affectionate hand on his wife's shoulder, thanks her, and plays back the recorded session while the day's celebrities sit round-eyed at the miracle of hearing themselves talk.

Benita's brothers write a murder mystery and put her in charge of sound effects, a single gun shot fired at a critical moment. When the signal comes, she slams down the Bible on a nearby table. The smack brings her dad rushing to the doorway, his eyebrows arching upward until it seems they might escape his forehead entirely. 'Just a minute here, young lady! Find yourself another weapon besides the Holy Book.'

He never manages to sound cross enough to scare anyone away. Even when neighborhood kids wear a path shortcutting through their yard, he shrugs philosophically to Marcella. 'You can't hurt grass. It'll grow back. Kids don't.' Every month, he takes his daughters and his paycheck and walks to a downtown restaurant where he treats them to tomato soup and oyster crackers.

Another prized possession, and a rarity during those Spartan times, is their set of olive green World Books. Marcella invested in the 1919 edition when she was teaching in the country school. What did it matter that they were over twenty years old? They're packed with exotic, timeless information that Eldon feeds to his children in daily portions. After reading aloud for ten or fifteen minutes, he quizzes them.

What is the most beautiful building in the world?

The Taj Mahal.

And where is the Taj Mahal?

Agra, India.

Who built it?

The Emperor Shah Jahan.

Why?

As a tomb for his beautiful wife.

One day, Benita's father fools his children by presenting a complete Catechism lesson, 'The Purpose of Man's Existence," as one more clever quiz.

1. Who made us?

   God made us.

2. Who is God?

   God is the Supreme Being, infinitely perfect, who made all things and keeps them in existence.

3. Why did God make us?

   God made us to show His goodness and to share with us His everlasting happiness in heaven

4. What must we do to gain the happiness of heaven?

   To gain the happiness of heaven we must know, love and serve God in this world.

5. From whom do we learn to know, love and serve God?

   We learn to know, love and serve God from Jesus Christ, the Son of God, who teaches us through the Catholic Church.

When I'm among the children who stray into these activities, I return home wishing that my parents, *like* Benita's, would play games in the yard, that my dad would read aloud to me from a World Book, that my mother would pitch horseshoes across the yard. My mother does display a talent for pitching things, which I witnessed during a passionate euchre game at the kitchen table. My Uncle John dealt; my mother gathered up her cards, frowned, fanned them out for all to see and demanded, 'What kind of a hand is this, not a face card in the whole works?' Without waiting for a second opinion, she flung the cards across the table and called for a new deal. 'Anne!' cried my stunned dad. 'You have to play the cards you're dealt.' *Maybe not,* was her feisty message. For a woman who touted the proverb, 'Actions speak louder than words,' her gesture was clear. She was a renegade in a milieu that saw God's will in happenstance and resignation as the proper response. Defiance was her act of hope.

My mother decides I'm old enough to take the piano lessons she was deprived of as a child. To reach the music room where elderly Sister Dolorosa teaches, I must travel from school to convent through an underground tunnel. Along the way, this passage widens into a dim, humid inner sanctum smelling of starch and damp cotton—the nuns' laundry room. There, dangling from clotheslines by their arms and legs, like criminals condemned to death by hanging, are the shadowy undergarments of the nuns. I flee past, sensing myself on the brink of a secret I'm not prepared to know.

Benita wants to take piano lessons, too. Maybe next year, her parents say, maybe they can afford lessons then. Whenever I complain about practicing, my mother reminds me of the 'financial sacrifice' they are making for me. Money is a paradox we encounter at every turn. It doesn't grow on trees. It's the root of all evil. Time is money. Fools soon part with it. It can fill a cavity in your molar, put a car in the garage, pay the light bill and exert influence, but it can't buy happiness. And yet the economic downturn is called a 'depression' not a gala, and money is precisely what everyone seems to want.

That other bothersome desire—sex—belongs to the store of forbidden knowledge owned and operated by grownups who turn over that information to God, osmosis and due time. But my weekly subterranean journey through that tunnel full of cloistered undergarments is a chance to find something out. I screw up my courage and tarry in the shadows of the laundry room in order to collect answers to the questions burgeoning overhead. What kind of underwear do nuns wear? Do they wear brassieres? How big? Or do female appurtenances shrivel up if you don't use them? Which bloomers belong to Sister Augustine, Katie wants to know. Do nuns wear nightgowns to bed? Silky or flannel? Did I notice any blood-stained rags thrown over the line? Dummy, Mary Jane retorts when Sally asks that question. Nuns don't have babies. Babies are what make you bleed. Elaine says her mother heard about a nun who had a baby. It happened because she secretly married a priest.

We apply group research to questions surfacing above ground. Is the stubble visible along Sister Sophia's temples gray or brown? Sister Josephine's is red, Teresa is sure of it. Benita wonders if nuns shave their whole heads or just to the edge of the veil. Katie promises to find out the next time Sister leans over her desk. Are nuns regular women? Do they itch and sweat and bleed? What is it they really *do* as the Bride of Christ? That's what we want to know.

Mary, the ultimate model held up before female eyes is not a regular woman. She's a virgin. Immaculately conceived. That means she managed not only to become a mother without the usual subversive activities, but she also escaped original sin, that tainted state Adam bequeathed to the rest of us by giving in to Eve's badgering. The idea of an innocent woman bothered the men in charge of truth. They said Christ died for everyone because everyone had sinned. Leaving Mary out of that threw the whole plan off. What the Immaculate Conception meant to us was a free day from school. On December 8, 1941, the observation of that feast day got mixed up with everything else happening in the world. Did we go to Mass that Monday because it was a holyday of obligation? Or because on that date, the day after Pearl Harbor, the United States declared war on the Axis powers? Just as my dad suspected and Roosevelt predicted and the Nazis intended all along, the European war had developed into a war for world dominance. Now the primary concern, the subject of every adult conversation, switches from money to war.

Gradually, our town is emptied of young men. Mingling with the uniforms we know and trust is the imposing uniform of war as ordinary boys are transformed into the commanding figures of United States soldiers, sailors and marines. Left behind are the old and the ineligible, farmers, clergymen, women and children.

Blue stars begin appearing on small flags in the living room windows I walk past on my way home from school. Inside lives a proud family notifying the world of a son serving in the United States military. Whenever Benita brags at school about her handsome, dark-haired brother, Richard, who is eighteen years old, a senior in high school and sure to become a soldier soon, I wish my brother was old enough to go to war, too, so we could put a blue star in our window and I could tell my classmates about him.

The role sugar or meat or tinfoil or nylon stockings played in defeating the Germans is a mystery to us, but mystery is part and parcel of our Catholic world. The purpose of the grease we collect from housewives on Saturdays is a mystery, too. We pull our little wagons through the neighborhood, hearts humming triumphant tunes as we trustingly pick up ingredients for explosives. The fistful of patriotic red and blue tokens we carry to the corner grocery store gives us a sense of participating in some grand vague effort.

"Hello, Mr. Craney," I call to our parish priest, when I encounter him on one of those mornings as I rattle along the street with my wagonload of cans holding second-hand fat. His neck stretches higher above his collar, his beak-like nose pecks the air like a hen alert to a fox sneaking toward the coop. Without looking directly at me, he lands a fierce reprimand into the core of my being. The fox behind my cheeky greeting is my brother, John, who dared me to commit the egregious sin of poking fun at a priest, specifically *this* priest. As an altar boy, John suffered from Father Craney's wrath—a physical chastisement one morning after serving Mass, a psychological battering another day in front of his fourth grade classmates. The priest's meanness motivated him and plenty of other boys to defect from the parish high school.

Random evening air raid practices keep us thinking of war. At the menacing wail of a siren, we race through the house to switch off lights, then huddle in the dark living room and imagine enemy planes swooping, bombs exploding, the havoc of hatred bursting around us. My father stations himself before the tiny amber glow of the radio dial as if trying to guard us from the world's bad news. And then he's gone, too.

Standard Oil Company, where my dad has worked for over thirty years, has relocated him to Mason City, Iowa, two hundred miles across the state. It's a ploy, he says, moving a sixty-one-year-old man so far from his family, a plain and simple attempt to provoke him to quit before his pension is due. Once each month, he takes a night train home, arriving Saturday morning and leaving Sunday evening. Between visits, his 1936 Chevrolet sits forlornly in the garage. My mother, like most women of her generation, has never learned to drive. Marooned with three children, eight, ten and twelve years old, she is thrust into the dual role of father and mother, a demand that taxes her physical and emotional resources.

'Stop, or you'll really get it!' she cries one day as she pursues me around the dining room table. Something I've said or done sent her marching to the yard for a switch from the lilac bush and now, armed, she intends to deliver a few desperate lashes meant to convince both of us that she's in charge. I confound the plan by running. She chases me until it appears we might end up like the tigers contending for Little Black Sambo's lovely clothes, a puddle of *ghee* on the floor. At that point, she gives me a choice. *Stop, or you'll really get it.* I can't win. I don't remember the outcome, only the paralyzed terror.

A few days later, after she regains benevolent control, she explains the basic problem. Every so often I simply needed a spanking 'to clear the air.' Her revelation casts me into a state of hypervigilance. What deed, gesture, smirk, comment, resistance, hesitation or joyous outburst will put me over the line? I send my dad painstakingly printed letters telling him how much I miss him. I tell him I'm doing well in school. I leave out the chase around the dining room table. He writes back in his childlike hand that education is important and he's glad I'm working hard. He says this with the conviction of a man who has spent his life in manual labor.

CHAPTER THREE

Anyone knocking on the Kane front door on a random early evening in the fall of 1942, after Benita and her sister, Irene, have finished the supper dishes and before Eldon catches the bus to work, will find the family on their knees in the living room reciting the rosary. Marcella Kane grounds their family life in prayer: daily Mass, the rosary, the 'offering up' of onerous tasks and petty frustrations.

My mother sprinkles religion into daily life the way she sprinkles holy water through the house during thunderstorms. She reads the diocesan newspaper, *The Witness;* she tucks blessed palms above the picture of the Sacred Heart; she fastens a crucifix above her marital bed and pins a pouch of medals to her nightgown before entering it; and certainly, she prays for her brothers, Joe and Tom. On Fridays, she attends the Novena to Our Sorrowful Mother at St. Patrick's church. I think she likes the evening out, the chance to put on her 'good dress,' powder her nose, and take the city bus to another part of town. Sometimes I go along. I like to hear her sing the closing song. 'Good Night, Sweet Jesus, guard us in sleep. Our souls and bodies, in thy love keep.'

One of Benita's ongoing frustrations is the sight of her brothers tossing a basketball around outside while she stands at the sink doing dishes. When Richard finishes high school, he takes a job at the arms depot in Savannah, Illinois, an hour from Dubuque. He comes home on the bus and arrives long after they've finished the rosary. Left without a basketball partner, Walt spends the interim between supper and the rosary reading at the kitchen table while the girls do dishes.

Benita proposes a plan. 'Mom, why not have Walter wash the dishes and lead the Hail Marys and Irene and I can dry and answer them.'

Her mother rolls her eyes in a silent, inflexible *No.*

'It would save time,' insists Benita.

'Since when is *your* time so valuable?' taunts Walter. The issue dissolves when he takes a job at the bus garage, where he works from four p.m. until the last city bus comes in at midnight. He has renounced sports for the sake of earning sixteen dollars a week. He's saving to buy a car.

Marcella says maybe she should go to work, too, like Richard, like Walter, like Mrs. Heri over on Rowan Street, who cut her hair as short as a man's and bought herself some coveralls and is making her own money.

Eldon chuckles. 'Have you nothing to do here, is that it? Or is it coveralls you're wanting?'

'A car is what I want.'

'You, too? Just when the President is telling everyone to quit the joy rides, you and Walter pine for cars.'

'I want to drive to the country for our own Sunday picnics again. I'm tired of begging a ride with Joe Strub and his family. What good does it do me to know how to drive if I have no car?'

'You don't like riding with the chief of police? Now, a lot of people would be grateful to ride to a picnic in his shiny car. Better than having him haul you off to jail.'

'Oh, sure! Me, a criminal, who doesn't go anywhere she can't walk. From my kitchen to the church, that's where I go.'

Underneath his bantering, Eldon bridles. The only car he ever owned he sold years ago. Money. It's always money. A man has to deny his family a simple picnic in the country because of money.

What Marcella wants is a reprieve. An outing in the autumn countryside near New Melleray, where she and Eldon were married. Just their family, sitting on the creek bank, dipping their toes into the muddy stream, eating peanut butter and jelly sandwiches, drinking lemonade. What she wants is a few peaceful hours, an escape from war, the day after day talk of war, everywhere war. Every front-page headline on every newspaper in the country proclaiming the intensity of the fighting, the number of deaths, the progress of war.

Every morning after Mass, Marcella goes up the aisle to the bank of vigil lights, lights a candle and kneels to pray for a host of needs; lately, she's been focusing on her sons and the war. She asks God for good will on earth; she asks Him to keep her sons safe. She prays for the family over on Bluff street who were informed their son is missing in action. Richard has begun to talk of enlisting in the army. The draft threatens; his hours at the arms depot are long and tedious; the army offers an alluring alternative—good pay, adventure, purpose.

'Eldon, listen to this!' calls Marcella one mid-January afternoon in 1943 as she unfolds the *Telegraph Herald*. The urgency in her voice stops him mid-flight on the stairs. He turns and comes down and stands listening on the bottom stair as she reads the headline aloud.

U.S. NAVY CONFIRMS DEATH OF FIVE BROTHERS.

She spreads her fingers over her mouth and reads on in anxious silence. 'They're from Waterloo,' she says finally, looking up.

'The Sullivan family. Their sons went down on a ship. They're gone. Every single one." She gives Eldon a wounded, baffled look.

Don't ask me to explain the mind of God, his eyes say in return.

For the Sullivans, the three-month anguish of waiting is over. Now, they can stop haunting the mailbox, stop pretending they didn't hear the rumor spreading around town: *the Sullivan boys are dead. Their ship went down.* Alleta Sullivan, the boys' mother, had written to the Navy, asking 'Is it true? Are they dead?' The military reply, 'Missing in action,' withheld the truth from both the Sullivans and the enemy. Now the word is official: all five of their sons are dead. They were aboard the Juneau when it was torpedoed during the Battle at Guadalcanal. As the wounded ship limped toward shore, a Japanese submarine struck again. The fuel oil and ammunition flashed and exploded. Four of the brothers were gone. The oldest lingered on, calling to his brothers from a lifeboat; sometime later, he was killed by a shark. Of the seven hundred men on the Juneau, eleven survived.

"An entire nation shares your sorrow," wrote President Franklin Roosevelt in a letter to the Sullivan family. Pope Pius XII sent a silver religious medal and a rosary with his message of regret. Newsreel men from Chicago came to film the family home and to record the American flag with five gold stars hanging in the window.

Five gold stars. Marcella imagines the window where they hang, but she cannot imagine a mother's heart able to contain the grief they represent. Newspaper articles extol the "Fighting Sullivan Brothers" and describe the family that raised them. Reading these stories, Marcella sees an Irish Catholic family much like her own, everyone pitching in to keep things going, playing sports with neighbors on the vacant lot next door, going to Mass as a family. But tucked away in one article is another tragedy. They also lost a five-month old baby girl, one of two daughters; she died of pneumonia. Seven children in all. Only one left. How do parents endure it, Marcella asks Eldon. He sometimes has trouble himself holding onto the idea of a good God who delivers so much random cruelty to His creatures.

A few months later, another news article reports that Thomas and Alleta Sullivan have begun visiting war plants and shipping yards to speak on behalf of the war effort. They hope their message will prevent the loss of other American boys. That's how people endure, Marcella decides, by putting their suffering to work for others with the Spiritual Works of Mercy—counseling the doubtful, comforting the sorrowful, bearing wrongs patiently, forgiving all injuries—that's what the Sullivans are doing, she tells Eldon. That's what keeps them going.

"And I respect them for it," he says. 'But I'd just as soon God didn't put *me* to that test." He knows his test will come soon enough. Richard has enlisted in the army and is waiting to be notified of his departure date. Soon Eldon will be telling his oldest child goodbye.

I'm glad now that my brother is only thirteen and too young for war. He's an irritant in my life, but he's teaching me to ride a bicycle. I don't want him to end up as a gold star in our window. Or to find myself sitting between my parents at a funeral Mass some day with his flag-draped coffin in the middle aisle, like the picture I saw on the front page of the *Telegraph Herald*. Until now, the war has been far away across the ocean. Suddenly, it's here, here in Iowa, less than one hundred miles from Dubuque, where it has devastated a family.

The war is not going well in June of 1943. Terrible battles are being fought on three continents; nearly one hundred thousand Americans are dead. Families of military men approach the mailbox with dread, open it with trembling hands, fully expecting bad news, the only kind war can generate. An empty mailbox is an ominous thing. An unexpected knock on the door in the middle of an ordinary afternoon means Western Union and a dreaded message.

Richard leaves for the Army on June 27, 1943. His weekly letters are Marcella's mainstay. If the week stretches to eight or nine days, her imagination goes to work. She scans his letters quickly, sitting down to savor them only after she's satisfied that he's safe and well. When he writes that he's been selected for Officer's Candidate School, both she and Eldon credit Providence. They pull chairs up to the dining room table, as they do every Sunday afternoon, and write to him. Marcella congratulates him and thanks God. Eldon asks him if he thinks Walter should enlist, too, or take his chances on the draft. Either way, soon Walter will be a blue star in the living room window.

In truth, Eldon Kane, veteran of World War I, father of two young men, is heartsick. Concern for his sons, for the son lost by Bea and Ralph Roscoe who live across from school, for sons everywhere, is a weight he carries inside his chest. He lugs it along on his beat every night and feels himself growing wearier with every passing day. The only outward sign of this burden is the hand he places over his heart now and then and the deep, anxious sighs he breathes out when Marcella isn't near. Walter, who finally owns his coveted car, is entering his senior year and has signed up for the Navy. In the spring, he will graduate and be gone.

On the homefront, an outbreak of polio compounds the worries over war. If a child seems lethargic, or fiddles with his food, or complains of a vague ache, parents' own hearts clutch. The epidemic delays the opening of school and gives an odd rhythm to our daily lives. It's like being on vacation in a dangerous town, where murders have been committed and muggers are known to lurk and you can't let your guard down.

The Kane children play games in the empty lot. Their dad, who has stayed home from work the past several evenings, observes from the yard as Walter tosses a football back and forth to his sisters.

'Teach me how to throw a spiral,' commands Benita.

'If you make me some fudge,' says Walter.

'Hey, dad! Come join us,' calls Irene.

'Maybe later, honey.' Eldon goes inside and drops wearily onto a chair in the kitchen where Marcella is sewing. He watches the skilled movements of her slender fingers and smiles. 'You are so beautiful,' he begins, but she interrupts the predictable, 'And I am such a lucky man,' with a vigorous shake of her head. 'Eldon, I think it's your eyesight that's ailing you.'

Something is ailing him, some vague distress migrates from his jaw to his neck to his arm, serious enough to cause him to call Joe Strub the other night and say he wasn't up to walking his beat.

'This war. What's to be gained by fighting?' He grimaces. His hand shoots to his face. 'That molar's acting up again,' he says when Marcella catches his eye.

She stops her sewing. 'Are you going to call the doctor? Or will I have to do it?'

'Tomorrow, if I'm not better.'

The next day the doctor deduces from Eldon's complaints that what's ailing him is teeth and recommends a visit to the dentist. The dentist sends him back to the doctor who this time diagnoses indigestion, maybe the start of gall bladder trouble, and advises a bland diet.

Marcella continues to walk to early morning Mass, where on a weekday there is never any danger of a crowd. When the bells for consecration tinkle and Father Dunn elevates the host, she bows her head in silent confession, My Lord and My God. The sacred moment brings strength and a simultaneous premonition that she will need it. After Mass, when she lights the vigil candle, she includes the health of Eldon and her other children in her petitions. As she kneels before the flickering flame, she asks Jesus and his mother, Mary, to protect her family from the dangers of illness and war. 'Thy will be done,' she whispers and blesses herself. The distress in her eyes says she hopes God agrees with her.

Maiming and death, the harvest of war and polio, hovers over early September, marring its beauty. With children home from school, daily schedules are in turmoil. For many families, the thud of the *Telegraph Herald* landing on the front porch late every afternoon gives the day its only shape. Mothers enjoy a few moments of respite while kids read Li'l Abner or Boots and Her Buddies. I'm living through Boots, whose life is littered with handsome, worshipful men, while in real life, even plain, lackadaisical men have become as scarce as sugar.

In a community of church-goers, the local Sunday newspaper arrives considerately, early in the morning. After Mass, while the woman-of-the-house makes breakfast, the kids read the comics and the man-of-the-house shakes out the front page and scans the world news. On Sunday, September 12, 1943, the men in Dubuque read this front page headline:

ITALIAN BATTLE FLEET DELIVERED

Heavy Fighting Around Salerno, Captured by Allies

Looks like things might be starting to turn around in Europe, they call into the kitchen to their wives who mutter varying replies of hope and disbelief. Next the husbands turn to the obituary page. There they see a photograph of a man with lively Irish eyes gazing good-naturedly from beneath the visor of his policeman's hat. The caption says:

DEATH CLAIMS ELDON W. KANE

Dumbfounded, the men summon their wives. *Agnes! Eldon Kane is dead; Margaret, look at this! Bernice, did Marcella tell you*

Eldon was sick? And Agnes and Margaret and Bernice hastily wipe their hands on their aprons and hurry to their husbands' sides and read the article with their own astonished eyes.

Patrolman Eldon W. Kane, 47, 1125 Cleveland Avenue, a member of the Dubuque Police Department for 15 years, died Saturday morning, at 2:30 o'clock at Mercy Hospital after an illness of 16 days' duration. The remains are at the Hoffmann Mortuary where friends may call beginning Sunday afternoon. . .the funeral will be held at St. Columbkille's Church. . .burial will follow in Mount Olivet Cemetery. Chief of Police, Joe Strub, described Eldon Kane as a man who would be deeply missed by the department, an efficient officer who had been paid high tribute on many occasions 'for his courtesy and consideration displayed in the line of duty.' Mr. Kane was a life-long member of the Catholic Church and an attendant at St. Columbkille's parish. He was a member of the Holy Name Society of that church. . .a veteran of the first world war. . .on April 16, 1923, he was married to Miss Marcella Mary O'Brien, who survives, as do the following other close relatives: Three daughters, Irene Kane, Benita Kane, and Carol Kane, all at home; two sons, Private Richard J. Kane, New Orleans, La. and Walter J. Kane, at home.

"Poor Marcella, what will she do?" they ask one another, shaking their heads at the dreadful news. Between the lines of the twelve-inch news column that summarized Eldon Kane's life, the people in our parish read a grim prognosis for his family, the oldest child in the army, the youngest barely two.

The discomfort that had been roaming through Eldon Kane's jaw and neck and shoulder had culminated Friday evening in excruciating pain. The tightness in his chest left him pale and sweating, nauseous, gasping for breath. Walter helped his father up the stairs and into the nearest bed. Marcella called the doctor and the priest.

Why had they been put to bed in their parents' room,

two-year-old Carol asked Benita that night. And why was their daddy in their bedroom, where he never, ever slept? His moaning confused and frightened them. Ten-year-old Benita lay still, trying, over the pounding of her heart, to make sense of the sounds below. Her mother's frantic murmuring into the telephone, followed by a cry of distress to Walter. "I can't reach Dr. Lynn! What am I going to do?' More telephoning. Interludes of silence. Footsteps on the stairs. Up and down, up and down. The front door opening and closing. A heavy-footed someone on the stairs. And then, the door opened to their bedroom and a slender figure appeared in the doorway.

"Are you Dr. Lynn?" asked Benita, sitting up, pulling the quilt around her shoulders as she peered into the dark. She made out a white collar, a skirted cassock, the pastor, Father Dunn.

"The Anointing Set," he said in a hoarse, hurried whisper. "Your mother told me it's in here, that you could find it for me."

"Why?" cried Benita. The priest here and asking for the Anointing Set with its candles and crucifix meant only one thing. Someone was dying. 'I want to see my daddy,' she said, and scrambled toward the edge of the bed. 'C'mon, Carol. Let's go see daddy.'

'Daddy,' said Carol and reached for Benita's hand.

'No, no, you girls are not to leave this room." Father Dunn extended imploring, nervous palms. "Now, will you get the Anointing Set for me, Benita, like a good girl?'

Persuaded by her awe of Father and her desire to be good, Benita got up, went to the closet, retrieved the item requested and presented it to him. As soon as the door closed behind him, she crept back beneath the quilt, where, for the sake of the little sister lying wide-eyed beside her, she swallowed back her tears. For what seemed to her a very long time, she lay quietly and listened to the footsteps moving up and down, up and down the stairs, the odd, shuffling sounds from the other side of the wall, the strange voices speaking in low, anxious tones.

Walter had helped the emergency team carry his father from the bedroom and down the steps. At the bottom, they set the stretcher down and angled it to negotiate the turn into the dining room. 'Walt,' whispered Eldon. "Take care of the girls.' Walter nodded, tight-lipped, then helped lift his father through the doorway, past the table, through the living room and the gaping doors of the waiting ambulance. Marcella got in and sat down beside her husband. A few hours later, Eldon looked up at her from his hospital bed. Suddenly, the pain clouding his blue eyes cleared; an expression of surprise overtook his face. He reached out to his wife for the last time.

Marcella is dazed and depleted and forty-one years old the Tuesday morning she stands with her children and relatives and fellow-parishioners in Mount Olivet cemetery south of town. September 14, 1943 is a day tender with autumn and azure skies, the Midwest's pacific passage to the gray siege ahead. She receives the flag that was draped over her husband's casket; she watches his body being lowered into the grave. When the bugler sounds the mournful notes of taps, she leans into the strength of the sons at her side, Richard, nineteen, home on emergency furlough, and Walter, seventeen, a high school senior. Benita clings to Walter's hand. Next to them is Irene, fifteen, holding two-year-old Carol, who is searching the faces of her siblings for the meaning of their sadness. Not until the last lonely note trails into silence and the first shovelful of dirt thumps against Eldon's casket, does Marcella turn and fall sobbing against Richard's chest. He holds her through the ominous salute of guns. The dead have been cared for, announces the battlefield tradition. Now the soldiers can go back to their fighting.

'We prayed for Eldon Kane at Novena,' announces my mother the following Friday when she returns home from the weekly service. 'Poor Marcella, what will she do?' Her sigh says she knows what it means to be alone, has felt firsthand the endless cycle of days when no one comes home, no husband arrives to separate day from evening with supper at the kitchen table. We miss the familiar rustle of newspaper pages turning, my dad in front of the radio talking back to the President. But we know his absence is temporary, and his care constant and tangible, and that he will return.

What *will* Marcella Kane do? Beyond the loss of her life's companion, the predictable loneliness and heavy responsibility, she faces a stern financial reality. The family's circumstances, never easy, are now precarious. The board and room paid by the relatives she puts up during the school year barely covers the cost of their keep. They will have to manage on her husband's pension as policeman and World War I veteran, meager amounts compared to their real need. Marcella casts about in her grief for explanations, weeps into her pillow at night, cries inwardly by day, questions God and laments fate—and finally, exhausted, she does what widows must do. She resigns herself to God's will and goes on, counting on her faith, prayer, God, and the church that mediates His grace, to see her through.

For a few weeks, she considers the possibility of going back to work as a school teacher and broaches the idea with Father Dunn who reminds her that she has a two-year-old child, that now more than ever, her other children need her reassuring presence in the home. And that's where her children find her when they come home from school day after day for the next years, intent at her sewing machine in the too-dim corner of the kitchen, earning a pittance as a seamstress. She alters hems and sleeves, repairs coats, fills orders for dresses and blouses and skirts. At one in the morning, when Walter comes home from his job at the bus garage, she is often still at her machine finishing a garment that someone wants at noon. She looks up and smiles, her eyes dull with grief and fatigue and worry. 'You're still up?' Walter asks, then starts toward the stairs, stops, turns back to the silhouette caught in the kitchen's lonely light. 'Mom, you should go to bed.'

What will *Benita* Kane do? That's the question on our minds when school finally opens that fall. I wonder how she will act, if she'll talk to anyone. I wonder what I should say to her, if I should tell her I'm sorry, or try to pretend her dad isn't dead. Talking about death feels risky; you might give God another bad idea. If Benita's dad could die at age forty-seven, what might happen to mine, who is sixty-two? I wonder if she'll play hopscotch or jump rope anymore, if, in fact, any of us ever will play with abandonment again, for, like so many adults in our world, we are now in uniform, too. Fifth grade is the demarcation line when girls are ordered out of worldly civilian dress and into plain, long-sleeved navy blue serge uniforms with detachable white collars and cuffs. Except for the bright red bow at our throats, we look like an army of juveniles in basic training for the nunnery. Benita's older sister, Irene, is relieved. No longer will she be humiliated by a free-spirited sister going to school in polka dots and plaids, looking as quaint as a Hutterite dressed for town.

Benita returns to school earnest and subdued. At first, the nuns lavish her with more kindness and patience and opportunity than they offer the rest of us. They pay her to do errands in the outside world. They arrange for her to take piano lessons in exchange for cleaning the music rooms. This gives her access to my exclusive route, but our bad experiences with nuns above ground has eroded our interest in their hidden life below. Among the kids, Benita's role is unchanged. She has always been a class favorite, the one we want on our side in games, as a guest at our birthday parties, for class officer, as our Valentine. But her saucy enthusiasm is gone. Every knock on the door of our classroom makes her eyes round with anxious conclusions. She fully expects that God, in his merciful, loving, mysterious way, will call her mother next. Sister begins to grow weary of her tragic outlook, to suspect that it's a way of getting more than her share of attention.

In August of 1944, three months after Walter graduates from high school, Marcella accompanies him on the bus to the train station across the river in Illinois. There, Walter boards the zephyr for Chicago where he will be processed into the Navy. As the train slides out of the station, Walter waves to his mother and hears his dad's whispered words, 'Take care of the girls.' He remembers his own silent nod. *I tried, Dad. I did what I could.* After Eldon Kane's death, Walter's boss at the bus garage had raised his salary to eighteen dollars per week; Walt gave ten of that to his mother. In the spring, he sold his car and gave her the cash. But, as it turns out, he can't keep the promise he made to his dad. He can't watch over his sisters.

Marcella waves until the train disappears. Walter is gone. She's alone with her three daughters, a family of women in a time of war. She turns and walks to the bus stop on the corner, waits for a few minutes, then sets out walking. She walks through East Dubuque, a seedy, tiny town of night clubs and bars where Iowans go to drink. The mid-morning streets are abandoned and silent except for the flutter of empty cigarette packages and candy wrappers dropped on the sidewalk last night. She keeps going, up over the bridge, across the Mississippi toward Iowa. Walking and crying and praying for her sons. *Lord, please watch over Walter. Please keep Richard safe. Please, Lord, bring my sons home.* Praying and crying as she goes up Dodge Street and as she climbs the short, steep street to Cleveland Avenue and home. When she goes inside to her daughters, she is out of tears.

The nuns teaching us in fifth and sixth grades seem hand-picked to test our mettle. They set out to rid us of our deadly, incipient sins. With frowns and chastisements and rulers and frantic punishments, they hone us for the cruel reality outside our childhood borders.

Everyone hold out their hands. Whenever Sister Josephine's mouth clenches and her steely eyes accuse us of perverse con-nivance, we prepare for wholesale punishment. We wince, slide sideways glances at one another and persevere knowing that after school, we will get revenge by belting out our version of the currently popular tune, 'Pistol Packin' Mama. *'Lay that ruler down, Jo, Lay that ruler down, ruler packin' sister, lay that ruler down.'* Now, Sister makes her way down each aisle with her three-sided ruler, delivering a blow to each palm. One of the boys extends his hand and gazes at her with expectant, long-suffering eyes, but as the ruler descends, he suddenly retracts his hand, causing her to lunge awkwardly, angrily, into his desk. It's a terrifyingly delightful sight. Roger may have taken things too far the day he anchored a yardstick across the aisle, near the floor between two desks. Sister steamed down the aisle in red hot anger over some mischief occurring somewhere, hit the yardstick and flipped forward. Roger helped her up, apologizing, swearing his innocence, explaining that he was conducting an experiment, that he wanted to be an architect. Aside from his inability to read, his future at that moment seemed too brief to accommodate any career.

All right. All of you will stay after school until somebody tells me who threw that eraser across the room. Sister Josephine stands before a roomful of ten-year-old kids devoted to team play and social cooperation and challenges them to narc or confess. The standoff reminds me of the day my mother and I turned to *ghee* in the dining room. Yet someone must have given in that day at school, or we'd still be there, locked in the stale prison of group guilt.

Write three hundred times, I will not chew gum in the classroom. Hand it in tomorrow. We figure out how to hold two pencils and write two lines simultaneously, a feat that takes longer, is more difficult, and looks exactly like what it is, but supplies the thrill of mutiny. We are eleven years old now and beginning to deal with the mutiny of our bodies, the physiological revolution within.

Mary Ann discovers an art book on a shelf in the back of our sixth grade classroom; inside are glossy pages of nudes, frolicking, reclining, brazen, somber, full-bosomed, round-buttocked people—primarily female people—with absolutely nothing on. It's a feast to share and Benita is among the first invited. Sister Philomena grows suspicious and saunters ominously over to the site. Her face goes scarlet; she puffs up like a ruffled hen. Whenever that happens, we know we're in for it. She thrashes us verbally for our prurient interests and orders Benita to the cloak room. We hear the furious reprimands, and then brisk, slapping sounds. The unseen assault stuns and somehow includes us. Bereft, fatherless Benita, our favorite classmate, has been chosen by Sister to be the sacrificial lamb. A dangerous new front seems to be opening up in a battle we don't understand.

My desk is across the aisle from Tommy Frey, whose presence has begun to affect my heart rate. He likes me for my spelling abilities, but I'm hoping to teach him to appreciate my dimples as well. I look over, whisper something irrelevant and smile. Sister Philomena sees me with the eyes in the back of her habit and whirls around. 'Virginia Holmberg!' she cries in outrage from the front of the room. A doomed stillness grips the class. 'Since you like Tommy Frey so much, just go over there and sit down in his desk with him.' I freeze in fear while she strides toward me. She stops beside my desk. I look sideways at the big, black rosary beads swinging from her belt. 'Up!' she orders. I stand. 'Now, sit down there with him.'

'I don't want to.'

'What? You don't *want* to? I'm telling you to. Now sit!' She points at the desk and Tommy cringing at the far edge. I bite my lip and shake my head *No*. 'Do as I say!' she shouts. 'Sit with him!' I don't move. She hits me and shoves me against the blackboard and begins slapping me about the neck and face. My barrette pops open; my hair tumbles over my eyes. I turn away. She yanks me by the hair and turns my face forward, thumping my head against the hard surface. The white collar of my uniform unsnaps and twists sideways. My red bow comes undone. I'm crying now. She steps back, florid-faced, nostrils flaring, and thrusts me back into my desk, then walks back to the front of the room.

I circle my arms on my desk and bury my face in them. A few minutes later, I wipe my eyes, straighten my collar and sit up. Mary Jane's eyes catch mine in a moment of bewildered empathy. I feel Tommy Frey's unstrung silence a few feet away. I lower my eyes in shame.

I have no memory of reporting to my mother the humiliating experience of that sixth grade day. But those vicious outbursts could not have continued if more mothers responded with the clarity and nerve of Hilda Saul, whose streak of assertiveness was displayed whenever she lit a cigarette or got behind the wheel of the family car. The day Sister Philomena caught Mary Jane and Benita talking in class and kept them after school to deliver her usual enraged walloping, Hilda saw the mark on Mary Jane's face, called the school and put Sister on notice: 'If you touch my daughter again, I'm coming over there and you'll take off that habit and you and I will settle the score.'

In the World War, the U.S. Army has suffered a serious reversal in its sweep from Normandy to the Rhine. Hopes for a quick end to the war have been dashed by stubborn German resistance. Now the Battle of the Bulge is raging, fierce and massive. Marcella opens her weekly letter from Richard with a premonition of bad news. *They're pulling the new guys out of OCS,* he wrote. *They need us in Europe.* She boosts Carol to her lap after supper and shows the girls the letter. She reads his signature aloud. *Lots of love to you and all the family, Rich.* She folds the page, chews on her lower lip and closes her eyes against her tears.

'Mom, he'll be okay, I know he will,' says Irene.

'Daddy will watch over him,' says Benita.

In April, Benita brings one of Richard's letters to school. The return address is 'Somewhere in Germany.' His note says, *Sure wish these Germans would break it up soon.. Would save a tremendous amount of everything, especially lives and wounds.* Benita tells the class that enemy soldiers are trying to kill her brother. That spring, she begins to plan her own death.

Because of the host of gruesome tales we've been told about martyrs, those courageous, holy men and women battered and scourged and slaughtered for their faith, Benita has come to believe that this ultimate sacrifice will be required of her. The war is turning around, which causes her to imagine that the Germans and Japanese will exorcize their leftover hatred by torturing Catholics. She is certain she lacks the necessary saintliness to endure. Therefore, she will preempt the dilemma by taking charge of her own demise. On April 30, after two weeks of mental preparation, she will lie down and expire. The designated day comes and goes and although she does lie down—for over an hour, in fact, utterly still and with her eyes closed—she fails to die, or even to go to sleep. Her Catholic upbringing has conquered her will. The air we breathe, the ground we walk upon is charged with the hidden presence of a God who has created all life and instilled in us a longing for it.

Ellen, one of the older girls in our class, gets her period. She doesn't tell us; we see the spot on her skirt. Seeing it makes me curious, then gloomy. Blood-stained rags loom in the future of every girl, it seems. Other than my lengthening legs, my body shows few signs of growing up. I'm contented in my puerile state, but now pressure to mature has begun. A new girl, two years older than the rest of us, joins our class. Her small head is set atop a gangly body. She has a wandering eye and a limp and carries her right arm in front of her like a paw. Her deformities fascinate us. She instructs us in sexual matters with an eager carelessness we mistake for expertise. Her description of 'fucking in the hay' makes the whole business sound disorderly and unromantic. I take my confusion to my brother, who is fifteen and has a paper route and a bike and easier access to forbidden knowledge.

On a Saturday morning he offers to take me on his bike to Grandview Park. I can ride myself by now, but I have to wait until Christmas for my first bike, a second-hand boy's model with a new coat of red paint. I clutch his forearm and boost myself up, balancing sideways on the bar between him and the handlebars. 'Keep your feet out of the spokes,' he commands. We ride down the gravel path between beds of blooming peonies into the park and the wooded area where John stops and points out where last night's lovers have been. 'See this?' he says, poking a stick into a thinnish, papery fragment lying in the grass. 'It's a rubber.' I find a stick and fasten the thing beneath it and push it around on the ground, while John presents an overview of the birds and the bees. The word for semen is 'jazz,' he says, then warns me never to utter it in front of our parents. The next evening, as we say goodbye to our dad at the front door, I blurt it, for no reason beyond an inability to contain it. John blanches; my knees go weak. Our dad says, 'You kids help your mother while I'm gone.'

Glorious news! Cantankerous Father Craney has been transferred to another parish. The reverence due him as Christ's representative requires us to restrain our exuberance. The question on our minds now is who will be our next priest? Who will teach religion? Coach football? Deliver sermons at Sunday Mass? Who will tell us how to behave and what to do to save our souls?

'You'll like the new priest,' Marcella promises her daughters when she returns home from early morning Mass in August. 'His name is Father Dunkel. He's young. Probably not much older than Richard.' Father Dunkel had emerged from the sacristy just as she finished her morning prayer before the vigil candle. When she stood, he approached her, holding out his right hand, smiling straight into her eyes. 'He looks kind,' she tells her daughters.

'What does your husband do, Mrs. Kane?' Father Dunkel had asked after they introduced themselves. The sudden tears pushing for release surprised Marcella. Meeting someone who didn't know about her loss revived it and caught her off guard. 'He's a policeman. I mean, he was. He died. Two years ago.' Father had taken her hand in both of his. 'I'm so sorry. That must be very hard. And. . .do you, are there children?' She told him about Richard and Walter, still in the service, and her three daughters at home. While she talked, he held her hand. When she finished, he said, 'A four-year-old child? You have a heavy responsibility. If there's ever anything I can do, Mrs. Kane. . .'

'What else does he look like?' asks Irene.

'Hmm-mm, well, I'd say about as tall as your dad. A nice smile. Brown hair. He was ordained just last month.'

On Sunday, Benita is standing with her mother and the rest of the congregation when the new priest enters the sanctuary with the altar boys. The people kneel while he places the covered chalice on the center of the altar, opens the Missal and returns to the foot of the altar. He makes the sign of the cross and says the opening words of the Mass. *Intro ibo ad altare Dei.* I shall go unto the altar of God. *Ad Deum qui latificat, juventutem meum.* To god the joy of my youth. She follows his movements during Mass. She sits close to her mother through the Gospel and sermon but her thoughts are on her dad. He loved the rhythm of Latin, the solemn ritual of Mass, even though he was never solemn himself. Right in the middle of Mass, he would wink and grin at Benita until she smiled back. Mary Jane liked to tag along with them on Sunday for the sake of that wicked smiling moment in church.

At Communion time, Benita kneels beside her mother at the rail and opens her mouth to receive the host on her tongue from Father's hand. After Mass, she kneels with her mother at the bank of vigil lights. When Father comes from the sacristy, Marcella rises and nudges Benita to stand, too.

'Father, I'd like you to meet my daughter. Benita. She'll be in seventh grade this year.'

Father Dunkel smiles down at Benita and puts his hand on her head in a priestly gesture of blessing.

'Benita. That's a name I've never heard before.'

'Her middle name is Ann,' Marcella says quickly, fearing

Father will think she ignored the church rule that said children should be baptized with a saint's name. She tells him about the bright, pretty girl she and Eldon met in Dubuque long ago, a charming girl from Mexico whose name was Benita. 'Right then and there, I decided to give that name to my next child. If it was a girl.'

'And she *is* a pretty girl,' says Father.

Benita blushes, lowers her eyes, drops her head and studies her feet. Her eyelids slowly lift and she risks an upward glance into his waiting blue eyes. He smiles.

First Communion, June, 1941

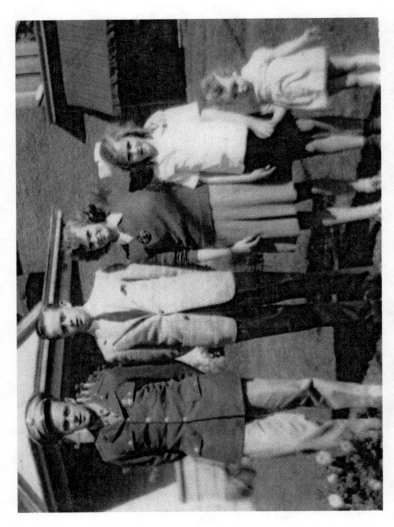

Kane children after their father's funeral: Richard, Walter, Irene, Benita, Carol

Age ten, 1943

Age eleven, 1944

Age twelve, 1945

Age thirteen, 1946

PART TWO

This isn't wrong

CHAPTER ONE

Testing the fortitude of teachers is an aptitude our class displayed early and refined throughout grade school, so that by the time we reach seventh grade and Sister Isidore, neither teacher nor students expect an easy alliance. Worse, she seems to dislike kids our age, especially girls, who spend sinful amounts of time smiling before mirrors. Every morning, she crosses her arms and plants herself like a hapless general in front of a feckless army of sixty twelve-year-olds. She tucks her plump, dimpled hands into the spacious sleeves of her habit, narrows her small, suspicious eyes on us and issues threats disguised as instruction. She is probably much younger than her pallid, moon-shaped face suggests, younger than her habit allows anyone to see, younger than we think it possible for any nun to be. She may drop into bed at night in tears or throw herself onto her cot in despair; she may beat her pillow out of frustration, or nip alcohol at midnight in the convent kitchen. Her anguish is not our concern.

We are under assault by our inconstant passions. Our bodies are spinning out of control; hair sprouts in odd, embarrassing places; pimples rage across our foreheads and over our enlarging, worrisome noses. Our blue and white uniforms announce that we are students at St. Columbkille Catholic school. Our Girl Scout uniforms say we are members of Troop 35. Our report cards rank us academically and evaluate us behaviorally. We're part of a family, a school, a parish, and, most significantly, a belief system. But suddenly, we've been thrust from that anonymous security onto a stage to perform before a fantasy audience. Applause, both real and imaginary, is the measure of our self-worth.

Sister Isidore does not appreciate our performances, nor does she reward them with applause. She claps her palms together often enough, but only as a cue that someone is about to be hustled off stage. (Clap!) *Sit down and behave yourself, Ellen.* (Clap!) *You girls over there, hush up and do your work.* (Clap!) *Mary Ann, go out to the hall and don't come back until you can quit distracting others.*

Father Dunkel, to the contrary, enjoys our theatrics. More: he enjoys *us*, the clamoring, unglamorous seventh grade girls. He's twice our age and good-looking in a sturdy, German way. Nothing is more flattering to our pliable, poetical souls than to be noticed by this young priest. Unlike the boys in our class, he generously and openly gives back the attention we lavish on him. The minute we spy him in the hall, or on the playground or the sidewalk in front of school, we flock to him, hungry pigeons in an Italian piazza competing for cast off crumbs. We watch his pale translucent blue eyes circle the group. Isabel thinks he's cute. Katie likes his heavy-lidded smile that seems to see straight into our souls. I admire the *oh* of his mouth as he exhales smoke rings. Often, as he stood smoking on the basketball court, we would close in on him with our unrehearsed routine, giggling and nudging each other out with blurted questions.

'Why do you smoke Philip Morris, Father?'

'Are they better than Lucky Strikes?'

'Father, can I have a cigarette?' Benita's voice.

Mary Jane jabs her with an elbow. '*May* you have a cigarette. *Can* means 'are you able?'

Father cocks an eyebrow at Benita. 'So *are* you able?' Without waiting for an answer, he puts his hand into the pocket in the sideseam of his cassock as if he means to comply. Instead, he keeps it there, fingering the outline of the pack while he looks at her. 'It will stunt your growth.'

'I'm as tall as I want to be.'

He brings out his cigarettes and shakes one out, but keeps his hand close to his waist and his eyes on her. 'Are you old enough to smoke?'

'I just want to see what they taste like.'

Elaine says, 'I want one, too.'

'Who else wants one?' he looks around wide-eyed at our stunned faces, as if he plans to dole them out.

'Damn dirty cigarettes,' my dad grumbles into my ear all the way from Mason City, Iowa. I put my hands behind my back, but several other girls hold theirs out.

Father gropes into his hidden pocket again. 'Any of you girls have a match?'

Shamefaced, we look at one another.

'Well, neither do I, so it looks like you're out of luck.' He slides the pack slowly back into the recesses of his cassock.

'We could light ours from yours.' Benita again. 'Like they do in the movies.'

He tilts his head and lifts an eyebrow at her. 'And what would your mother say if she found that out?'

'She doesn't have to find it out.'

He drops the half-inch butt onto the ground and rubs it out with his heel. 'But she would. . .' He smiles strategically.

Benita has begun to dally deliberately after school so that she'll arrive home after the country cousins have gone upstairs to do their homework. Yesterday when she came home, Father was sitting at the table, drinking coffee and chatting with her mother as she sewed a button on the jacket of his clerical suit. 'There's that girl of ours,' he said as she set her books down on the table. 'And what mischief has kept you so late?' He flicked ashes from his burning cigarette into their best ashtray that she had to wash with the supper dishes.

Marcella dislikes smoking in general, but classifies smokers according to their situation. She considers smoking by married men a frivolous use of money; any woman who puts nicotine to her lips marks herself as loose and unsavory (with the exception of Hilda Saul, her good neighbor); priests who smoke—and many, if not most, do—deserve special consideration. Few people, especially a devout woman like Marcella, would ever presume to judge a priest's habits. Men who have forsaken the comfort of a wife and family deserve some indulgences—fine whiskey, gourmet food, tobacco, and in the case of the archbishop, even a collection of fine art pieces (eventually sold to help pay off notes he'd signed in the name of the archdiocese in a dubious gold-mine scheme; it turned out to be a scam costing the diocese half a million dollars).

'Will you teach me to blow smoke rings?' I ask Father now, surprising myself and him with my ill-timed question, inserted out of a desire to be in on the wrongdoing, or at least, the attention.

The other girls break into self-conscious tittering.

'I'll teach all of you in high school,' he responds solemnly and pauses for effect as he gazes around the circle of incredulous eyes.

'You will?' blinks naive Eloise behind her heavy glasses.

'Honest?' says Mary. She and I are the youngest in the class, but her small stature and long curls give her the advantage of being presumed innocent by nuns.

'Sure. I'll teach you Latin. And religion. And maybe P.E. But smoking isn't on the curriculum.'

'Smoking is an extracurricular activity,' retorts Nancy. She's worldly-wise but diminutive, and like Mary, treated more temperately by the nuns who seem to assume docility in a girl who is small or quiet.

Father throws back his head and laughs appreciatively. 'You girls are too much for me.' His tone says he enjoys being overwhelmed by us.

We watch for opportunities to hang around him, improvising scenarios to gain his attention. He's never difficult to find. He hovers on the brink of our activities.

'Today's my birthday, Father.'

'Well, so, Happy Birthday! How old are you?'

'Twelve.'

'You look older.'

A burst of giggles.

'How old are *you*, Father?'

'Old enough to know better.'

'But too young to do it,' mouths Nancy to the group at large.

A wave of laughter rises and subsides into awkward silence.

Eloise comes to our rescue. 'Did you ever have a girlfriend, Father?'

'Never.'

'Not even one?'

'Nope.'

'Oh, I bet,' comes a chorus of voices.

'How much?'

'I bet a quarter you had a girlfriend in high school.'

'I wanted to be a priest.'

'Does that mean you couldn't even *like* a girl?'

'It means you owe me a quarter.'

The fascination we imagine in Father's eyes during those playground encounters makes it easier for our awkward, uncertain, pubescent selves to imagine the charming, savvy females we someday will be. In a world before Beatles, he is our swaggering hero whose approval makes our dreams plausible. When his glance begins to fall more and more often on Benita, we're disappointed and envious, but not surprised. The hint of melancholy in her eyes ever since her father's death is a mystery only a priest can understand.

Perhaps our daily dramatics are what inspired Sister Isidore to challenge us with a bona fide on-stage opportunity. She announces that our class, in conjunction with the sixth grade, will present a musical version of the play, *Tom Sawyer*. A certain few students are always chosen for leading roles; another predictable set fills in the supporting cast; the leftovers are disposed of in crowd scenes or as stage hands. Sister tries to inject a note of equality by mixing one or two class favorites into the crowd scenes. But the musical aspect of *Tom Sawyer* requires kids who can and will sing solo on stage.

Boldly, I begin hoping for the role of Becky Thatcher, Tom's girlfriend, partly because that would mean daily proximity to the most sought-after boy in seventh-grade, David McCann, who has been selected for that role. David is smart, athletic, good-looking and self-confident, a powerful combination that alternately draws me to him and frightens me away. There is also the matter of Benita. She and David have a crush on one another. He sends notes up the aisle to her during class. She reads them with a sly smile and scribbles a reply. Every evening he walks his neighbor's dog the six or seven blocks from his house on South Grandview

Avenue past her house on Cleveland Avenue. And every evening, just as he happens to stroll by her front door, Benita happens to come out. After they say a surprised, 'Oh, hi!' they stand on the sidewalk and talk while the restless dog sniffs and pees and wanders the circumference of their flirtation.

Obviously, pretty, blonde Benita is the logical best choice to play Tom's pretty, blonde girlfriend, Becky. Even so, I go to bed at night imagining myself singing sweetly onstage to my boyfriend, Tom. When Sister names me to play Amy Lawrence, the neighbor girl who gets to sing a solo but *doesn't* get Tom, I feel disappointed relief. Benita doesn't get him, either. A sixth-grader does. Benita flits in the background as one of a dozen Sunflower girls, tilting their faces to the bright side of life on the Mississippi.

Two more classmates get the 'curse.' All of the girls seem to be developing breasts. I turn around and around with dismay before the bedroom mirror at night, posing from various angles, trying to determine if the hesitant swells on my chest will ever amount to anything. I discover a collection of tiny lumps beneath the nipple area and report that fact to my mother who, true to her Irish heritage, assumes the worst and takes me to a doctor. He taps and pokes and frowns over the relevant territory.

'Her nipples are inverted.' He addresses my mother as if I'm either deaf or disconnected from the diffident nipples under discussion. 'Nothing here to worry about, though.'

Nothing here?

He chats on, oblivious to the bruising effect of his callous words. If my current shape is predictive, I will never be as well-endowed as the other Virginia in our class, whose curving femininity has begun to strain against the strict seams of her school uniform. The boys pretend to avert their eyes when she walks past, but I've seen their quick, fascinated glances and the grins they toss to one another. 'She's beginning to develop, that's all,' the doctor reassures my mother as I button my blouse. Giddy with hope, I take his promise home to my mirror.

Benita has helped her mother with the laundry often enough to see and suspect the long, narrow bloodied rags washed and spread out on the grass to bleach in the sun; she's asked her mother about them. 'You'll find out when you need to know,' came the reply. The rags are an outward sign of an unspeakable inner mystery. We've been immersed in mystery from the moment the priest poured water over our infant heads and transformed us into children of God and heirs of heaven. We're awed by mystery at every Mass when the bells ring and the priest says 'This is my Body, this is my Blood.' We approach mystery with every trip to the Communion rail. But the mystery staining these rags is specific to female bodies; this blood is the sign of genital organs and sexual impulse and the whole tale of the corrupt human condition. The mystery of menstrual periods is called 'the curse.'

Benita decides to forego the process. Nor does she intend to bother with breasts. With them comes a division of roles that she deeply resents—an indoor life of housekeeping for girls, while boys go right on playing basketball outside. For an intelligent girl like Benita, with long, shapely legs, a fetching face and a desirable boy doting on her, it's easy to dismiss the importance of a bosom.

Until we're fully, flagrantly female we can carry on as carefree outdoor kids. We imitate the man who walks down the boulevard every Monday afternoon, pausing at each telephone pole to introduce himself and circle it twice. If a car slows down and the driver cranes his neck to puzzle over our activity, we wave and go around the pole again. On Halloween, we climb trees in the yards along Grandview and pitch apples at passing cars. When Benita lobs one through an open window and hits the woman passenger, we drop to the ground and scatter into the nearby bushes. In winter, we tow sleds and skis to the golf course and squeal with terrified delight as we speed out-of-control down steep hills. In spring, whenever we have ten minutes and nine girls, we dash to the empty lot across from school for a game of baseball. We scream and yell like savages protesting the restrictions looming. One Saturday afternoon, we hear the sound of nuns playing ball behind the hedge of the convent lawn, no doubt the robust, young farm girls who grew up chasing cows and stacking hay. Imagining it repels us. The idea of a nun hitching up her habit, of Sister Isidore or Sister Josephine running and shrieking and playing with abandon is as disgusting as the slightest hint that our parents engage in sex.

Whenever we wish to practice our feminine wiles, we turn to Father, our reliable, ubiquitous testing site. He shows up after our Girl Scout meetings, on the playground at recess, whenever and wherever two or three of us are gathered together. Our Girl Scout leader is a puppeteer and suggests a marionette show as the entertainment for the annual dad-daughter date night. We work for weeks, making our own puppets, designing and sewing their clothes, learning to maneuver them with strings and finally practicing the show on stage in the parish hall. I know my dad can't come across Iowa on the train for a Girl Scout puppet show on a random Wednesday evening, but I feel entitled to verbalize my self-pity. 'Take your brother,' my mother says, fed up. Only if she had tossed out 'Take Edward Beach,' our elderly, reserved English neighbor, could she have been more convincingly obtuse. I cannot imagine sitting with my brother, John, across the table from Mary Jane and Katie and Sally and their dads, dignified, full-fledged men. I feel as forlorn and fatherless as Benita.

Father Dunkel senses my woe. On an evening when we're rehearsing our puppet show, I exit the stage and encounter him in the doorway of the abandoned parish kitchen. 'Hey, Virgie,' he says, gently. No one has ever called me that. It sounds grown up, slightly naughty, meant for someone else. He catches me by my left shoulder and restrains me against the doorframe as he talks to me, his earnest blue eyes looking for a long minute directly into mine. Then his hand drops lower and stops where the girlish swell of my breast begins. He keeps it there and keeps on talking while he presses his palm against that tender, beating place. I look back at him, trying to comprehend his words while my body struggles to understand the language of his hand. Part of me is reluctant to stir; another part wants to flee. Footsteps move closer. He lets me go. I wonder about this, but not from the angle of sin. Sins are something we commit and priests forgive. Father had rested his hand close to a forbidden zone, but it was possible that, like the doctor, he thought there was nothing there to worry about. Or maybe his hand slipped there by accident. In any case, whom would I have told? And what was there to say?

One morning after early Mass, Marcella expresses to Father her sadness that Benita is the only Girl Scout without a dad to invite to dad-daughter date night. Immediately, he volunteers. Each Girl Scout is responsible for preparing the box lunch for herself and her dad, but Father is no ordinary dad, Marcella reminds Benita, and therefore, she will fix the lunch, which will not be ordinary either. She will make the special minced ham sandwiches that Eldon had loved.

Father loved them, too. He told Benita so at the supper. He leaned over and whispered, 'And you're the prettiest Girl Scout here. The smartest, too, I bet.' He told her how lucky he was to be her date for the evening. She's still glowing when we meet backstage to put on our marionette show. She manipulates the strings confidently, as if her puppet is the star. Father claps and smiles and nods approval. When he takes Benita home, he tells Marcella he's never eaten better minced ham sandwiches. 'Your husband was a lucky man, Marcella. And so am I. Anytime Benita needs a stand-in dad, let me know. I'd be honored to help you out.'

Marcella is delighted at this news. No one will ever fill the void left by Eldon, but here is a priest, someone she can turn to with trust, offering help. Marcella assumes her children want to be good and will be, if she gives them guidance and appropriate rein, which the neighborhood of like-minded people helps implement. Mrs. Kennedy has told her that Benita, David, Mary Jane and Tommy met one Saturday afternoon on the city bus and went downtown to a matinee. The McCann's are an admirable family; David is a good boy and Benita is in no sense a wayward girl, but she's reached that restless age when one word from a father can be more effective than two hundred from a mother. Marcella counsels her from her sewing machine, looking up with pins in her mouth and weariness in her eyes as she tries to hear her daughter's girlish concerns over the anxieties blaring in her own mind. But Benita's young heart contains more questions than she has time or energy to answer. Now Father, a man of God, is holding out a guiding, fatherly hand. He's the answer to her prayer, someone who will help steer Benita along the right path.

The next dad-daughter affair is a breakfast sponsored by the Holy Name Society to be held in the parish hall after Sunday Mass. My loyal, law-abiding Catholic dad belongs to this group, of course, and luckily, the breakfast is scheduled on one of his rare weekends at home. I look forward to the sound of his deep laugh and the rough feel of his big, working-man's hand around mine. After nine-thirty Mass, my sister and I go off with him to the parish hall. We're hungry. We've been fasting since midnight in order to receive Communion. As we push through the buffet line and heap scrambled eggs and pancakes onto our plates, the door opens and in comes Father Dunkel with Benita. There she is, twelve years old and entering the crowded parish hall with a man whose sturdy shoulders were draped moments ago in regal vestments. The priest who stood in Christ's stead at the altar and in His name said the words of consecration over the bread and wine, *This is my Body, This is My Blood* is now cast as Benita's dad.

I want to sit at the table with them. 'No,' says my dad. 'I can't stand being around those damn cigarettes.' He motions us to a nearby table. *Damn* is a word he uses to spice up his sentences; I like the earthy, masculine sound of it. *Goddamn* bursts out of him only when he's trying to fix the lawn mower or my bike and frustration temporarily wins out over his promise to the Holy Name Society. He is not clever mechanically. Nor is he skilled at interpreting the emotions of adolescent daughters. I sulk through breakfast; Anne Marie grumbles at me for wanting my own way; our dad asks between bites, 'What's wrong with you girls?'

At the table where I long to be, Father Dunkel hooks his arm around Benita's chair, leans over and says into her ear, 'You're the prettiest girl here. And I'm a lucky man to be in your company.' Afterward, they walk the two blocks to her house and he thanks Marcella for loaning him her daughter for the morning. 'She's a very special girl, Marcella.' Benita watches her mother smile and nod at Father in eager agreement. She liked hearing her dad say these words but Father's praise makes her stomach tighten.

'Marcella Kane's older son is home,' my mother says one summer day in 1946. 'Bernice McCleary said she saw them walking down Grandview the other evening.' Marcella's prayers have been answered. Richard is safely home but with him has come a burden of distressing memories. He had been among the troops under General Bradley's command during the continuous offensives that crushed the remains of the German forces in the Ruhr. He'd helped mop up after that attack, taken part in the battle of Leipzig, gone on to meet the Soviets on the Elbe River.

On those long summer evening walks with Richard, Marcella listens as he describes his terrified weeks in a fox hole, the sound of shells whistling overhead, bombs exploding nearby, men crying out in panic and pain. He had experienced a dread so constant that he began to long for the certainty of death. He had witnessed a hunger so devastating that he feels obligated to reprimand Benita and Carol for the least sign of waste. Walter was on a destroyer in the Caribbean near Guantanamo, Cuba when the war ended. He returns in July in a calmer frame of mind, eager to rekindle his romance with Jo, the girl he left behind.

Richard and Walter often accompany their mother to morning Mass. She introduces them to Father, the man her letters taught them to appreciate. 'The new priest isn't much older than you, Richard,' she'd written. 'But he's like a father to Benita. So kind and solicitous. She's getting back some of the sparkle she lost when your dad died.' When she wrote to Walter that Father loved minced-ham sandwiches, his worries subsided; his dad's dying request, 'Take care of the girls,' was being answered by a priest. As Marcella's sons shake hands with Father, they thank him and say how hard it was to leave their mother and three sisters alone to fend for themselves. They tell him his kindness was an answer to their prayers.

One Saturday evening, Walter asks Father to join them for a family penny-poker game. Father arrives after he finishes hearing Confessions, notifying them apologetically that he won't be able to stay long because he has early Mass the next day. Yet, he stays on, laughing and relaxed, a cigarette constantly smoldering in the ashtray next to him. When Walter opens a beer, Irene asks Father if he'd like one. A beer would be great, but a bourbon would be even better, if they have any on hand, replies Father glancing from her to Walter to Marcella and stopping his eyes on Benita. He smiles at her. She looks back soberly and says, 'I'd like a beer.'

'Benita!' Irene's eyes widen in alarm. Her brothers laugh. Father says, 'Beer is not a drink for young girls, Benita.' She wrinkles up her nose.

A few weeks later, Marcella invites Father to come along with the family on a Sunday afternoon picnic in the country. 'Only if you promise to make those minced ham sandwiches,' he says. He arrives at their creekside site dressed in his black clerical slacks, but instead of his usual Roman-collared shirt and suit jacket, he is wearing a snug white T-shirt that shows off the muscles in his shoulders and arms. His appearance flusters Benita; he looks part priest and part man and acts like part of their family. He tells Marcella he'd love another sandwich; he asks Walter for a second beer and winks at Benita as he opens it.

Late one Sunday afternoon, he pulls up to the Kane household with a woman in the front seat of his car. He's brought his mother from the family farm near Dyersville to meet Marcella, who would have been honored to meet the mother of any priest, but is particularly thrilled to meet this mother of eleven who has raised this good and generous man. Just as Father predicted, the two women form an immediate friendship. A bond is developing between their sons, too; Father is priest, big brother and friend to Richard and Walter. By winter, the man telling Benita regularly how special she is to him, is special himself to her entire family.

My dad retires and returns home from Mason City that same summer. I'm twelve now and my mind is on eighth grade. He lingers at loose ends in the kitchen and watches our daily routine as if it's a parade passing by. He reads the newspaper while I practice the piano. Afterward, he claps in an obligating way. He nags my sister to work harder in school. When I sit with a book in the living room, he asks what I'm reading, but doesn't listen for my answer. He and my mother drive to daily Mass. Afterward, he makes coffee and takes up his post in the kitchen. There's an air of resignation about him, as if he has no hope of marching in step with us again.

Benita is glad to have her brothers home, even though it means ironing their shirts and crowding back into the bedroom with Carol and her mother. When the country cousins return in the fall, they take over the 'girl's' bedroom vacated when Irene left for nurses' training.

Richard and Walt regularly invite Father to join their family poker games. He maneuvers to sit next to Benita. In the guise of instructor, he rests his arm on the back of her chair, cups his hand around his mouth and leans close to whisper strategy into her ear. Richard and Walter consider him the ideal male advocate for their mother and sisters. His attentiveness frees them to look forward again, to get jobs, enroll in college, court girls and resume their own lives. When Carol starts kindergarten in September, Marcella applies for a part-time job doing alterations at a downtown clothing store.

For her thirteenth birthday, August 4, 1946, Benita receives a five-year-diary. The squat, missal-sized book consists of a few blank lines designated for each day from eighth grade through high school. It is a prescient gift in which she records her fears and dreams.

The tall, slender, intelligent nun who is our eighth grade teacher is our reward for surviving the three previous demoralizing years. Sister Edward finds joy in teaching and worthy traits in thirteen-year-old students. She likes us with a disarming straightforwardness that encourages us to see ourselves less like troublesome rowdies and more like real people with potential. She demands our best, which implies a core of good exists, which, in turn, inspires us to work to uncover it. The kids abandoned as unteachable since second grade are moved to the front of the room and attended to. She drills all of us in our native tongue; we compete in spelling bees, learn parts of speech, diagram sentences that grow in complexity until they spill off the page. She asks the class, even the girls, what we want to be some day. Most of us change our minds every other week, but Benita answers consistently and with conviction, 'I'm going to be an astronomer.' In that case, says Sister, plan to go to college.

'Mrs. Swift called,' Marcella cheerily tells Benita one evening that fall. 'She asked if you were available to clean her house. I told her yes, you were very good at cleaning.' Benita's mouth drops open. 'You told her I would? Without even asking me? Mom, I don't want to clean Mrs. Swift's house!'

'Why not? She'll pay you well. I don't understand. It's a chance to earn. . .'

'I don't want to be Mrs. Swift's maid. I don't want to clean her house.'

Marcella sighs. 'I'm sorry, honey. I thought. . .well, now what will I do? I'll have to call her and tell her . . .'

'Never mind. I'll *do* it. Just don't take any more jobs for me.'

Sister Edward is as wan as Sister Isidore, but we've come to accept pallor as natural to creatures who dwell indoors and tunnel between buildings. Some of us suspect that sex is what puts color into a woman's cheeks. That, or rouge, neither of which is permissible, or available to nuns. Their commitment to self-denial is their business, but their compulsion to impose it on us makes us bristle. Girls in our school are not allowed to wear makeup of any kind, even in high school, not the slightest trace of lipstick, certainly not mascara or eye shadow. No painted hussies will stalk the halls of St. Columbkille's. Women make themselves up for one obvious reason: to incite male desire. If we learn only one thing in this school, it will be the undesirability of sexual desire. No one says that in those words, but the implication is omnipresent. Desires of the soul and mind for God are encouraged as good. Passions of the flesh are a menace to fear, a powerful, seductive force that makes men weak and causes them to lose control. Orgasm (another word that no one says) is the prime example. Woe to woman, provocateur of desire, who confounds man's reason and robs him of power.

Woe to us, then, because our first boy-girl social has been scheduled, a Halloween costume party and dance to be held in the parish hall. Dancing complicates things. Now I must design a costume that will attract both boys and prizes. I convert a suit box into a three-dimensional playing card with an elaborate crayon drawing of the Queen of Spades on front and back. The costume encases me from neck to knees. Mary Jane and Benita outfit themselves as matching dice. Their square white boxes with painted-on black dots end at their thighs, revealing long, shapely legs sheathed in black stockings for all the boys to admire. A cumbersome Queen has no chance of competing with those leggy dice. I give my costume to Mary Ann and become a Hawaiian dancer in a hastily constructed crepe paper grass skirt. I stumble around the dance floor twice with a boy who is not Tommy Frey. Mary Ann wins the prize for 'most unusual costume.' Benita and Mary Jane are the evening's popular, dazzling duo.

Just before Thanksgiving, Benita gets the 'curse.' Her mother explains the long, narrow rags she's seen on the lawn and gently shows her how to use them. But unlike the other girls, Benita does not come to school and excitedly announce her plight to us over lunch or whisper it to a friend in the cloakroom. She stands as pale as a nun on the sidelines at recess and watches us with the doomed eyes of a saint fated to tangle with lions. A sprinkling of pimples decorate her chin.

Father catches her by the shoulder in the hall, touches a fresh, plump pimple with his index finger and asks, 'Where'd you get the hickey?'

'Hickey?'

He touches another spot. 'Here, too.'

She chews on her lip and looks away.

'You'd better not be sneaking off with that Grandview Avenue boy,' he says and walks away.

She feels exposed and ignorant. Does Father know something about her that she doesn't know. 'Teresa!' she calls and catches up to her friend. 'What's a hickey?' she whispers.

'Something you get from kissing. I *think*. Want me to ask my sister?'

'No! Don't say anything to anybody.'

'Why? Did David kiss you?'

'No! All we do is talk.'

'Even in the movies? When it's dark?' Teresa lives three doors down the street from Benita. She knows about Benita meeting David on the bus for the matinee downtown. Somebody told her that David put his arm around Benita in the darkened theater. Somebody else said they'd kissed.

'Just forget I asked. Okay?'

'Okay.'

'And don't tell anybody about the, the. . .'

'The hickey?'

'Teresa! Shhh-hh!' Benita looks around.

'Jeez, what's wrong with you anyway?'

'It's a zit. And I don't want to talk about it. Okay?'

Benita's permanent fatherless condition earned Father's attention in a way that my temporary deprivation never did. In eighth grade, he is again her lucky Girl Scout dad. He uses the occasion to tell her, with an arm around her shoulder, how fortunate he feels. 'You're the prettiest girl here. And the smartest, too, I bet.' Gradually, it becomes clear that they have sealed a pact, more personal than his role as family friend. His eyes search her out, stop on her, follow her down the halls of school.

She mulls over the issues of Father and kissing and zits in her diary.

Kissing is becoming a popular subject. People either have been kissed or pretend they have. During lunch hour one day, Patty says casually that Father Dunkel tried to kiss her. That's Patty. Her imagination brims with strange stories brought home by her dad, a traveling salesman who ventures regularly into the flat, foreign, non-Catholic country unrolling from our lofty locale.

Kissing is on my mind as I ride my bike down Rowan Street after school a few afternoons later. According to my calculations, I've been kissed once, in second grade, when Donald O'Shea suddenly leapt from his desk, bussed my cheek and sat back down. Whether desire or dare inspired this act didn't count. I slow in front of Tommy Frey's house and toss the *Telegraph Herald* onto their front porch. My brother has hired me to help him carry his paper route, a lucky break for me because it takes me by Tommy's yard every day and I'm waiting for him to happen to come out the way Benita does when David walks by. But he never does. Boys don't choose girlfriends because they've won spelling bees, I'm finding out. And they don't want to walk very far to see them, either. If only I lived near the school, so my house would be more convenient. If only I would get the 'curse,' so I would have some shred of hope for my future as a woman.

Because I live so far from the center of things, spontaneous peer gatherings often occur without me. I learn about the excitement later, for example, the Saturday morning when Benita and several other girls encountered a group of boys making their way home from altar boy practice. The girls dared the boys to knock on the door of a Protestant minister's house across the street. The boys embellished the dare by shouting, 'Come out, Reverend, and hear our confessions!' The minister telephoned our pastor, Father Dunn, who had a reputation—and a talent—for subduing rambunctious boys in the rectory.

Missing out on the trouble is disconcerting to me; missing out on boy-girl encounters is a calamity. How will I ever become the object of some boy's crush, living as I do on the fringe of everything? Then, miraculously, one winter evening, several of the boys from my class make their way down Grandview Avenue to my house. They gather under the street light, jostling and joking, while my heart cheers them on from my bedroom window. I hear the window in my parents' street side bedroom slide up. I hear my dad bellow, 'Hey! You guys out there! Move on!' The window goes down with an emphatic *wham*. The boys scatter. My dad grumbles to my mother, 'They're like a damn pack of dogs after a female in heat.' I fall onto my bed in embarrassed outrage. My dad has shattered my romantic hopes and coarsened my emerging desires.

That spring, my friends and I begin committing another sin he reviles—smoking—although no one has mastered inhaling yet so perhaps it isn't a full-blown sin but only an occasion of one, except that our method of obtaining cigarettes may have broken a commandment or two. Usually Sally crosses the street from her house to Sullivan's grocery store and charges a pack of Camels to her dad's account. If the regular trusting grocer isn't on duty, she slips a few cigarettes from her dad's pack on the buffet. Or Mary Jane eases a pack out of the middle of her mother's carton, then shakes the rest into the extra space. As a last resort, Benita forages for the long, snuffed out butts left in the living room ashtray by her brother, Richard, a chain smoker.

Clutching our illicit goods, we run to the south edge of town and the pastures where Catfish creek meanders. There, we sit in a circle, like Buddhists at meditation, and light up. We're determined to learn to inhale. Week after week, we gulp and choke and make ourselves dizzy, then dig a hole and bury the remainder of the pack, set a rock on top and arrange a few branches over the site and go home. Sometimes we hold contests to see who can smoke the greatest number of cigarettes. The winner is automatically our president. When the June sun warms to July, Mary Jane dares Eloise to take off her clothes and jump into the creek. She does, then dares Mary Jane back and soon, all of us are splashing wickedly naked in the muddy water, 'Here come the boys!' someone screeches and we scramble to the bank for our clothes. In spite of our hopes, the boys never show up.

Even during the summer, the school and church function as our gathering place because that's where we can find Benita doing her cleaning. Often Mary Jane is there, too, helping a nun make hosts for Mass. One afternoon, as we stand on the basketball court making plans for a venture to Catfish Creek, Father Dunkel pops up, dressed as usual, in his cassock.

'So you girls are sneaking off to smoke?'

We look at one another and shrug, deadpan.

'Where are you getting your cigarettes? '

Sally begins making a circle in the gravel with the toe of her tennis shoe. The rest of us watch her.

'Holmberg!' He turns stern eyes on me. 'Do you smoke?'

I hate being called by my last name. 'Virgie' appeals to me more, but he no longer calls me that. 'Me? My dad would kill me, Father.'

'And you?' He turns to Benita. 'Does your mother know what you're up to?'

'Sure, Father. My Mom knows everything.'

'Oh?' His tone says he knows better. The rest of us take advantage of his distraction with her to scurry off with our guilt.

As I get on my bike to go home, I can see Father in his long skirt and Benita in her rolled-up jeans standing together. A few feet away lingers Teresa, waiting to walk home with Benita. When Father and Benita set out toward the rectory, she waves and goes on her way alone.

I pedal off, too, but I'm uneasy thinking about Benita in that dimly-lit, fearsome rectory where boys are punished for teasing the Protestant minister.

As Teresa passes Benita's house, Marcella calls from the front door. 'Is Benita coming?'

'Yeah, pretty soon. Father's talking to her.'

Marcella smiles and closes the door.

Two blocks away, in the low light of the rectory parlor, Father faces Benita. 'I'm concerned about you. You're a special girl to me, Benita. You know that.'

She fastens her gaze on the floor.

He cups her chin, lifts her face until she meets his eyes. 'What

I'm saying is, I'd hate to see you get hurt.'

'Hurt? Why? Who would hurt me?'

'Those kids with fancy addresses think they're better than the kids on Cleveland. I've warned you about them before.'

'They're my friends, Father. We have fun.'

He leans closer and peers at her neck. 'Another hickey, I see.'

Benita pulls away. 'It's a zit.'

He gives her a gloating look. 'I saw you swinging your hips in front of that McCann boy.'

Benita shifts from one foot to another but says nothing.

'What would your mother think?'

'But I didn't. . .I don't. . .she doesn't think that.'

'Just remember what I said.' He keeps his eyes on her for a long, silent moment. Then he slides his hand into his pocket and takes out his pack of cigarettes. He slips one out, lights it and offers it to her.

She backs up a step and shakes her head.

'You don't want it?' He puts it between his own lips, shakes three cigarettes from the pack and hands them to her. 'Here. Take these. Now quit stealing cigarettes. It's a sin.' She looks at him and hesitates. He pushes them toward her. 'If you need money, I'll arrange a job for you.'

'You will? What would I do?'

'Clean. You'll help clean the church.'

Father reaches for her hand, turns it palm upward and closes her fingers around the three cigarettes. He keeps her hand in his and says gently, 'Let's keep this between us. I don't want you to get into trouble with your mother.'

Benita tells her diary that night that Father gave her three curlers, our code word for cigarettes, and that he has promised her a job cleaning the church. Now she won't have to be some lazy, rich woman's servant.

When she brings her own Philip Morris cigarettes to Catfish Creek, we wheedle for her source. 'They're a gift,' is all she'll say.

CHAPTER TWO

Veni, vidi, vici, declared Julius Caesar when he returned triumphantly to Rome after his decisive victory over the king of Pontus at Zela in 47 BC. We hear these words for the first time as fourteen-year-old high school freshmen in Sister Agnes' Latin class. To our dismay, Father Dunkel is not teaching first year Latin. That makes the religion class he does teach much more significant. We vie for conspicuous seats in front and solicit attention with flamboyant questions. *God made us, but who made God? Could God build a mountain so high he couldn't jump over it? Was Jesus a Catholic?*

Until our sophomore year, we are subject to Sister Agnes' metal ruler and her deadly rendition of Caesar's conquests. Far more intriguing to us is the popular love song, 'These Foolish Things,' which translates the emperor's bellicose boast into the language of sweet surrender. We thrill knowingly at the image of a cigarette bearing lipstick traces; we imagine being overtaken and swept away even though that nebulous, climactic event is beyond our repertoire of experience. Our yearning girlish hearts feed on the promise that some day, inevitably, we will be possessed by the love of a powerful man. The culture has told us that passivity and surrender are the essential ingredients of romantic love, indeed, of religion itself. Submission to a higher power, whether to God, a guru, the patriarchy, a lover, a cause, or simply fate, is the way to holiness. Happiness, too.

All that emphasis on acquiescence implies an oppositional tendency in women, a trait that needs to be quelled. Yet, metaphorically and literally, most women of that era were transported through life as passengers in vehicles driven by men. Otherwise, they did what my mother did: walked, took the city bus or stayed home. When Father stops fourteen-year-old Benita after school in the early fall of ninth grade and asks if she would like to learn to drive, she thinks she's misheard.

'Me?' Her voice breaks with surprise.

He nods and smiles straight into her eyes. 'Yes. You. If you want to learn, I'll teach you.'

'Am I old enough?' She tries to feign calm even though her imagination is leaping to the glory ahead. Father is offering to teach *her*, Benita Kane, to drive his new 1947 Dodge, a splendid cream-colored car with red wheels.

'Not yet,' he says. 'But you will be. By the time you learn, you will be.' He lights a cigarette, takes a few puffs, narrows his eyes on her. 'We'll start today. After school.'

'I can't. I have to clean the stupid music rooms after school.'

'I can arrange that.' Father reaches out and rests his hand on her shoulder. 'So. It's settled. Meet me at 3:30 at that empty lot near the corner of Cleveland. As soon as I stop, jump into the car and get down so no one will see you.'

She hesitates. Sneaking doesn't appeal to her.

'Don't worry. Everything will be okay.'

Her concern pales before this astonishing opportunity. She gives him a shy smile. 'I do want to learn.'

After school, she flees the rest of us and goes up Holly Street, then left, around the corner and down the hill to the place he'd assigned for their meeting. Within seconds, the Dodge appears. Father is in his clerical garb. He opens the door. 'Hurry.' He half pulls her onto the seat. 'Down!' he commands. 'Put your head on my lap.' They drive away.

Her cheek is pressed against his thigh, into the black serge pungent with cigarettes and that same spicy male odor that drifts through the confessional screen. She wonders if he can feel her heart thumping. 'Keep down until I tell you to sit up,' he says. 'Are you okay?' he asks when she doesn't respond. Her 'yes' is muffled against his leg. He lifts one hand from the wheel and waves. 'Your brother's girlfriend.' Benita goes weak. She's sure Jo can see her curled up on the front seat of Father's car. Father lights a cigarette. 'I bet you want one, too.' Before she can decide what to say, he says, 'Maybe later. After your lesson.' From the corner of her eye, she alternately watches the blue September sky going by and his black oxford pivoting from the gas pedal to the brake. They drive for what seems a long time before he stops. 'You can sit up now.' She is tousled and disoriented, too embarrassed to look at him. The white water towers she sees in the distance tell her they are in the countryside west of town. A scary thrill goes through her.

Father, calm and officious in his black suit and Roman collar, pushes back the seat, spreads his legs wide and pats the space in between. 'Sit here in front of me.' She hesitates. 'C'mon,' he says. She slides along the seat and works herself over his right thigh. He takes hold of her shoulders and settles her between his legs. She puts her hands on the wheel, aware of the warmth of his body, of his breath, of the sureness of his hands as he puts them over hers. He keeps his foot on the gas pedal. 'One thing at a time,' he says. 'First, you need to get the feel of steering.' He guides her hands on the wheel. 'Think of a clock. Right hand on the four, left hand on the ten.' He helps her ease into 'drive' and they glide away from the side of the road and go slowly, slowly, along the gravel road, right at the junction, down the next road. They drive past the water towers and over a rough stretch of gravel that jiggles the wheel and her hands, too. Benita giggles. 'It tickles.' He grips her hands tighter. The road tunnels through ochre-colored fields of corn nearly ready to be harvested. They pass mailboxes along the road with family names scrawled on the side. Meyers. Link. Gassman. Schmit. Hardworking German families settled this land but their orderly habits have given way to a clutter of buildings and the stench of pigs. Father stops the car by an empty field but keeps his hands over hers on the wheel. Sitting there in front of him in the stillness of the turned-off engine, she suddenly feels trapped. She tries to slide forward, but she's cinched between him and the steering wheel. He gives a little laugh, eases over just enough to allow her to scoot across him into the passenger seat. She looks at him expectantly. 'Did I do okay?'

'More than okay. You learn fast, Benita.' He smiles. 'Haven't I been telling you you're smart?' He works his hand into his pants pocket and gets out his cigarettes, lights one, inhales deeply. He appraises her as he exhales. 'And pretty, too. Very pretty.'

Her face goes hot. 'Thanks, Father,' she murmurs. 'For the lesson, too. Driving is fun.' Her stomach growls; she slaps her palm against it and giggles. 'I'm hungry.'

'And I'm going to take you home. So your mother doesn't worry.'

'She'll be surprised when I tell her about my lesson.'

'I was thinking. . .' He puts the cigarette to his lips and squints.

Benita watches his profile and the faint rhythmical movement of his Roman collar as he smokes. The scent of tobacco tantalizes her.

'Why not surprise your mother? You could learn to drive first and then ask her to go for a ride.'

Benita beams. 'I could take her to the country. She loves

going there. Except we don't have a car.'

'As long as I'm around, you do.' Father turns the key in the ignition. 'Will your mother wonder where you've been this afternoon?'

'I hardly ever go straight home from school.' Like other neighborhood children, Benita freely roams the blocks around the parish, riding her bike, playing basketball in the street or on the court at school, avoiding the houseful of cousins while her mother assumes her whereabouts and safety.

'We need to keep these lessons between us,' says Father. 'Your brothers might tell your mother and ruin the surprise. And other people. . .well, they wouldn't understand.' He steps on the gas pedal; the car begins to move. 'Okay. Take your position.' For a second, she's befuddled and simply looks at him, then drops down with her face against his thigh. Only once during their return does she lift her head. 'You didn't give me a cigarette.' He takes his hand off the wheel and playfully pushes her back down. 'You didn't ask. Ask and you shall receive. You should know that.' A little later, he says, 'I'll let you out on Curtis.'

Curtis Street is six blocks from her house. Father drives around the block to make sure no one is out walking or waiting for the city bus. As she gets out, he says, 'Remember. Keep this quiet.'

Benita runs the first blocks, terrified of meeting someone she knows. Mrs. Flynn or Mrs. McCleary. Or worse, Mrs. McCann. As she nears home, she slows to a walk to catch her breath. When she reaches the kitchen, her mother is leaning close to her sewing machine, stitching slowly as she guides a sleeve of heavy tweed beneath the foot. Benita stands in the doorway and watches.

'This job will be the death of me,' mumbles Marcella. 'I'd rather sew two new jackets than alter one.' She comes to the end of the seam, lifts her eyes toward Benita and sees the clock on the wall above her. 'Oh, my goodness. Five already. You've been at school all this time?' Without waiting for an answer, she stands up. 'I'd better get supper going.'

The fall school term has brought a new set of country cousins, once again claiming the girl's bedroom and crowding around the table at suppertime. Boarding these students brings Marcella a little income, but essentially, it's an act of charity. She is making it possible for them to attend a Catholic high school and simultaneously helping to fill the empty desks left by parish students who have switched to private high schools. David McCann now goes to Loras Academy, a Catholic military high school for boys. Hilda Saul has transferred Mary Jane to the Immaculate Conception, a Catholic girls' academy on the north side of town. Some people see this defection as a blatant statement of superiority. Father has told Benita this is one more sign that David McCann thinks he's better than the kids at St. Columbkille's.

'I'll set the table, Mom,' says Benita and opens the dish cupboard.

'Thanks, honey.'

Benita gets out a stack of plates and starts around the table. One slithers from her fingers and shatters on the linoleum floor. Benita's eyes fly to her mother's face. 'Oh, Mom, I'm sorry. I didn't mean to. . .honest. I'm sorry. I don't know what happened. I'll buy you another one.' She's on the verge of tears.

'Benita, for heaven's sake, it's only a plate. Now get the broom and sweep it up and finish the table.'

At supper, the mashed potatoes run low in the bowl and Marcella signals to Benita not to take any. As soon as the dishes are washed, Benita picks up her basketball and goes outside. She dribbles it along the sidewalk and into the street, then pitches it through the makeshift hoop, an old laundry basket fastened to a telephone pole. She catches the ball and slams it against the pavement. She resents giving up her share of food. She's tired of the constant confusion of extra people in their house, the daily worry about money, the cheery pretense. Sometimes she wishes her mother wasn't so kind, so. . .so noble. She grips the ball, aims, and tosses it easily, smoothly through the basket again. Even without a decent hoop, she's good at this. Father has told her so. He's the freshmen girls' basketball coach.

She's his special Holy Name daughter again that year; he's the revered priest with whom she enters the parish hall while the rest of us watch and wish and wonder. Father uses every occasion to tell her, sometimes aloud, sometimes with his eyes, sometimes with a hand on her arm or a pat on the back, and sometimes with a strange, possessive innuendo, how fortunate he feels, how pretty and intelligent she is, how much he enjoys her company. Sometimes she deliberately seeks him out for the sake of that admiration, even though gaining it leaves her with a commotion of feelings.

'Meet me at four tomorrow. On the same corner,' he tells her the following week after religion class. As the other students filed out of the room, he had beckoned her to his desk on the pretext of explaining an assignment. As soon as everyone cleared out, he switched to the subject on his mind. Benita feels skittish this second time but even more excited. Father is a few minutes late; she worries that someone will see her standing there. When she sees his car round the corner, she moves to the curb and leaps inside the second he flings open the door. She drops down low on the seat with her head on his lap.

'Good girl, Benita,' he says and strokes her hair. 'I'll tell you when to sit up.' She feels the starts and stops and turns through town, then the glide of wheels on the highway and finally the bumps and pings of gravel. 'Okay, the coast is clear.' He brakes to a stop. When Benita sits up, she recognizes immediately their location. South of town, just past Key West, in front of the wrought iron gate to Mount Olivet cemetery. She knows by heart the narrow roads that wind around the tombstones. She could walk blindfolded to the grave where she has stood so often with her mother to pray.

'Ready?' asks Father now and signals for her to sit in the space he's made between his legs.

She points to the open gate. 'We're going in there?'

'Sure. Why not?'

'It's a cemetery.'

He laughs. 'All the better. Nobody in there will gossip. C'mon, move over here.' He reaches an arm around her shoulder.

She hesitates, then clambers across his leg and puts her hands on the wheel. He shifts himself to accommodate her and puts his hands over hers. This second lesson proceeds much as the first, his foot on the gas, his voice directing their progress along the gravel tracks leading through the cemetery. 'Take that road to the right,' he points. It leads past her dad's grave.

'I'd rather go straight.'

'You're in the driver's seat.' He pauses. 'Just don't forget. My foot's on the gas pedal.' He tousles her hair. 'Have it your way. But don't hit that tree ahead.'

They follow the circuitous tracks around massive, deciduous trees and a century of tombstones, some squat and resolute, others humble rectangles, still others tall and slender with a cross jutting from the pinnacle, like small church steeples. They drive south past the unconsecrated section of the cemetery, an open grassy slope sprinkled with small white crosses marking the graves of unbaptized infants. When they reach a barbed wire fence, they stop. Grazing the lush pasture on the other side are a few Holstein cows. They look up and chew their cuds and ponder their visitors. Father turns off the motor.

'Another good job, Benita, my girl,' he says as she scrambles over him to the seat. He unhooks his Roman collar, slides it off and sets it on the dash board, then lights a cigarette and arches an eyebrow at her. 'So?'

For a minute she feels ignorant, unsure what he's asking. Then she remembers. 'Can I have one, too?'

He holds onto the cigarette. 'I don't know. Are you able?' Before she can answer, he hands it to her and flicks his lighter. She pretends to inhale but ends in an embarrassing coughing fit.

'Watch me.' Father takes a long draw on his cigarette, tilts his head back, closes his eyes, holds the smoke deep inside his throat for what seems forever to her, then slowly exhales, opening his eyes as he does so. She watches in awe. He turns toward her, touches her mouth, says 'Open.' She parts her lips and he inserts the cigarette between them. 'Now do what I did.' She tries, but once again, sputters and chokes. He shakes his head and chuckles. 'It looks like you'll need smoking lessons, too.'

Through the balmy fall season, Benita eagerly scampers off to whatever random meeting place Father selects. He notifies her in a curt murmur on the playground. 'Meet me on the corner of Rising Avenue at four.' Or takes her aside in the gym. 'After practice, walk over to Booth Street and wait for me.' Or she smells the tobacco-scented cassock behind her in the hall and hears the low-toned directive as he passes. 'Thursday at four. Be at the empty lot by Kenneally's.'

She gives him a code name in her diary. He's Fr, short for Father, but mostly for Friend, the person who gives her 'curlers' and tells her how special she is to him.

It's obvious to us that Father prefers Benita, but that's understandable. Her curly, silken blonde hair, her blue eyes, her academic and athletic talent impress us, too. We've elected her freshmen class vice-president. Also, we're accustomed to teachers favoring certain children, the shy girl who says she wants to be a nun, the boy who lost his mother in a fire, the awkward, freckle-faced kid whose businessman dad is a friend of the archbishop. Now and then Teresa does wonder if Benita is under some kind of spell, especially when Father comes by the playground and

Benita drops out of our games and tells Teresa to go ahead home without her. But prudent Teresa keeps her imagination in check and her thoughts to herself and her hands out of the path of rulers.

When Mary Jane notices the cream-colored Dodge parked more and more often in front of the Kane home, she thinks Benita is lucky; no priest visits their house or plays poker with their family. None of us, not Sally or Katie or Mary Ann or Eloise or anyone, imagines the truth, that Benita is meeting Father regularly at a designated site, that she's climbing into his car and ducking down with her head on his lap while he drives into the lonely countryside where he is teaching her to drive. As a bonus, he is showing her how to inhale.

After one driving session, he tells her to stay seated in front of him. He reaches around her with a cigarette, puts it between her lips, lights it. 'Draw in.' The feel of his chest rising and falling with each breath, of her hips curved against his groin, of his hands cupping her shoulders, unnerves her. She begins coughing and wiggles free, telling Father she needs fresh air. 'No, no, no,' he says as she tries to open the door. 'Don't give up. I have another idea. I'll inhale and then blow my smoke into your mouth. That will make it easier.' But when his bulging mouth approaches hers, she turns away. 'I don't think that will work.'

Mary Jane is the first to master inhaling. A savvy upperclassman at Immaculate Conception academy has spent two weeks of lunch hours tutoring her behind a tombstone in the cemetery adjacent to the school. Mary Jane passes on her knowledge to Benita, who teaches Teresa, and so on, until our entire group has acquired the skill. But my dad's relentless, outspoken disgust for cigarettes and those who smoke them has made it impossible for me to light up without a cringing conscience.

Winter and the first wet snowfall claims Catfish Creek and enforces a hiatus on our escapades. Inhaling has hooked Benita on cigarettes; she wants to smoke regularly. Sometimes Father supplies cigarettes, but knowing Marcella's opinion of females who smoke, he slips them to Mary Jane or Teresa to divvy up with Benita. Once, he invites the three of them to go for a ride in his new Dodge; as soon as they sink giggling into the spacious back seat, he hands cigarettes over his shoulder and they all light up. One Saturday afternoon when Mary Jane and Teresa meet Benita in front of church after her cleaning chores, Father ambles along. 'Follow me and we'll have a cigarette together.' He leads them around the church to a door in the back, then down through the dark on a set of narrow, wooden steps, and into the boiler room deep underground. When they finish their cigarettes, he says, 'You girls keep this quiet if you want to come back.' Another day, he opens the door to the auxiliary confessional room and says to the three of them, 'C'mon in and have a cigarette with me.'

Winter curtails Benita's driving lessons, too. Father compensates by dropping into church on Saturday mornings when she's there cleaning. He stands in the dim light that drifts through the stained glass windows and watches as she dusts the long rows of oak pews. After awhile, he approaches, gingerly touches her cheek or her neck, claims to see a hickey and shakes his head disparagingly. 'When are you going to quit hanging around that boy?'

Even though David McCann is no longer her classmate, he continues to saunter past Benita's house and to call her on the phone. They make dates to meet on the bus for a matinee downtown. He invites her to roller skating parties at the Knights of Columbus where his dad is a member. She goes with him to the Loras Academy Homecoming bonfire, to football and basketball games. They're a lively, handsome pair, the object of peer admiration and envy. They did seem to be one of those occasional young couples meant for one another, who meet as school children, marry young and persevere through life in ostensibly harmonious, gratifying marriages.

Late one Sunday afternoon in early April when the country

cousins are off at a movie, Benita opens her Latin book at the kitchen table. She intends to work on her assignment but instead she daydreams about David. No matter what Father says, she likes David. His eyes smile even when his mouth doesn't; his voice is deeper than some of the other boys; he's cute and smart and they have fun together. And no matter what Father thinks, they never do anything wrong. She hears the Dodge stop in front of their house; Father knocks on the door, opens it a few inches and calls in, 'Marcella?'

Marcella hurries through the living room, welcomes him and begins quizzing him about his wants. 'Are you hungry, Father? Would you like a sandwich? Or coffee? What can I get for you?'

'I do have a favor to ask,' he says and extracts a pair of new black slacks from the bag he's carrying. 'Unhemmed,' he says with a helpless shrug.

'Oh, that's nothing. I can do that in no time. Come into the kitchen.'

Benita stands out of respectful habit. Marcella sits down at her machine and begins to rummage in her sewing basket. Father lights a cigarette and sits down at the table. He pats the space between his legs and winks, "Sit down, Benita.' She feels her face go hot; her eyes shoot to her mother, who is absorbed in her search for a tape measure. 'I'm glad to see you're working on Latin,' says Father. 'Maybe you'll earn a front seat in my class next year. That's where I put my best students.'

Marcella stands and dangles the tape measure against the inseam. 'Thirty-one inches, isn't it, Father, if I remember correctly.'

'You're going to sew on Sunday?' asks Benita.

'Not on the machine. Hemming a pair of slacks by hand isn't manual labor.' Marcella glances toward Father. 'Is it, Father?'

'It would be for me,' he laughs. 'But with your skill, I'd call it recreation.'

'Benita, get Father an ashtray,' says Marcella. 'And then run out to the yard and check on Carol.'

'I want to see that little rascal, too,' says Father and follows Benita out the door to the sandbox. Carol looks up long enough to solicit praise for the castle she's constructing.

'Meet me tomorrow at six. On York Street,' says Father to Benita as they return indoors. She nods, but this bold gesture, barely out of her mother's earshot, makes her stomach clench.

'Will you stay for supper, Father?' asks Marcella. 'Richard and Walter and their girlfriends are coming by. We could have a game of penny-poker.'

'Only if Benita promises not to torment me.'

Marcella laughs. Twice during their last game, Benita correctly called his bluff.

At supper, Marcella announces that starting next week, she will be the seamstress at Kaybee's Dress Store. 'Part-time,' she says and beams at the prospect of having a bona fide job downtown.

After the poker game, as Father leaves, he says, 'If you ever need a ride to work, Marcella, just give me a signal when I pick up my car.' He is now renting the empty shed on their lot for his garage. For a dollar a month, he has purchased shelter for his Dodge a few yards from the Kane back door.

'That's good of you, Father,' says Richard.

'Yeah, Father, thanks for helping Mom out,' Walter adds.

Father arrives promptly on York Street. He takes the highway south out of town and at Key West, goes left toward Bellevue. He turns off the main road that follows the Mississippi and onto a gravel country road. He drives another mile or so before he stops. Benita sits up, moves over and grips the wheel. Father puts his hands on her shoulders, then slowly slides his palms down her arms and fastens her hands beneath his against the wheel. 'Are you mad at me?' he asks and nuzzles his face into her neck.

She arches her back. 'I thought you were going to teach me to drive.'

'Okay. Okay. Don't get huffy. Find the gear.' She shifts to 'Drive' and they move down the gravel road toward the trees that define a river in the distance. When he pulls off the road and stops the car, Benita begins to ease free of him. Father says, 'Wait! Don't move yet. Look!' He points toward the west and the red-streaked horizon. 'Look over there. You can see Sirius.'

'Who?' Benita tries to locate the object of his pointing finger.

'Sirius. The brightest of all the stars.'

'You know about stars, too?'

'Yeah, a few things. When I was a kid, I liked to lie on the grass on summer nights and look up there and. . .' She quits listening. She doesn't want to think of him as a kid. He's Father. Her teacher, older and wiser.

'I'm going to be an astronomer,' she says.

'You are, are you?' He gives her a quick hug from behind. She works herself back to the passenger seat. He reaches over, takes her face in his hands and holds it until she looks at him. 'Then we'll need to come out here more often. But right now, I need a cigarette. How about you?'

He lets her out on Plymouth street. Enveloped in darkness, the trees along the boulevard become ghostly shapes snatching at her as she runs the ten blocks home. She arrives breathless at her front door.

'What kept you so late?' asks Marcella. This time, she listens for an answer.

'I was at Eloise's house working on a science project.' Benita feels the lie surface in her eyes and sit there for her mother to examine.

'Is that cigarette smoke I smell?'

'Maybe. Her dad smokes.'

Marcella studies her for a moment, turns and walks back to the kitchen.

Don't tell anybody about this or it will be all over, Father had said when he dropped her off. He issues that same warning each time. *Keep this a secret. You must never say a word. No one will believe you. You'll be in trouble.* She hates sneaking and lying to her mother. One lie has led to another, until the truth is tangled inside. But only with Father does she feel grown up. Important. In her diary entries, she tries to straighten all this out.

With spring comes the annual three-day retreat required for all high school students at St. Columbkille's. It's like a spring housecleaning of the soul, using the tools of silence and prayer. We go to school as usual, then immediately turn around and file down the sidewalk to the church where we sit in rows, as stern as Quakers. On the left, beneath the statue of the Blessed Virgin Mary, are the girls in uniforms and white veils. On the right, under the gaze of St. Joseph, the carpenter, sit the boys, bareheaded and in civilian dress. Our imposed silence and supposed prayer is punctuated by fiery sermons from a zealous, circuit-traveling retreat master, a priest skilled at terrorizing teen-agers into chastity. He tells a spellbinding story about a teen couple who are going steady, which we all know is an occasion of sin because it so easily leads to the sin of petting which we all know means any touch or kiss that rouses sexual excitement. At this point in the priest's talk, many of us drift into introspection, pondering the various and vague stirrings of our own bodies and trying to determine demarcation lines. Meanwhile, the priest goes on with his story of the couple, who also go on, and on, until they've gone too far and committed the dreaded mortal sin of sexual intercourse. That very night, the girl is killed in a car wreck. At her funeral, as classmates grieve and console themselves that this good, innocent girl surely is in heaven, her sobbing boyfriend endures as long as he can, then bursts out, 'No! She's in hell!' We sit stunned at the overwhelming odds: the world, the flesh and the devil, all scheming our ruin.

Father regularly shows up in Marcella's kitchen, wanting coffee or a button replaced, soliciting a request to stay for supper. She responds with routine invitations to family meals and penny poker on Saturday evenings. Sometimes on Sunday afternoons, he brings his mother by to visit.

As spring warms to summer, the Kane family often goes to the country for the Sunday picnics Marcella loves and so carefully prepares. Frequently, Father goes along. Usually, their picnic includes a swim in the muddy creek, or more accurately, a session of splashing and screeching and shouted warnings that the dense water harbors snakes and bloodsuckers and every sort of predator, eager to feast on human flesh.

On this Sunday, Benita is wearing her new red swimsuit. When she wades into the water toward Walter and Jo, Father follows, scooting his hand over the surface and splashing water on her back. She pushes off on her toes, swims a few strokes and stands up. Something pricks her ankle. She yelps. Father bursts through the murky water, laughing. 'Gotcha!'

'No, you didn't.' She scoops water toward him and swims away.

'I will. Wait and see,' he calls after her.

'Hey, Father!' Walt bats a yellow ball across the creek. 'How about a game of water volleyball?'

Later, as Benita towels dry and eyes the minced ham sandwiches her mother is setting out on the blanket a few yards away, Father comes up behind her. 'Wear that swimsuit on our next drive.'

She wraps herself in the towel and steps away.

'C'mon, can't you take a joke?' he says.

Their 'next drive' is always unpredictable. Sometimes he tracks her down twice in one week and notifies her where to meet him. Other times a week, two, even three go by before he seeks her out. Just when she begins to feel ignored, or think she isn't important to him after all, he calls or shows up.

She wears jeans the next time, even though a swimsuit might have been more practical. The weather is Midwestern hot, as humid at eight in the evening as it was mid-afternoon. Father has told her to meet him on Booth street. She's happy to escape the house. Satin and net and pattern tissue are scattered everywhere. Walter and Jo have set their wedding for August twenty-eighth, four weeks away and Marcella is in a frenzy of sewing a volumi- nous bridal gown along with elaborate bridesmaid dresses.

'We're going north this evening, up towards Sageville,' says Father looking down at Benita, concealed on the front seat with her head in his lap. 'I know the perfect place to watch the stars come out.'

'What about driving?'

'That, too.'

After he stops and she takes her position behind the wheel, he directs her to a remote gravel road and up a steep hill. When they reach the top, he says, 'This is the place.' She moves back to the driver's seat, he lights a cigarette for each of them, and they sit smoking. 'Look! There's Orion,' he says. 'Let's get out.' As she stands beside him, he puts one arm around her shoulder and points with the other. 'There. See? The bright star on the left. See it? That's Betelgeuse.'

'Beetle Juice? That's a weird name for a star.'

Father laughs and spells it out. 'It comes from an Arabic term. Having to do with a hand. Although the star is actually on the hunter's shoulder.'

'What hunter?'

He traces along the sky. 'Orion represents a hunter. There's his arm, holding a sword. His head is. . .there. Those three stars are his belt. His dogs are at his heels. Over there. See? Canis Major and Canis Minor.' She stands in silent fascination at the constellation, but at his knowledge, too. His arm drops to her waist. He pulls her closer and whispers, *Benita. That's the name of my star.'* She lets herself lean into him, lost in the enchantment of the moment.

A week later, on Benita's fifteenth birthday, her family gathers for supper and birthday cake. Father had gotten word of it and finagled an invitation from Marcella. She thinks of him almost as a member of their family, except that he's a priest. They always address him as 'Father.' So does his mother, Marcella's friend, Mrs. Dunkel. Father's gift for Benita is a dainty sterling-silver rosary in its own velvet-lined case. Marcella notes and appreciates this subtle message to her daughter, lately so vocal in her complaints over their nightly family rosary. The gift pleases Benita, too, who, despite her protests, does look to the woman, Mary, for guidance.

'See Father to the door, Benita,' says Marcella, when he gets up from the table, explaining that he has a sick call to make. 'Meet me on Burns street in half an hour,' he murmurs as he goes out.

Excused from the dishes by the occasion, Benita tells her mother she's going out to meet her friends. 'I hope those girls aren't smoking,' Marcella calls out as Benita closes the front door.

'Where did you tell your mother you were going?' asks Father after Benita settles down on the front seat.

'Out with my friends.' She lifts her head. 'That's a lie, isn't it?'

Father pats her shoulder. 'You're with me. And I'm your

friend.' He glances down. 'Right?

'Sister Edward told us a lie was any intent to deceive.'

Father shrugs. 'Well, today's a special occasion. And I brought you a birthday treat.' When they stop, Benita sits up. They're on top of the same remote hill where they stood the night he explained Orion.

Father reaches into the back seat and retrieves a slim paper bag. He lifts out a tall bottle. 'Jim Beam. In honor of this event.' He opens it and tilts it toward her. She hesitates. 'Go ahead, try it.'

She sputters and coughs. It feels like learning to inhale all over again. 'Yuk. What is it, anyway?'

'Bourbon. I thought you'd like it.'

'Should I try some more?'

'Sure.'

She sips again and this time swallows a little and doesn't cough, but the tang makes her wince. She hands back the bottle to Father. He puts it to his mouth and drinks down an inch. Benita watches in astonishment. He swipes his hand across his mouth, puts away the bottle and smiles at her. 'Let's get out for awhile.'

From the hilltop, the countryside defies the stereotypes of Iowa. Instead of flat, confined fields of corn and cows, green hills, darkening in the dusk, roll off toward the horizon. Thick groves of oaks and maples promise a spectacular autumn. Now and then a light flicks on in a farm house.

Father stands close behind her. 'Heaven on earth. Right here,' he says. He takes her by the shoulders and rests his chin against her head. She points. 'Is that Sirius?'

'Very good. You're a smart girl.' He drops his hands to her waist. 'Beautiful, too.' His arms go around her and his hands clasp in front of her. She stands motionless, unsure what to do with her own hands and arms. She points again. 'I think I see Beetle Juice, too.'

'Betelgeuse,' he chuckles and squeezes her to him. 'Listen for the difference.' He says both versions.

Benita repeats them and this time captures the subtle distinction.

'Ah, Benita, my precious girl.' His arms tightens around her. Whiskey lingers on his breath.

She stands still, telling herself his breathing hasn't quickened, that he isn't pressing warm and swelling against her, but her fast-beating, excited heart recognizes something enticing and danger-ous here, as if she's a child about to dash across a busy street.

'This isn't wrong,' whispers Father.

Whirling before the mirror on the morning of Walter and Jo's wedding, Benita observes with pleasure her grown-up glamour. The curving bodice and elaborate, billowy skirt of the pink bridesmaid dress, the single string of pearls, the subtle dusting of face powder and bright touch of lipstick have transformed her into an almost-woman. Later, she slowly walks up the aisle with the bridal party and enters the sanctuary where she encounters Father's admiring eyes. He's wearing a lace-trimmed surplice over his cassock and kneeling at a nearby praedium. Monsignor Dunn is the officiating priest. It's a feather in any family's hat when mul-tiple priests inhabit the sanctuary for their weddings and funerals. Throughout the Nuptial Mass, whenever Benita glances up, she meets Father's eyes telling her she's precious to him. His precious girl. She feels a rush of joy.

In sophomore Latin class, we learn that the Latin root for 'precious' is *pretiosus*, derived from *pretium*, meaning 'price.' Benita likes Latin and discovers she has a talent for it. Her front and center seat makes it clear that she's Father's star pupil. I'm in the middle row. I respect Latin as a linguistic tool, but I prefer spoken languages and recklessly lapse into English during class. *Latin is a dead language, dead as dead can be. First it killed the Romans and now it's killing me,* I mutter to Mary Ann, next to me.

'Holmberg!' Father spews my name as if it were an epithet, 'You're being disruptive. Out in the hall! And don't come back until Friday.' I sit in the deserted morning hallway, ruthlessly banished for four days from Father's kingdom, for that's what his classroom is to us. He's our priest and confessor, our religion teacher, our volleyball and basketball coach, and now our Latin teacher. He's young. Vigorous. He can infuse life into a dead language and still toss a football around the field after school. His male energy captivates us as adolescent girls, especially those whose homes lack that force. To be castigated and rejected by him is far more devastating than to be exiled from Sister Isidore's seventh-grade classroom.

Fortunately, my confidence as a female is waxing. I'm fifteen and five feet six inches tall and now have hard evidence that I'm normal. During the lethargic days of the previous summer, away from school and the anxious influence of the three other non-menstruating girls in my class, my first menstrual period has occurred. Thus reassured, I set out with Sally on Friday evening excursions to downtown Dubuque, where we stroll Main Street and corner glances at passing cars. When boys honk or call out car windows to us, we feign disinterest. Two boys—young men, in fact, for they're twenty, out of school and gainfully employed—challenge our act and coast to the curb in their 1949 Oldsmobile, to flirt at closer range. Despite their curious biographies—they're vague Protestants roaming through life without parish roots—they're as unsophisticated and innocent as we—fortunately—for after a few curbside rendezvous, we begin to ride around with them, and to pair off.

I sit in the front seat with Dan, who owns the Oldsmobile; Sally sits in back with Bob, his disarming buddy. Our mothers, had they known, would have been needlessly apoplectic, for nothing even venially sinful happened through that next summer, other than the subterfuge of where we were going and where we had been. To report honestly would have been to confess that we were testing the waters outside our parochial world. Literally, for Bob owned a motor boat and took us for deafening jaunts on the Mississippi. Shy, good-hearted Dan capitulated to my plea for a land-based adventure. *Sure, I'll teach you to drive.* He pulled to the curb and we switched seats and he became my passenger. I wanted to learn to drive before my mother found out.

The following spring Dan produces a flashier mode of travel. A motorcycle. I meet him at the corner, a block from my house, and hop on behind him for a rousing ride around town. I revel in the rush of wind through my hair, the aggressive roar of the motor, the wondrous sense of my body clinging to his, *his*, this Dan, the slight, unassuming fellow who garnishes my sixteenth summer with one timid kiss, my first, in fact, unless I count Donald O'Shea.

'What do we mean when we say *Outside the Church there is no salvation?*' asks Father Raftis of the sixty-two sophomores slouched before him in religion class. He's new at our parish, newly ordained, tall and boyishly handsome with a shock of jet black hair and blue eyes that crinkle with his easy grin, but he lacks Father Dunkel's magnetism. Or perhaps the difference is in us, now guileless girls of fifteen. He interprets our mask of boredom as disinterest in religion, when in fact, we're brimming with questions. His query rouses us to attention.

'It means you have to be a Catholic to go to heaven,' says Delores, who has an aggravating habit of answering a teacher's question before anyone else digests it.

'It means you shouldn't sit outside in your car during Sunday Mass,' says Willy, who, since first grade, has maintained his illiteracy and his back row seat. He's describing his dad.

'I think it means the Catholic Church is the only true church. So if you want to go to heaven, you have to join it,' says Vincent. He's one of a dozen or so students who came from other parishes to economical St. Columbkille's, the only Catholic co-ed high school in town.

'Close,' says Father. 'Anyone else?'

Silence. Nancy lifts her desk top, as if she means to look inside for the answer, but we recognize the strategy. The desks open upward and create a shield for us to hide behind, a place to snack, write notes or study for our next class. She bites into her peanut butter sandwich.

'It doesn't mean *anything*,' says Benita.

Heads turn.

'I'm not sure I understand,' says Father.

'It's just the Pope, going around telling people that if they want to go to heaven, they have to be Catholic. How does he know?'

'He's infallible. He doesn't make mistakes.' Delores again.

'Who says?' asks Benita.

Father spells out the qualifications for papal infallibility. The pope must be defining a doctrine of faith or morals, speaking as head of the Church, with the clear intention of binding the whole Church.

'So what about Mrs. Kennedy? Does that mean she's going to hell?' asks Isabel who lives next door to Episcopalian Mrs. Kennedy.

Father braces for a revolt. The Catholic church is the one true church, he explains, because it was founded on the apostle, Peter, and you could trace right down the line from him to the present pope. God commanded everyone to be a member of this true Church. That means anyone who deliberately disobeys that command, or remains outside the Church through his own fault will not be saved. He sounds as if he's reading from a book.

'Mrs. Kennedy sends her girls to Catholic school,' says Rita.

'I don't see why she has to do that either.' Benita's heathen cynicism makes Delores' eyes pop.

'Because if she wanted to marry Mr. Kennedy, she had to promise she would,' says Marie. 'That's the rule.'

'Let's leave Mrs. Kennedy out of this,' says Father. 'What it comes down to is this. Somebody might not know that God has commanded him to belong to the true church. Or there might be a reason why it's impossible for him to be baptized. If he loves God above everything else, if he's sorry for his sins and longs to do what is required for salvation, then he receives what we call Baptism of desire. Or Baptism of blood.' His eyes go to Benita. 'In other words, the deep, inner, secret longing he feels entitles him to possess heaven, the same as baptism by water.'

'Do girls ever feel that way?' asks Nancy.

Father frowns, sensing a trap.

Elaine puts up her hand. 'You mean if you really, really want to be a Catholic, that's the same as being one?'

'No, no, no, no. Just think about it.' He runs his fingers through his thick, black hair. 'Even though people outside the church can be saved, they don't have the infallible Church to guide them about what to believe and do in order to serve God. They have to live without the sacraments. Without Mass and Holy Communion and all the sources of grace the Church supplies for actual members.' He scans our faces. 'It would be like wanting to graduate from high school without having any school or teachers or books. You kids are lucky. You already have the truth. Just remember. Faith is a gift. Don't take it for granted. You could lose it.'

Benita is gazing out the window and chewing skeptically on

her lower lip, as if she might be thinking up another question. Or maybe of David McCann, a more likely scenario in my mind, which more often than not is on boys and my prospects with them. What she's thinking about is her own insides. Her gut is gripped in a vise of menstrual cramps. Her monthly periods are fraught with distress. Raging headaches beforehand, horrible cramps when the blood begins. Lately, the headaches come more often and make her cross and restless.

That evening, Marcella, who's had her share of female woes, commiserates with her daughter. She excuses her from the supper dishes and the rosary and suggests a glass of warm milk and an early bedtime, a routine that consoled Benita as a child.

'Will you read to me, too?' Benita is only partly jesting. 'The poem about the gingham dog and calico cat. That was my favorite.'

Marcella tracks it down and sits on the bed next to her daughter. 'The Duel, by Eugene Field,' announces the former school teacher, ceremoniously.

Benita nestles closer. 'The gingham dog and the calico cat,' begins Marcella, then stops and sniffs. Benita freezes. She'd smoked a cigarette in the backyard before her mother got home from Kaybee's, but afterward she brushed her teeth and chewed cinnamon gum.

Marcella clears her throat and goes on. 'Side by side at the table sat.' The poem proceeds through a series of terrible spats in which the air is littered with bits of gingham and calico while the animals employ tooth and claw until both disappear without a trace. Marcella pauses dramatically before the concluding verse. 'But the truth about the cat and pup is this: they ate each other up! Now what do you really think of that?' She closes the book. 'That's not a very happy ending. I wonder why you were so fond of it.'

'Mmm-mm' says Benita behind closed lips. She's afraid

speaking will set off her mother's sniffing again. What she liked best as a child was hearing her mother's voice without the accompaniment of the sewing machine.

Marcella sighs and slowly gets up.

Benita catches her hand and strokes her fingers. 'Are you tired, Mom?'

'A little. I've been up since five-thirty. I spent the entire day putting a new lining in a wool coat with the most beautiful fox collar. It reeked of cigarette smoke.' She takes a few steps toward the door, then turns. 'Smoking is such a disgusting habit.' Benita makes no reply. A fence has gone up between her and her mother and she's caught on its barbs.

Father catches up with Benita after school a few days later. 'Meet me Thursday at seven. On Burns Street.'

They drive out past Key West where he tells her it's safe to sit up. All around them are the erotic shades of autumn: blood red, lush bronze, deep gold and juicy wine, trees, fruit and fields oozing color beneath the blue aphrodisiac of sky. Seductive September, luring Midwesterners into the woods and hills to absorb enough warmth and beauty to sustain them through the brooding winter.

Father drives through the waning light toward New Melleray and stops on a side road a few miles from the Trappist monastery. Respectfully, she tastes the bourbon he brings out, even swallows a little, but wrinkles up her nose and contents herself with a cigarette. He takes a drink, puts away the bottle and lights a cigarette. 'Let's go for a walk,' he says. He tugs off his clerical collar and tosses it into the backseat, then takes her by the hand and leads her along the faint tracks of a vehicle into an opening in the trees. A church bell bongs in the distance. He stops, pulls her closer until he's standing behind her, his arms around her, his fingers interlocked at her waist.

'Where's Orion's belt?' he asks.

Benita searches the navy blue sky with her finger. 'There's Orion. And. . . there's his belt! There. Those three stars.'

'A-plus. Now tell me what *desiderare* means.'

'It's Latin. I know that much.'

'Think about it. *De* means 'from.' *Sidus*, or *sideris* means 'star.'

'So it means from the star?'

'*To await from the stars.* People used to watch the stars for signs. Sailors looked to them for direction. It's the Latin root for . . .you tell me. What English word?'

She leans into him and looks up, lost in thought. "Decide? Destination?'

'Good guess. The answer is. . ." He tightens his embrace. 'Desire.' He drops his head against hers. His mouth moves along her temple. 'What a treasure you are. *My* star. The one I've waited for.' Slowly, his palms creep upward, pause on her ribcage, then slide up and stop on her breasts. His breathing quickens. His fingers begin a gentle, rhythmic pressure. 'You're developing nicely,' he murmurs. A sickish feeling of bliss immobilizes her. And then a faraway feeling, as if she's somewhere else, watching. 'Don't worry,' he whispers. 'This isn't wrong.'

That evening, as I finish my piano practice and stand up, I see a girl across the street. She's walking fast in the direction of St. Columbkille's. As she passes beneath the street light, she breaks into a full run, as if someone is chasing her. For a second, I think it's Benita and open the door to call out to her. But no, Benita wouldn't be there on my street, more than a mile from home on a school night, alone in the crisp autumn dark.

Father had dropped her off at Mt. Carmel, the cul-de-sac at the far end of South Grandview. As she got out, he issued the usual warning, but in a sterner voice, 'Don't tell anyone about this. And don't worry. This isn't wrong.' She disliked being let out so far away from home, but Father said it was a nice night, people might be out walking and see them. As she ran, she tried to think of something to tell her mother that wasn't exactly a lie. Her mother is growing more suspicious, not about Father, but about cigarettes. And Benita doesn't want to give up either one. She clings to Father's words. What they do isn't wrong. He's a priest, he knows about right and wrong. That's what she tells her diary that night.

CHAPTER THREE

The trees shed their leaves to reveal sinewy, reaching branches that seem to plead mercy for the people required to trudge through Iowa's gunmetal winter. Sally and I transfer our romantic energy from our town boyfriends to boys within the walls of school. The object of my crush is a senior who passes me unnoticed in the hall between classes.

Lucky Benita, to be doted upon by David McCann, and consequently, invited to the Loras Academy Military Ball in February. Being asked to a dance at Loras is a coup for girls from St. Columbkille's. Usually that honor goes to girls from the nearby Visitation Academy, 'Viz girls,' we call them and mimic their uppity ways. Their dads are doctors and lawyers. The Military Ball is particularly thrilling because the boys wear their ROTC uniforms and look grown-up and breathtakingly commanding. To date such a boy is to be in the presence of a budding hero who has tasted the games of war in ROTC. He has crept on his stomach, crawled on his hands and knees, learned to keep his head down or get 'killed.' Supposedly, all that fun has made him courageous and patriotic.

Benita wears the pink bridesmaid gown. 'Wow!' says David

when he sees her. He looks dashing himself in his uniform. He presents her with a corsage of six full-blown scarlet roses. As they go out the front door, Father backs out of his garage.

'You kids need a ride?' he asks, poking his head out the window. 'Or you could borrow my car and Benita could drive.'

Benita's heart speeds up.

'No thanks, Father, my brother's taking us.' David points to the Buick at the curb. As they get into the back seat, he asks Benita, 'Can you really drive?'

'No. That's just Father, trying to be funny.'

The evening opens with a Grand March that gives import to everything that follows. That 'everything' reportedly includes lingering embraces, kissing, even drinking and smoking during intermissions. Unlike our nuns with their prim impositions, the priests in charge of Loras have weightier matters on their minds than policing the inevitable. But Benita and David aren't among the group huddled on the fringes in a cloud of smoke. He holds the same opinion of cigarettes as her mother. When Benita is with David, she's an innocent, carefree girl who neither smokes nor drinks.

When the band announces the last dance, *Goodnight Sweetheart,* the imposing soldiers become yearning boys. Benita watches an upperclassman put his arms around his girlfriend's waist and pull her close; the girl circles her arms around his shoulders and the two of them move to the music as one. David and Benita dance at a virtuous distance, confidently pacing their feelings for the long term.

At the front door, he invites her to the spring prom in May, then leans to kiss her goodnight. Just as their lips meet, Father pulls into his garage and floods them with his headlights. David jumps back. 'We'll finish this later,' he says and squeezes her hand.

Father did that on purpose, she's sure of it. But his meanness doesn't quash the song in her heart as she goes upstairs to her room. *David McCann. David McCann. Mrs. David McCann,* it says. She hears it again on Valentine's Day, and at her brother Richard's February wedding to Ruth Eckstein.

Later that month, as the students exit the room after Latin class, Father beckons Benita to his desk 'Are you planning to take Latin next year?'

She nods. 'Senior year, too. I like it. I might major in it in college.'

'You're planning to go to college?'

'If I can. If it doesn't cost too much.'

'If you keep up your grades, you could get a scholarship.'

She gives a cynical snort. Her grades are sliding and he knows it. So is her conduct mark. The A that had been a fixture since first grade has skidded to B. Too many questions in religion class, too much gazing out the window in Math, too much dissonance between word and deed.

'Maybe you need someone to put in a good word for you. Or help you out financially.'

She watches his face, the metallic blue gaze, the tight little discomfiting smile.

'You're special to me, Benita. That smart-aleck boy will go off to some fancy college and forget all about you. Remember that.'

On a windy, mid-March Saturday hinting of spring, Father phones her at home, early in the afternoon. 'I'll pick you up tonight after I finish hearing Confessions. Eight-fifteen. Corner of Booth and Curtis.'

'Who was that? asks Marcella.

'A wrong number.'

Benita wears a light jacket over a pullover sweater and jeans. She's going next door to Mary Jane's, maybe from there to

Teresa's, she tells her mother.

She hunches against the wind and waits in the shadows just outside the circle of light falling from the corner streetlamp. She's relieved to see the Dodge and to drop her head into the warmth of Father's lap.

'I know a protected place, out of the wind,' he says. They drive for awhile and stop. They're parked in a dark grove of trees near a creek, an area she doesn't recognize.

'Can I drive here?'

'Let's skip the lesson tonight. I have another idea.'

He reaches over the seat and retrieves a six-pack of Schlitz from the floor behind them. 'You didn't seem to like bourbon so I brought this.' He opens two cans and hands one to her. The sweet, yeasty flavor appeals to her. He lights a cigarette and gives it to her, then lights one for himself. She crosses her legs and taps the ashes into the tray on his dashboard. He drinks thirstily, tosses the empty can out the window and opens a second beer. 'Let's get out. I think we can see Leo tonight.'

They stand side by side in front of the car while he finishes his beer and points out the stars comprising the lion of Greek mythology. She shivers and pulls her jacket closer. He drops the empty can, wraps both arms around her and clasps her to himself. 'Is that better?'

She nods against his chest. He slips his hands inside her jacket and along the small of her back, then lifts her sweater and walks his fingers along her bare skin until he finds the edge of her bra. He traces along it to the cotton cups, presses a palm over each, flattening her flesh beneath the fabric. He abandons her breasts, drops his hands to her waist and pulls her closer.

'I'm not sure if this is. . .'

'Sh-hh. This isn't wrong. Not for us.' Something clicks off inside her. She's dangling like a puppet at the end of the strings

he manipulates. Now he's clasping her so tight she finds it difficult to breathe. He puts one hand behind her head, brings her
face close and kisses her, and then again, this time thrusting his
tongue between her lips. His body presses hard against hers; his
tongue searches her mouth. She feels suffocated, then limp. He
withdraws his tongue and moves his lips along her face and neck.
'Are you awake yet?' he whispers.

She's the ignorant girl again, unsure what he means, but sensing she *should*.

He kisses her again, more gently this time, then lets out a
long, exhausted breath, as if he's just exerted a great force of will
and releases her. She steps back and wipes her lips with her fingertips.

He tilts his head and looks inquisitively at her. 'Why so
somber? This isn't wrong. God wants us to be happy.' When
they're inside the car again, he turns to her. 'Don't breathe this to
anyone. You'd ruin your reputation.' She runs the entire seven
blocks home, trembling with dread as she flees past the living
room windows along Grandview. She can feel the eyes on her,
Mrs. McCleary watching from behind her curtain, taking notes
to tell Hilda Saul tomorrow. At home, she pauses on the doorstep
and catches her breath before opening the front door.

Marcella looks up from the magazine in her lap and gives her
that long, hard, 'I-hope-you-haven't-been-smoking' look. Benita
feels a flash of anger. Smoking is all her mother worries about.

As March melts into spring, the sun regains its vigor, turning
vagrant patches of gray snow into oases of grass and flowers.
April's sweet showers bathe the neighborhood in sumptuous
scents—tulips and iris and violets and the promise of peonies for
Memorial Day. Father suggests a Sunday afternoon fishing outing. He'll bring the equipment and teach Benita the proper tech-
niques.

Sitting with him on the creek bank in the warm sunlight of

that Sunday afternoon and the others that follow, she feels disconnected from the guilty, frightened girl scurrying home through the shadows. There in the daylight, she can smoke and drink beer with him without the hovering fear of darkness. Even when he puts his arms around her and pulls her close, or fondles her breasts, or kisses her, working his tongue deep into her mouth, she feels separate from the worrying, apprehensive girl in town. Only when he whispers, 'Are you awake yet?' does she lapse into that old, troubled ignorance. 'Don't worry about this. It will all come out in the wash,' he says one day when he drops her off. That remark baffles her, too. As a twelve-year-old, when she asked her mother about the blood-stained rags spread out in the sun, her mother replied, 'You'll find out when you need to know.' Therefore, Father's enigmatic statements will be resolved, too. But a reality nags at her: despite all the hard scrubbing, despite the careful arrangement of the rags in the sun, telltale brown traces always remained.

Early one Saturday afternoon in late April, Father comes into church. 'C'mon in here and we can smoke,' he says, gesturing to Benita from the confessional room sequestered between the central and east vestibules. She's eager to put down her dust cloth and follow him. She's been alone working since mid-morning, polishing row after row of oak pews in preparation for tomorrow's Masses. In an hour, Saturday Confessions will begin. She's scarcely lit up when he begins to stroke her hair, to fondle her, saying over and over, 'Benita, my precious girl.' A dreadful joy possesses her. He takes away her cigarette, snuffs it out, begins kissing her. Her knees go weak. She feels dizzy, hopelessly caught in a whirling magnetic force. Demanding, agitated kisses, one after another, his tongue thrust into her mouth. His hands move from her waist to her breasts. His breathing grows louder, expels the odor of cigarettes. He's held her and kissed her like this before, but today the rough urgency in him makes her heart pound with fear. Or excitement. She's not sure which. He tightens his grip, pins her between himself and the wall, begins pushing rhythmically against her. She holds onto him and tries to keep her balance. She wants only not to fall. He lifts her blouse and explores the tender flesh beneath. He pushes up her skirt until he can access the panties underneath. In one gesture, he pulls them down and in another, unzips his fly. *No, stop. No. Don't. Stop. I don't. . .* He pulls her closer, closer until he is pushing inside her, pushing and panting, out of breath, his heart pounding with effort as he thrusts harder, deeper, harder and deeper, hurting her. The piercing pain makes her cry out. He covers her mouth with his hand. 'No. Sh-h-h. Be still. I love you. You're mine.' His thrusting becomes more rapid and frenzied, he's working frantically, the sounds coming from him low and groaning, then more and more desperate until he lets out an agonizing moan that quickly dies to a simpering sigh. He collapses against her, sweating, exhausted. 'Did you come?' he asks and with a peaceful sigh lets her go. She untangles herself, straightens her clothes and bursts from the confessional, her eyes wild, a damp ache between her legs.

She darts through the shadowy vestibule and swings open the door. Her head whirls. Her clothing is in disarray. She races across Rush Street and up Holly to the corner of Cleveland Avenue where she turns right. Her heart hammers. Her mouth is dry. 'Oh, God, please, please, God, don't let anyone see me.'

In front of her house half a block away, a car is parked. Uncle Larry, her dad's brother from Minneapolis, spies her and beckons. She combs her fingers through her hair, smoothes her skirt and glances down, fearful that the smelly wetness between her legs is leaking through, trickling down her thighs.

Her uncle calls out, 'A-ha! Here comes the girl we've been waiting for.' He turns to his sister-in-law. 'Marcella, your wandering child has returned. Now we can be on our way. '

'Uncle Larry's taking us to visit your daddy's grave,' says Marcella. 'After that, we're going to stop at the monastery at New

Melleray for a while, and on the way home, he's treating us to ice cream.'

Seven-year-old Carol is bouncing in the backseat of the car. 'C'mon, Benita, we're gonna get ice cream. C'mon, Mom. C'mon, Uncle Larry.'

'I need to change my clothes.' Benita starts toward the house.

'You're fine the way you are. C'mon, honey, you're keeping everyone waiting.' Marcella opens the passenger door.

'I want to put on jeans.' Benita hurries into the house and up the stairs to the bathroom. She lifts her skirt and takes off her underpants. Splotches of blood. Something has broken inside her. She felt it give. That awful burst of pain when Father said he loved her. It still aches. She sits down on the toilet and looks for more blood on the tissue. There's only the slightest trace of pink. It's not her period, then, coming early. She stands, turns on the faucet and tries to scrub out the blood, first flooding it with hot water, then cold, frantically trying to recall which her mother said worked best. Why is blood so stubborn?

'Benita! For heaven's sake, what's taking you so long?'

'I'll be right down.' Her breath is shaky. She wrings out the panties and hides them at the bottom of her dresser drawer. Her hands tremble as she zips her jeans, but the solid, enclosed feel of denim calms her. She would like to check herself in the mirror, but she can't meet her eyes. She takes a deep breath and goes down the steps and out to the waiting car.

'Almost six years, Larry,' sighs her mother after they finish their prayer at the graveside in Mount Olivet cemetery. They are standing side by side with their eyes fixed on the tombstone: *Eldon Kane, August 1, 1896--September 11, 1943.* 'I still argue with God about it now and then, I'm afraid.'

'God understands. There's a purpose in this, I know. It's just hard to see it from here. But someday we will.'

At first, their talk annoys Benita. The complacent assumptions, the weary cheerfulness, the groveling before God's cryptic will. Then, it disheartens her. *Why did they always have to be so sad?* Whenever Uncle Larry visits Dubuque, they come straight to this grave. Submission to suffering permeates their lives. In church, in this cemetery, and at home, where beneath the current of prayer and work lies the sediment of her mother's loneliness and grief. Now, deep inside her, the ache begins again, a burning wound in the secret place where Father has been. She feels wet, dirty. She wishes she could make herself invisible.

'He was such a good man,' sighs Marcella. 'Such a precious daddy.' It's a description she uses often. Nuns and priests use that word in religion class, too, but they always connect it to Christ's precious blood spilled for our sins. The first time Father called her 'his precious Benita,' she had looked it up in the dictionary. *Precious: of great price or value; of great desirability; beloved, dear.* There was nothing about Christ or blood or sin.

'You've had a hard, lonely job and you've done it well, Marcella. Eldon would be proud of you,' says Uncle Larry. He puts one arm around Carol, the other around Benita and hugs them to him. 'I bet he's smiling down on these little girls right now.'

Carol yanks on his hand. 'Can we go get ice cream now?'

'First the monastery, *then* the ice cream,' says Uncle Larry. He knows how much that stop means to Marcella. She and Eldon were married at New Melleray and ever since that April day in 1923, they returned regularly to visit Father Pius. As the children arrived, they took them along for his blessing. Benita always dreaded the place. While the monks fed them unpasteurized milk and warm cookies, her eyes would rove the dark walls and high ceilings where she imagined a menacing trap door about to spring open and swallow her up. Today, she longs to disappear.

CHAPTER FOUR

Two altar boys, gleaming with Sunday piety, precede Father Dunkel into the sanctuary for Mass. He is wearing a green chasuble, the color symbolizing the sacred season of hope and growth issuing from the death and resurrection events of Easter. Respectfully, the congregation rises. From their usual place on the left side of the church, Benita watches with Carol and their mother as Father places the covered chalice on the center of the altar, opens the missal and descends to the foot of the altar to begin the Holy Sacrifice of the Mass. *In nomine Patri, et Felii, et Spiritu Sancti, Amen.* He says the introductory Psalm 42, expressing trust in God, awareness of his own unworthiness, and the desire for all present to set aside daily distractions and prepare to offer the sacrifice of atonement.

Early that morning, before anyone else stirred, Benita wrapped the bloodied panties in layers of newspaper, but before she shoved the bundle deep down into the garbage can, she opened it and looked once more at the stain. A quiver went through her, like the thrill she'd felt the first time she'd swung out from a high tree branch and dropped into the creek. When she looked up to where she'd been, she was amazed at her nervy act. Now a dull heaviness draws her downward like gravity. She feels herself sink. She is underwater gasping for air.

Last night as she lay awake in bed, the ache between her legs brought back the misery of menstrual cramps. She flattened both hands on her belly, spread her fingers open and stayed perfectly still, listening to the sound of her heart pounding in her ears, blood in, blood out, blood in, blood out, blood spilled on her panties, water rushing uselessly over the stain. The steady thump of her heart soothed her finally to sleep. But an hour later, she woke in a panic. Something had happened to her mother. She was so sure of it that she got up, tiptoed into her room and stood near her bed until she saw for herself the rhythmic movement of the blanket.

She awoke this morning to an eerie calm, like the foreboding that had gripped the rooms the morning of her dad's death, except that this dread was inside her. It had begun yesterday at the cemetery when Uncle Larry and her mother talked so calmly about God as if they'd forgotten His cruel way of taking for Himself the people others loved.

Father bows before the altar and finishes saying the Confiteor; the altar boys take it up, repeating it in Latin on behalf of the people, confessing to Almighty God, to blessed Mary ever Virgin, to blessed Michael the Archangel and eventually to all the saints that they have sinned exceedingly in thought, word and deed. *Mea culpa, mea culpa, mea maxima culpa,* they say, striking their breast with each regret. The recitation ends with a plea for prayer to the same saints invoked before, and then to God Himself for mercy and forgiveness and remission of 'all my sins.' Father goes up the steps to the altar, kisses the place where relics of martyrs are cemented, moves to the right side of the altar and reads the opening prayer.

Through the Introit and Kyrie and Gloria and Epistle, Benita watches him. When he mounts the pulpit to proclaim the Gospel, she stands with the congregation. As he preaches the sermon, she looks up, deaf to his words, aware only of his eyes, waiting for them to turn toward her, longing for him to notice her, to single her out from the crowd and silently announce how much she means to him. After the Lavabo, the washing of the hands that marks the purity of body and soul necessary for the Holy Sacrifice, Father turns toward the people and extends his hands in invitation: *Oratre Fratres.* During the Secret, the silent prayers of petition, her hope leaks away. And when the bell rings three times, signaling the Sanctus, the coming of the Son of God to the altar, her heart thumps in fear.

Five times Father blesses the offering of bread and wine, five times in honor of the five wounds of Christ; next he says the words Christ himself said at the Last Supper, the transformative words, *This is my body. This is my blood.* The Altar boy rings the bell. Father elevates the host first, then the chalice, commemorating the lifting up of Christ on the cross of Calvary when he gave his life in sacrifice. Eyes lift in silent worship, hands touch chests. *My Lord and my God.* Heads bow in adoration. Silence overwhelms the church. *Oh my God, I'm heartily sorry for having offended thee.* The words of the Act of Contrition throb in Benita's ears, but hasn't Father told her over and over, 'This isn't wrong. Don't worry. In the eyes of God, this isn't wrong.'

Father is giving himself Communion, saying in Latin as he receives the host, 'The Body of our Lord Jesus Christ preserve my soul unto life everlasting. Amen.' Then he uncovers the chalice, genuflects, asks God, 'What shall I render to the Lord for all that He has rendered unto me?' He then receives the precious blood of Christ, saying 'The blood of Our Lord Jesus Christ preserve my soul unto life everlasting. Amen.' Next, he lifts the ciborium, turns to the congregation and elevates a host for all to see. 'Behold the Lamb of God, behold Him who taketh away the sins of the world.' He repeats three times the prayer of the centurion to Christ, 'Lord, I am not worthy that you should come under my roof; but only say the word and my soul will be healed.'

People begin to move toward the Communion rail. Marcella turns toward her daughters. Carol assumes the scrupulous posture of a fresh First Communicant and steps into the aisle. Benita hesitates. Her mother touches her arm, whispers, 'You look pale. Are you all right?' Benita swallows and nods. She longs to be Carol, seven years old again. No, she longs to be herself and seven years old again with her daddy in the church watching her walk up the aisle for the first time, her innocent heart yearning for Christ in the form of bread. *Oh Lord, I am not worthy, that thou shouldst come to me, but speak the words of comfort, my spirit healed shall be.* Those were the words we sang as First Communicants, a sentiment and melody that our souls would never forget.

As she kneels next to her mother at the ornate white rail, she feels Father approaching closer, closer, holding his host-filled gold chalice in his left hand, stopping now in front of her. With his right hand, he retrieves a host, holds it up between his thumb and index finger. His hand moves toward her. She closes her eyes, tips back her head, opens her mouth. He places the host on her waiting tongue. 'May the Body of our Lord Jesus Christ preserve your soul unto life everlasting. Amen.' But as he draws back his hand, he brushes his fingers slowly, lightly, slyly along her chin. Her gut contracts with alarm. A few moments later, as she kneels in the pew, head down in thanksgiving, elation sweeps through her. Now she understands. She is truly special to Father. His secret touch was his pledge.

The climax of the sacrifice comes with consecration and communion. After that, the denouement, the succinct unwinding of all good drama, in this case, Christ's Last Supper. People begin to gather up their things, missals, purses, jackets, to transfer their thoughts to one another and the chance to converse as they shuffle down the aisle.

'Another fine sermon, Father,' says Marcella when he joins the parishioners still milling about on the sidewalk.

'Father!' says Carol. 'Uncle Larry took us for ice cream yesterday. I had two scoops of strawberry.'

Father ruffles Carol's hair. 'Does that make him your favorite uncle?'

'Larry drove down from Minneapolis yesterday,' explains Marcella. 'We went to the cemetery.'

Father looks at Benita. 'Did *you* have two scoops of strawberry, too?'

'I wasn't hungry.'

'She's weird,' says Carol, hopping around on one foot, fidgety with joy.

Marcella gestures, open-armed. 'Isn't it a beautiful day, Father? I can't wait until it's warm enough for a picnic in the country.' She smiles at him. 'You're invited, of course.'

'And I'll *be* there, of course, but only if. . .' He arches an eyebrow and sends her an impish smile.

'I know. I know. Only if I make those minced ham sandwiches.'

'My other favorite uncle is Uncle Billy! He might come for my birthday,' Carol calls over her shoulder as they turn toward home.

'And I might push you on the swing if you come over to the playground this afternoon,' replies Father.

'Huh-uh! That's too scary!' Carol gives a sturdy shake of her auburn curls and skips up the sidewalk. Father had pushed her on the swing last week, but when she called down, 'That's high enough,' he ignored her plea and kept pushing, higher and higher, until she'd screeched with fear. He'd laughed then and let her go.

A few days later, Father approaches Benita after school and tells her to meet him at the boys' locker room, a place she's never been before. When the last boy clears out, Father calls her in. 'This isn't wrong,' he says again. 'Not for us.' It hurts less the second time.

'Meet me in the church kitchen,' he whispers into the telephone at eleven p.m. the following Friday night. 'Go around behind the church and tap on the basement west window. I'll let you in.' 'Mary Jane wants me to come over for awhile,' Benita tells Irene, who is spending the night with her younger sisters while Marcella visits country kin. She tosses a trench coat over her nightie, closes the door calmly behind her and flees, propelled by a dreadful excitement. Her loafers click against the sidewalk as she runs. Her legs seem separate from her body as they carry her over the two dark, terrible blocks to the window where Father waits. He opens it and she crawls through into the secret world where he's master and she is pretty and special and *his*.

Dancing in David's arms a few weeks later at the Loras Academy spring prom, she's a quintessential teenager in a charming homemade dress. She had requested a white formal, pure white, she told her mother, but contented herself with the fabric Marcella found on sale, white pique sprinkled with delicate red flowers. As Marcella basted the skirt to the bodice, she pricked her index finger. It flew to her lips and she sucked at the wound. 'Oh, well,' she said, 'The flowers are red, so a little drop of blood wouldn't be a disaster.' Yes, yes, it would, Benita had wanted to say. Someone would notice it. Someone was noticing now, as she dances. She could feel their eyes inspecting the stubborn stain soap and sun couldn't touch. The corsage David had given her matched, too. Six flaming red carnations. *Does he know about the blood?*

Afterward, at the front door, he moves closer to kiss her good night, hesitates, looks around. 'I'm a little spooked. Seems like he pops up every time I want to kiss you.'

'Who cares about him? He's not in charge of us,' replies Benita and closes her eyes for David's kiss.

Jotted in bold, black ink on the facing page of Benita's 1949 high school yearbook is this inscription: 'Don't worry. It will all come out in the wash, Fr. Dunkel.' That bewildering assurance became his mantra. *Don't cry out,* he had warned. If the awfulness of her deed didn't silence her, the futility of telling it would. *Who* would she tell? *What* would she say? She and Father know too much about each other now not to be conspirators. He is her connection to everything that matters in her life. Whatever thread of resistance she had clung to is gone. Now, like Caesar, he can boast, *Veni, vidi, vici.*

That summer, Bea Roscoe, the parish organist who lives across the street from the church, offers to teach Benita to play the organ, an opportunity she didn't extend to her own daughter, a year younger than Benita. Benita's assigned practice time is early evening. As she sits at the organ, alone in that dark, cavernous Gothic church, Father appears, as if by instinct, with his ravenous words and hands. *You're beautiful. You're mine.*

Throughout the summer and corn-ripening temperatures of autumn, they often drive to the country with a six-pack of beer. Sometimes, he brings along a blanket and they walk to a clearing in the woods. Usually, they simply use the back seat of his car. One pleasant Sunday afternoon, they go to the country to fish in the creek running through his brother's farm. Father brings along a seventh grade girl from the parish, a fatherless girl who needs an outing in the country, he explains to Marcella. He sits with the two girls on the grassy creek bank, listening to the gulps and whooshes of the muddy water; after fishing for awhile, he asks the girl to hold the fishing lines while he and Benita walk to the farm house to get some sandwiches. He knows his brother and sister-in-law aren't home and that their unlocked door is a standing invitation to come in and enjoy the beer and food in the refrigerator; a segue they may not have anticipated is his enjoyment of their double bed.

He continues to join Benita's family for Saturday night poker games, casually sitting down next to her where he can indulge in sexual innuendoes, pressing his knee against her thigh, nudging her foot with his. When the round comes to him, he invariably makes it Dealer's Choice. 'Seven-and-a-half to twenty-one, high-low hand,' he says, emphasizing the seven-and-a-half. The crude allusion that amuses him distresses her.

After school resumes in September, every chance passing in the church or school or gym is an opportunity to arrange a rendezvous. 'Wait for me at the empty lot tomorrow at four.' 'Meet me at the corner of Curtis and Bryant.' 'Be in the east vestibule of the church at seven.' Any spot that offers fifteen secluded minutes becomes a trysting place. Late one afternoon, Father and Benita exit the boiler room beneath the church and run into the tall, gaunt janitor coming down the steep, dark stairwell. 'You catch her down here again, Father?' he asks, tilting his head. He flashes a sly smile that unleashes a row of large, overlapping yellow teeth. 'Them girls and their cigarettes. I found two of 'em down here smoking one day last week.' He doesn't mention his attempt to tease kisses in exchange for secrecy. Now he looks down at Benita from half-closed eyes and snickers. 'She's a naughty one, that girl. But hell, they could be doin' worse things than smoking down here. Right, Father?' Father gasps in mock alarm and says he certainly hoped not and he's sure glad Ernie is helping him keep an eye on them. Ernie pauses at the bottom of the stairs and turns to watch the receding figures, the priest's cassock brushing along the concrete steps, the mid-calf length of the girl's uniform denying him the least glimpse. Ernie takes off his cap, scratches his head and frowns, then ducks through the low door into the boiler room.

Molly, the live-in housekeeper at the rectory, may have scratched her head, too, those mid-mornings when she noticed Father slip into the rectory office and close the door. She knew that behind it was Benita, practicing on the parish's only available dictaphone. Instead of sewing aprons in Home Economics with the other junior girls, Benita signed up for a second semester of typing. She wants to go to college and study Latin and astronomy and learn to be a teacher. Improving her secretarial skills is her insurance should those hopes fall through, hopes that rest entirely on a scholarship.

Or perhaps Molly went about her work trying to ignore the closed door and the uncharitable thoughts it set off. *That brassy girl. Chasing Father. What would her mother think?* Maybe she convinced herself that Father actually was helping Benita with her Latin. Like Caesar, Benita was ambitious. Most of us had had enough of Latin after the two required years. She liked languages, it was the only one offered, and she was among the few juniors in Father's class. What he's doing behind the door, in fact, is stroking her hair, caressing her breasts, kissing the back of her neck, telling her how much she matters to him, assuring her, when she tries to turn back to her work, that she needn't worry about either college or the Latin test tomorrow. He will leave the questions on the desk for her. 'Instead of studying tonight, meet me at. . .' She interrupts him with an indignant shake of her head. 'No, I don't want to cheat.'

Her extracurricular activities are taking an academic toll. The usual A's on her report card are interspersed now with B's. Her conduct mark, which dropped from A to B last year, falls to C in her junior year. For the first time in high school, she fails to meet the qualifications to be exempted from semester exams—a ninety average in academics and deportment, perfect attendance, no tardiness. Benita refuses to take the tests and announces her decision to switch to the public high school. Before she can set her plan in motion, Sister Gabriel, the principal, summons her. As Benita walks down Holly Street toward school, she sees Father exit the convent door. 'We've tallied up your grades again. You won't need to take the tests,' announces Sister, closing off Benita's escape route.

'Wait for me in the rectory office tonight,' says Father a few days later, waylaying Benita on the outside stairs leading into the school basement. She has a babysitting job, she says, and a history test to study for. She needs an A or there's no hope of a scholarship to Clarke. He bats the air with his hand, as if annoyed by a gnat. 'You don't need to worry about grades. Or the pittance you get baby-sitting, either. What is it you make? A buck an hour?'

'Fifty cents.' She lowers her eyes.

Father flings open a palm in impatient disdain. 'Look! If Clarke falls through, I'll get you into Mundelein.'

'In Chicago? That would be even *more* expensive.'

'Don't *worry*. You'll *go* to college. I'll see to that.' He takes her by the arm. 'Where will you be tonight?'

That evening, after making sure no neighbors are coming or going and the children are asleep in bed, Father taps on the back door of the home where Benita is baby sitting. In the time it takes him to smoke a cigarette, down a bourbon and copulate, she earns forty cents for college.

CHAPTER FIVE

In February of 1950, the Republican senator from Wisconsin, Joseph McCarthy, gives a speech to a West Virginia women's club, waving before them a fabricated list of 205 names of active communists known to the Secretary of State. What actually does exist is a reservoir of dread that began with the explosion of the first atomic bomb. It intensified when China fell to communist rule and the Soviet Union tested the atomic bomb. McCarthyism has heightened the sense of public vulnerability with shrill warnings that Communists are everywhere and each carries within him 'the germ of death for society.'

Catholic fear focuses on the aggressive, atheistic, materialistic character of Communism. Pius IX declares it 'absolutely contrary to natural law itself,' a system that would utterly destroy the rights, property and possessions of all men, even society itself. Catholics join study circles, attend conferences and lectures, take courses that promote a Christian solution to the certain loss of morality accompanying irreligion. They express their faith by an increased devotion to Mary and the rosary. This zeal began in 1917 when Mary reportedly appeared to three children tending sheep outside the small Portuguese town of Fatima and urged people to pray for peace and the conversion of Russia. In the decades that followed, as Catholics advanced their fingers along the beads, they imagined the transformation of Russian hearts and the retreat of Communism.

An ominous sign of the materialistic times is the appropriation of Victor Herbert's *Toyland* for commercial use. Now, instead of lyrics praising the mystic joyland of childhood, a prosaic verse promotes a spectacular new beauty product. *Dream girl, dream girl, beautiful Lustre Creme girl,* croons a male voice on radio commercials, *You owe your crowning glory tooooo, Lustre Creme Shampoooo.*

To be a dream girl is a noble secular goal in 1950. But this is Dubuque. We're Catholics. Our role was defined long ago in the fiery epistles of Paul of Tarsus. Man is the image and glory of God. Woman is the glory of man. A woman's long hair is a glory to her, conceded Paul, because it was given to her as a covering, a reminder that she is subject to man. She is also a temptress, an obstacle to devotion, a rival to the Church and the confusion of man. Woman is the perpetual Christian dilemma.

Required to cover her head, woman designs elaborate headdresses that hinder devotion; she attaches seductive veils to her mandatory Easter bonnet. She cuts her hair; she shaves her head; she grows her hair out and shampoos it with Lustre Creme. We contribute our bit to the rebellion by dropping into church to pray with a handkerchief pinned atop our crowning glory.

As Catholic females, we're both the source of male torment and the guardians of male chastity. Every year before prom season, Sister Gabriel rounds us up and spells out our responsibility toward the boys escorting us. With the renewed emphasis on Mary, whose virginal body was hidden beneath layers of fabric, come stricter standards of modesty. No bare backs. No uncovered shoulders. No plunging necklines or hints in that direction. Earlier that spring, Sister had called my mother to express concern about the formal I wore for a glee club concert, a pale cerulean blue gown with a sweetheart neckline that exposed my collar bones and their adjacent unholy flesh. Now, in case she's failed to hook our conscience, Sister Gabriel tosses in an appeal to our vanity. 'Wrap a towel around yourself and take a good look. Now what's pretty about it? Nothing! And that's exactly how a strapless dress looks.'

Because Marcella sews Benita's formals, she can manage their modesty, never a contentious issue with a daughter whose taste tends more toward sporty than sexy. But she cannot control her daughter in another realm. The trouble simmering there inevitably erupts.

Marcella had taken a job at Edwards, a downtown clothing store where she works longer hours altering more expensive clothes for more discriminating customers. Every morning, she boards the 8:40 bus and every morning, as soon as that bus leaves the curb, Benita lights up, smokes a quick cigarette and races to school before the final bell.

One morning, instead of getting onto the bus, Marcella yields to her misgivings and returns to the house. She opens the front door to see smoke streaming from her daughter's nostrils. 'Oh, Benita, no!' she exclaims. If her mother had yelled or cursed, if she had struck out at her or even fainted, Benita would have found it easier to bear than that pale, wide-eyed, interminable moment. Marcella strides across the room to the telephone and dials. 'Irene? Something terrible has happened. You must come home this evening.'

'It's bad enough for men to smoke. . .but for a girl? It's just so . . .so revolting! And it's making you dishonest' says Marcella that evening at the family conference. Her disillusioned eyes now recognize the evidence: Benita's sudden disappearances late in the evening; the scent of cigarettes on her clothing when she returns; the impulsive decisions to run over to school to play basketball or next door to Mary Jane's or Teresa's for awhile; her own perplexity as she stood at the window and watched Benita fleeing into the dark. 'Your hard-earned money is going up in smoke,' adds Irene.

Despite the discord caused by this discovery, it focuses Marcella's anxiety: *Benita smokes.* Marcella quits her subtle sniffing when Benita returns from a mysterious outing; instead, she glances at her daughter with candid disappointment, the flash of a camera illuminating the excruciating task of love.

Five days before their scheduled date for the Military Ball, David McCann telephones Benita at the home where she's babysitting and says he doesn't want to go with her. Those are his exact blunt words. Not 'I don't want to go,' but 'I don't want to go with *you.*' She, on the other hand, has her dress and her shoes and her heart set on going with *him.* She turned down two babysitting jobs that evening. Maybe Father was right about David all along. Maybe he does think he's better than she is and finally has gotten up the nerve to drop her. Or maybe he detected the scent of cigarettes on her breath the last time they went to a movie together, or heard something about her, some piece of gossip that makes her unworthy to be his date. Maybe his mother has seen her slip out of Father's car and break into a run. Something has happened, she's sure of it. Why, otherwise, did he call off their date and invite a non-smoking Visitation girl to the prom instead?

Marcella's disappointment is almost as great as Benita's. After all, it was Marcella who went shopping for the sky blue taffeta that matched her daughter's eyes; Marcella who hunted down enough matching net to make an overskirt; Marcella who'd been cutting and sewing in the kitchen all week. She'd just finished hand-stitching the hem when Benita came home, thin-lipped and stoical. 'I won't need that dress, Mom. David called. He doesn't want to go to the Military Ball with me.'

It's Benita who sits at the organ in the empty church those long winter evenings, intending to practice and pretending to, except that her tears blur the notes and her nose runs and it all seems so hopeless. It's David's fault. Mean, snobbish David. No,

Father is to blame. He ruined things between her and David. A sob breaks from her lips and echoes through the church. And then he's behind her, putting his arms around her, cupping his palms over her breasts, whispering, 'You're everything to me.' She leans into him. Just the two of them there in the dusky church. 'You're mine, my precious Benita.' There's nothing now except the turbulence between them, the storm that David McCann sensed and steered away from.

'Let's get a six-pack and go for a drive.'

Benita nods. She's thirsty.

CHAPTER SIX

ather adds a caveat to his routine reassurance: *There's nothing wrong with this, it will all come out in the wash.* Now he tells her she needs to go to confession, but not at St. Columbkille's. Benita turned sixteen in August and for all practical purposes, is a woman, and therefore, accountable. The onus of guilt is now on her.

Without transportation, stealing off to another part of town, to another parish and another confessional in order to seek forgiveness from another priest is a formidable requirement. Superimposed upon this quandary is another. Benita has been assigned as organist for early morning weekday Mass. Among the devout little group attending are her mother, Mrs. O'Brien, the Kurts, Mrs. Teeling, Bernice McCleary, Molly, the priests' housekeeper, my parents, and more often than not, me. This intimate gathering provides the ideal setting for her blossoming skill, but in her tainted spiritual state, it is the cause of intense distress.

As Communion-time grows near, Benita's mouth goes dry, her heart races, her fingers feel wooden on the keys. *Not* to receive Communion in that situation is to announce to her mother and neighbors the morbid state of her soul. *To* receive is one more mortal sin. When people begin to file up the aisle toward the

Communion rail, her struggle escalates. *Oh my God, I'm heartily sorry for having offended Thee, and I detest all my sins. . .*but an Act of Contrition is not sufficient to remove grievous sins. She has to confess them to a priest, promise to sin no more, do the assigned penance.

There were mornings in those high school years when I knelt next to Benita at the Communion rail, wrestling perhaps with my own jealous feelings toward her role as church organist, or as David's girl friend, or as popular, talented student, but never imagining her inner turmoil as she descended the steps from the choir loft and hurried up the side aisle to the altar rail. A tortured conscience was a predicament she could escape only when she was with *him*.

The approach of Easter heightens her dilemma. Among the six commandments of the church is the strict obligation to receive Holy Communion during the Easter season and to make a good confession within the year if you are in mortal sin. All who have reached the age of reason, usually considered to be age seven, are bound by this law under the pain of mortal sin. Anyone who knowingly receives Holy Communion in the state of mortal sin commits sacrilege. Sin upon sin upon sin. Benita is cornered.

On a dreary March Saturday afternoon, she puts on a storm coat and babushka and huddles on the rear seat of a city bus that takes her to St. Mary's church on the north side of Dubuque. In spite of the cruel wind, she gets off three stops away and rehearses her lines as she walks the remaining blocks. *Bless me Father, for I have sinned. It's eleven months since my last confession. I have committed the following sins.* Her legs feel rubbery; blood throbs in her ears as her lips move silently through the formula. She considers starting out with venial sins, maybe the priest will drift off and miss the worst. She puts up her collar and walks slower, slower, stops. She will wait until another day; she needs more time to think things through. She steps to the curb and watches for a homeward-bound bus, then abruptly turns and sets out toward the church again, walking rapidly now until she reaches the formidable main entrance. Inside, the darkness is blinding; the air stale with incense. When vision returns, she notices two old women in babushkas crouched in the back pews; further up, a white-haired man half- kneels and half-sits, elbows on his knees, head in his hands as if he is grieving. In a side pew a young couple kneels as one, earnestly whispering. She sinks to her knees for a few minutes, then stands and takes her pounding heart and soiled soul into the confessional.

The slide opens to a fleshy male profile tipped toward the grill and exhaling a peppery scent.

'Bless me Father.' She clears her throat, dislodging a jumble of words. 'It's been uh, well, quite a while since my last Confession. Almost a year, I think. Maybe not quite. I couldn't go because. . .because. . .'

'Yes. Because. . .?'

'Because I was afraid.'

'Afraid? And what are you afraid of?'

'Father said not to tell. He said it wasn't wrong. But he told me to go to Confession. I wasn't sure what to do. I need to receive Communion on Easter. With my mother. And I need your absolution.'

'For what sin? I need to know what sin is troubling you.'

She takes a deep breath. 'I've been with a priest.'

'You've been with a priest?' The shadow sighs heavily, shifts ominously nearer. 'What are you telling me, young lady?'

'I was. . .with Father. He did. . .we did. . .'

'What did you do?" An agonizing pause. "Have you committed impure acts with a priest?'

'Uh, I don't know.'

'You don't know? What is it you've done? Precisely, now.'

Silence.

'Have you tempted a priest?'

She nods, whispers, 'I guess so.'

'Caused him to fall.' A flat, accusing tone.

She nods again.

'How old are you?'

'Sixteen now. Fifteen then. Or. . .maybe thirteen. I'm not sure exactly. . .'

'You're not sure? What is it you're not sure of?'

'Fifteen,' she says quickly. 'I guess it was then.'

'This is terrible. Terrible. A very grave matter. A sacrilege. Do you understand that? A sacrilege.' He falls silent. She listens, trembling, to his reproachful breathing and then ventures more truth.

'I received Communion, too. Nearly every day. '

A profound sigh. 'That, too, is sacrilege. Did you not understand that you have been violating all that we hold sacred? Why did you do this dreadful thing?'

Benita chews on her lip to stop the spill of undeserved tears. She has earned this scolding.

'You must never do this again. Ever. Do you understand? You must promise. This man belongs to God. Forever. You have no right to him. Without sincere sorrow and a firm purpose of amendment, I cannot forgive you.'

Over and over she promises whatever he asks, until at last, the priest raises his hand in a grudging absolution. 'Go in peace and sin no more.'

She leaves, but not in peace. She has made promises she knows she won't—can't—keep. If she has to give up Father, she might as well be dead.

'I'm not going,' says Benita when her mother reminds her of the blue taffeta formal hanging in the upstairs closet. She'd hung it there after the aborted Military Ball, telling Benita she would be all set for the junior-senior prom at St. Columbkille's in May. The prom is the most anticipated social event of the year.

'But you're a junior. And one of the leaders in your class.'

'I don't want to go.'

'Have you even asked David? Maybe there was a reason. . .'

'I'm not asking him.'

'Some nice boy in your class, then.'

'Mom, *I don't want to go.*'

Marcella drops the subject. Benita would change her mind. Long-suffering was an unnatural trait in any sixteen-year-old girl, but especially in this popular, ambitious girl, the daughter whom Eldon, with his World Book and quizzes and affection, encouraged to be a star. When Benita says yes to a baby-sitting job the evening of the junior-senior prom, Marcella's worry intensifies.

When Benita returns from that baby-sitting job and Marcella detects the scent of cigarettes on her clothing and a hint of something on her breath—not bourbon, it couldn't be that, but something *like* that, a peculiar odor, in any case—her maternal conscience is in turmoil. She deliberately did not forbid her to smoke. To do so would have made every cigarette a sin of disobedience. Is there something behind the awful headaches that strike Benita like a weapon across the temple? The terrible pre-menstrual cramps? What should a mother do? What could she do? Maybe she should take her to a doctor. She wonders if Father has noticed anything wrong. She will talk to him. He is always willing to intercede on her behalf.

Father stops by one late May afternoon. Marcella is at the kitchen table clipping six inches from the formal Benita wore to last year's Military Ball. She gestures him to a chair, pours him a cup of coffee and sets an ashtray in front of him, then finishes trimming her way through the delicate red flowers blooming on the full white skirt. She lifts up the transformed dress for his appraisal. 'Do you think this is modest enough for Benita to wear to Mass, Father?'

He leans back and assesses it, then bends closer and runs his fingers along the edge of the fluttery cap sleeves. 'It's a very nice dress. You made it, didn't you?' He chuckles. 'Marcella, I don't think there's any danger of either you or Benita indulging in indecent clothing.'

'The real danger, Father, is the vanity of a seamstress with a pretty daughter. I do like sewing for her.'

'And has your pretty daughter sworn off proms, is that why you've cut off this dress? Or maybe she's finally given up on that McCann boy?'

'I'm worried about her, Father.' She puts down the dress and looks at him with weary eyes. 'I've been wanting to talk to you.' She pours out her concerns for nearly an hour when Benita arrives home from school.

'There's that girl of ours,' says Father.

In religion class, we learn that we can't always prevent impure thoughts and feelings from coming into our minds and bodies. Therefore, unless we keep them there and take pleasure in them—'entertain them' is what Father says—it isn't a sin. We also learn that the chief means of preserving the virtue of chastity is to avoid unnecessary dangers and to seek God's help through prayer, frequent confession, Holy Communion, attendance at Mass and devotion to the Blessed Virgin. Benita is seeking God's help in all the recommended ways, the daily rosary with her mother, daily Mass and the anguished Communion received from Father's hands when his fingers brush her chin with a promise. You're special. You're mine. His touch is her source of hope and survival, an outward sign of her inner worth. He is a necessary danger. She cannot give him up. What she does give up is the safeguard of 'frequent Confession.'

Frequent Confession is the recourse of many of us as young Catholics beleaguered by the temptations of the flesh. Attaining harmony between body and soul is difficult in a church that describes human sexuality in lofty language, but in practice, views it with suspicion and fear. The desires of the body are disconnected from those of the mind and spirit; the passions are controlled with draconian proscriptions. Benita's rationale is that as long as she does not find pleasure in what she does with Father, as long as her body remains numb, she will be free of sin.

In spite of the sincere rosaries storming heaven on behalf of peace, the newspapers once again tell of war. On June 25, 1950, Communist North Korea crosses the thirty-eighth parallel to invade anti-Communist South Korea; a week later Truman dispatches American ground troops. The Korean War marks the end of our junior year in high school and of our dreams, too, we fear. The boys we planned to fall in love with, marry and have children with, are being drafted and sent away. So are our brothers, including mine who finds himself in the Army immediately after graduating from the University of Iowa. The nation is in shock. U.S. soldiers are battling Communists in Korea; Russia is armed with the A-bomb. The idealized fifties feel more like a time of chronic international emergency.

The hedonism loosed by war may have prompted the summer plan in progress among a group of my classmates, next year's seniors. An excited buzzing begins over the planned week of swimming and beach-lounging at a rented cabin at Delhi, Iowa. Camp O'Delhi was a popular resort area an hour or so west of Dubuque, not far from Dyersville and the farm where Father grew up. Two rather nebulous chaperones would oversee the outing. Fiery sermons and threats of sin aside, unless Sister Gabriel was one of those chaperones, the prospect of seventeen-year-old kids hyped on hormones and stripped to swim suits lying day after day in the languid summer sun was not a parental sleeping potion. I didn't even bother to bring up the subject to my parents, specifically my mother, who applied her olfactory acumen to my every proposition. If she said, 'It smells fishy,' the deal was doomed.

Benita's stealthy smoking had damaged Marcella's natural tendency to trust her children. She now questions and warns and exerts unwelcome authority over Benita's life. Without proffering reasons, she tells her daughter she cannot join the group at the cabin. The pronouncement sets Benita wondering if her mother suspects her 'other' life. Is she plotting at this very moment to catch her in another guilty deed? She begins to watch her mother for signs of betrayal.

Father's family has a cabin near Hartwick, a site down the Maquoketa river from Camp O'Delhi. He invites Marcella and anyone she wants to bring along to picnic and swim there on summer Sunday afternoons. After early Sunday Mass, Marcella, Richard, Walter, Irene, their spouses and families, Carol and one or two of her friends, Benita and her friend, Teresa, even Great Aunt Maggie and Great Uncle Larry Maher on Marcella's side leave for the sandy beach. After the last parish Mass, Father joins them. The moment someone sights him, a shout goes up. 'Here comes Father!' Activities halt while they welcome him with waves and laughter. 'Hi, Father! Glad you could make it!'

If they'd had palm fronds in their hands, the scene would have evoked Christ's triumphant entry into Jerusalem. "Who is this?' the Jews began to wonder upon that occasion, a question no one in Benita's family found reason to ask on those Sundays in Iowa. This was Father, their parish priest, trusted family friend, the sponsor of their fun, the man who had upgraded their Sunday picnic site from a humble country pasture by the creek to a sandy beach on the river. He basked in their gratitude while watching for opportunities—the drive to the local grocery store to replenish the beer supply when he casually names Benita as his co-pilot, the games of beach volleyball when he collides with her in her swim suit, the moments of proximity he seizes to admire her figure or the color of her eyes.

Throughout the rest of the summer, his encounters with Benita are conducted with dispatch in homes where she baby-sits, his room in the rectory, the back seat of his car parked in an isolated country lane, the boiler room beneath the church, the choir loft, the confessional room. From time to time, he casually repeats the question, 'Are you awake yet?' As long as the question remains an enigma, she senses some bit of hope alive in her soul.

The convent tunnel that was the daring site of our second-grade voyeurism becomes, in our senior year, a potential bomb shelter. When China enters the Korean conflict late that year, an atomic showdown seems inevitable. School kids are taught to dive under desks in 'take cover drills.' People feel increasingly helpless in a world girding itself for apocalyptic confrontation. Our high school establishes 'Mary's Sodality,' a student organization centered on the Blessed Virgin. Benita joins the committee that meets regularly to recite the rosary for world peace.

On November 1, amidst ominous imaginings and pleas for prayer for the conversion of Russia, Pope Pius XII declares the dogma of the Assumption, the bodily transference of Mary into heaven. It is her 'crowning glory. . .to be preserved from the corruption of the tomb,' wrote the pope, 'and, like her Son before her, to conquer death and to be raised body and soul to the glory of heaven. . .' The critical theological distinction is this: Christ ascended to heaven by his own unaided power, while Mary was *assumed* into heaven, that is, passively drawn upward by the power of God. In a hierarchical patriarchy, it was the only way to go.

Regardless of her mode of transportation, Catholics rely upon Mary's status in heaven. Her function is summed up in the motto, *Ad Jesum Per Mariam:* a woman will listen when a man won't;

empathize when a man will judge; plead for mercy while a man will exact punishment. In other words, Mary is the one to approach if you wish to change the mind of God. This influential Virgin helps us feel better about ourselves as Catholic girls.

On December tenth, my seventeenth birthday, William Faulkner accepts the Nobel Prize for literature. In his speech, he speaks of the dread unleashed by the threat of nuclear holocaust. 'There are no longer problems of the spirit,' says Faulkner. 'There is only one question: when will I be blown up?'

Being blown up is an unsettling proposition for a Catholic girl in the state of mortal sin. Benita's last stronghold—the sexual impassivity that was the refuge of her conscience—has been conquered by Father. Now when he asks, 'Are you awake yet,' she can answer, 'Yes! Oh, yes!' Now when they set out together, she knows the pleasure awaiting and wonders how she did without before. The sex that thrills her body begins to fill her mind with the possibility of love. And then, with the awful futility of her situation. He is a priest forever. He claims her as his, but she can never claim him as hers. They can never be each other's. Yet, every time they are together, he says he loves her. If she falls in love with him, she's doomed. She isn't sure what love is. She wrestles with the question in her diary and looks for insight in popular music.

Love is a tender flower, a dewdrop of sweet surrender, comes the answer. Love is make believe, playing the fool, giving more than you get, risking a broken heart, a life of regret. Love bewitches, bothers and bewilders, the very feelings excited in me by the callow Loras college freshman I met that fall. I'm preparing to give my final piano recital in the spring but often, in the midst of practicing *Malagueña*, thoughts of him detour me to a pertinent piece of sheet music, *Too Young*. Hearing me play it drives my mother into a frenzy. Not only am I too young to really be in love, but I'm dangerously off course. The prospect of a botched recital, a botched life, takes her to the breaking point. She tears up my sheet music. By then, I know it by heart and go right on asserting my capacity for enduring love while out in the kitchen, she seethes and pares potatoes for supper.

Certain traditions mark our senior year in high school. Among them is a required essay on the vocation we feel called to by God. A nod is given to marriage and the 'single state,' but everything in our schooling says the highest vocation is the religious life. 'I desire the married life,' writes Benita in her essay, 'because I love children and know how beautiful family life can be from experience baby-sitting and also that of my own home. But there is one great drawback for me entering that life. I have no particular interest in boys. Maybe that will come later, but I have my doubts. From this obstacle to marriage along with a few other inclinations I feel, maybe I have a calling to the religious life, but I would dislike giving up my worldly pleasures. Another thing that holds me back is the question of who will take care of my mother. She would be the last person to hinder me, but I can't stand to think of her ever being lonely after all she has done for me. The only other road to consider is the single state, but from the advice of the church, I would like to avoid that because it might endanger the salvation of my soul. Right now I feel I could brave the temptations that would arise, but I do not know too much about the way of the world. With prayer and the sacraments and effort on my part, I hope God will help my unsettled mind and put me on the right path.'

Her unsettled mind, heart, soul. Her desire to pursue both worldly pleasures and the right path. As her guide, prayer and the taboo sacraments. An essay honed to meet the expectations of teachers and family. She designs social activities with the same intent—to present herself as a typical seventeen-year-old high school girl. When Greg Jones, a fellow-student in her fourth year Latin class, asks her to be his date for the annual junior-senior prom, her enthusiastic 'yes' is a cover-up. It's also a frantic unconscious grasp for release from her attachment to a man who plies her with forbidden pleasure while leading her further and further down the wrong path.

May is the month set aside by the church to honor Mary. Every year, our school holds a May crowning, a religious ceremony in which high school students—girls in pastel formals and white veils, boys in their best suits—march with folded hands from school to church. Behind them, garbed in a flowing blue satin mantel, walks the senior girl designated by the nuns as May Queen. Accompanying her are five senior girls selected to be her attendants. Among them that spring is Benita, wearing her pink bridesmaid dress. As the May Queen mounts the steps to Mary's statue and places a wreath of spring's most beautiful flowers on her head, the rest of us sing, 'O Mary, we crown thee with blossoms today, Queen of the angels, Queen of the May." The ritual concludes with a rosary led by Father from the altar. Afterward, he takes Benita aside and tells her she was the prettiest girl in the procession.

A week later, that same pious group of seniors change into blue-jeaned rowdies setting out for our final class event, a day long field trip to the country. Father is our chaperone. Out of range of Sister Gabriel's censorious squint, we frolic all day in swimsuits. We swim in the brown creek, picnic, play volleyball. Now and then, in the heat of conversation or games, Father sets his hand on a bare female shoulder or waist. When we gather on blankets for lunch, he sits down near Benita and reaches into her basket for the minced ham sandwich Marcella has secured inside for him. After the picnic ends and the others are gone, Father and Benita return to the picnic site and a sky full of stars. He holds her as she names them. He's never had a student like her before, he says. With her pleasure that evening comes a terrible fear. What if her mother could see her now? Or Richard or Walt or Irene? How would she ever explain herself?

"On the second day of June, the 1951 seniors will start the march toward uncertainty. For then a world of deceit will be our highway. But to pledge our safety upon the road, the rosary will be our constant guide." This is the somber challenge issued on the Foreword page of the 1951 *Bwan*, the St. Columbkille high school yearbook. Occupying the lower half of the page is a photograph of the 'Living Rosary,' a ceremony held on the high school football field. In it, sixty seniors stand in a circular formation lined up according to height, shortest to tallest, a progression imposed by nuns who seem unaware of the potential psychic damage to those of us at the extremes. Ten girls in blue school uniforms and white veils, each one depicting a bead, constitute one decade of the rosary. Ten boys in suits form the next decade and so on, around the circle. At five feet eight, I'm the last girl in the fifth decade and Benita, an inch shorter, is the Hail Mary in front of me.

Scattered throughout that yearbook are drawings connecting Mary's miraculous history to mundane school moments, sketches of her hovering in the skies of Lourdes and Fatima juxtaposed with illustrations of students studying, playing, praying. A large, painstaking drawing of the rosary is repeated strategically throughout the album. On one decade there are twelve beads. On another, thirteen. The illustrator was Benita, a tentative artist, who used the aberrant decades as a protest against Father, who she is certain manipulated her appointment as yearbook artist.

She receives the needed scholarship to Clarke. The Elks scholarship goes to her. She wins the watch awarded for perfect attendance, although it takes two drawings to make that determination. To Benita, every honor suggests a ploy, compounding her indebtedness and crippling her self-confidence. 'Teresa, what's with Benita and Father?' asks one of the losing contestants for the prize watch. 'You'll have to ask her,' says Teresa.

The morning after our high school graduation, Benita's sister, Irene, marries Don Breitbach at a Nuptial Mass in St. Columbkille's church. Afterward, Father, the celebrant, searches out Benita among the crowd socializing in the church hall. 'I wish this was our wedding,' he says as they stand silently watching the bridal couple greet well-wishers. She ponders his perplexing words on the last page of her diary, then buries the little book in her dresser drawer.

CHAPTER SEVEN

In college, we switch to filter-tip cigarettes, not out of concern for our lungs, but because we consider them more appropriate to the young sophisticates we imagine ourselves to be. We swing the long, slender cigarettes to our lipsticked mouths with the sullen chic of Marilyn Monroe. Benita smokes Kents; I prefer Winstons. My packs invariably last two or three days, more than twice as long as Benita's. Simply imagining my dad's mutters and glares and tallying up of nails being hammered into my coffin when I light up is enough to dampen my smoking pleasure.

In the hierarchy of nuns—and there is one, everything is ranked according to power or prestige, the parish, the school, the neighborhood, your house and attire, even the truth (the dogma of the Immaculate Conception, for example, is not an essential belief of the Christian faith, but the divinity of Christ and the redemptive value of his life, death and resurrection is)—the Sisters of Charity of the Blessed Virgin Mary are highly esteemed. They are intelligent, progressive, well-educated women who not only encourage us to achieve academically, but also approve of lipstick and designate an on-campus smoking site.

Emerging from twelve strict years, we are astounded at the

possibilities. In conjunction with a required liberal arts core—science, philosophy, history, language, art—we can choose poetry, drama, fencing, zoology, business, home economics. In theology, we are introduced to Plato, Aristotle, Augustine and Aquinas who give us reasons for the faith that is in us, although the idealism and dualism embedded in their thought does not work to our advantage as females. All of them were ambivalent toward sex and passion and its role in the 'fallen human condition'; none of them were able to resolve the conflict between the needs of the body and the needs of the mind and soul. Their deductions are our heritage: a religion that fears physical desire as a threat to spiritual yearning rather than intrinsic to it; a patriarchal institution that sees women as the problem in need of control. The priest who is our logic professor suggests that as women, we are incapable of fully grasping the subject, but he goes right on trying, while we put our energy into finding a personal patriarch who will direct our irrational tendencies.

Semester tuition in the fall of 1951, excluding board and room, was less than $300, the then-sacrificial price of a ticket into the WASP world. Catholic girls from Chicago and Des Moines and small towns dotting the maps of Iowa and Illinois arrive at Clarke with hopes of developing marketable talents and dreams of finding husbands who will make marketplace work unnecessary. Those of us who would have been deprived of college if it had required room and board somewhere are lucky to have Clarke in our hometown. We have the Catholic church to thank. In spite of the outraged rulers and outrageous tenets we encountered along the way from grade school to college, we arrived there because of devoted, flawed human beings working within a system dedicated to providing schools, hospitals and communities for uneducated minorities struggling to adapt to an antagonistic, often anti-Catholic society.

At the parish level, that system focused on equipping us with ammunition with which to defend our faith. Our high school course in church history argued a continuous line of popes, beginning with the moment Christ said, 'Thou art Peter and upon this rock I will build my church,' on through the present time. Concealed behind that impregnable surface were political intrigues, foul play, threats, bribes, papal mistresses and papal children (one of whom provided the model for Prince Machiavelli). The bulk of available resources was spent training us in the creed and conduct of being Catholic. Consequently, we finished high school with no exposure to the classics or art or any foreign language other than Latin, not even a basic course in U.S. Government.

Benita encounters the effects of this lopsided education with the assignment of the first term paper in our freshman year at Clarke. She appeals for help to Sister Edward, that inveterate advocate of language skills who was our eighth grade teacher. Her assistance expands into mentoring and a friendship that gives Marcella hope, even a little relief regarding her enigmatic daughter.

As full-time alteration lady at Stampfer's department store, Marcella works in solitude which allows her mind to wrestle with concerns beyond the projects in her hands. Carol is a happy-go-lucky ten-year-old with a bevy of fifth-grade friends. Benita, at eighteen, is still besieged with migraine headaches, torturous monthly periods, and a vague brooding that Marcella's prayers and worry and consultation with Father have failed to resolve. David McCann has broken her daughter's heart. But there's that nice Greg Jones from high school. And James O'Neill, from a good family in the parish, a friendly Loras College boy with curry-colored hair and matching freckles and an obvious interest in Benita.

My mother's strategy toward my romantic adventures continues to be resistance. For awhile, I date a passionate Italian boy, an indifferent Catholic confounded by my virginal commitment. Next there is a brawny fullback, also Italian and mysteriously still in college at age twenty-five, or six, or seven. My mother swears twenty-eight. His unpredictability and swarthy good looks keep him on my mind, and on my mother's too, but for a different reason. My parents keep a vigil at the front door; my dad watches us go out, politely refraining from saying what he is thinking about banana peddlers; my mother and the porch light wait for me to return home. My vigil is at the telephone, where I wait in a tormented charade of the popular song, 'All In The Game.' The lyrics start out philosophically and trill through misunderstanding and misery to a joyful reunion. My real-life romance simply fizzles out.

Outwardly, Benita appears typically collegiate, a long-legged girl in a belted straight skirt, trim turtleneck sweater, penny-loafers, walking from class to class with a stack of notebooks and textbooks pressed to her chest. Among them is Spanish Grammar I. Four years of high school Latin whetted her appetite for languages. Spanish Grammar is among the books I carry home each night, too. We take several of the same courses and between classes, hurry to the 'Union' for a quick cigarette and a round of bridge; at day's end, we often ride home on the same bus; we study together for exams. Sometimes, after cramming into the wee hours, I spend the few remaining hours of the night in the upper bunk in her bedroom. We continue to be in each other's presence at daily Mass where she plays the organ and I kneel with my parents in pew fifteen. She and I often kneel side by side at the Communion rail.

Inwardly, her entanglement with Father has left her as vulnerable as a china cup at a children's party. The tension between inside and out is what Marcella senses and frets over. Had this concern provoked her to repeat the surprise attack that documented Benita's smoking, she would have slipped away from work and taken the bus home in the middle of some random afternoon. As she stopped inside the front door to take off her coat, the sound of someone in distress would have beckoned her through the house and up the stairs, tracking the moaning through Carol's empty bedroom and on to its source, Benita's closed door. She may have stopped to knock, or simply turned the knob and finding it locked, frantically called out, 'Benita! Are you all right?' Or she may have burst in on them without warning and cried in outrage and despair, 'No! Oh, Benita! No!'

On any random day that semester, a bus could have brought Marcella home to a scene of sexual passion worked into Benita's freshman class schedule. Or to its tranquil aftermath, the satiated murmuring of a man making impossible promises. But Marcella spends her day at work while her home serves as a venue for assignations. The neighbors pay little attention, accustomed as they are to Father's car coming and going from the 'garage' he rents so frugally there.

What the neighbors do notice early that winter is Father's sudden absence. He has been transferred to St. Joseph's parish in Chelsea, Iowa, a hamlet of fewer than three hundred people west of Cedar Rapids.

'What's Archbishop Binz thinking of, wasting a young priest in a place like that,' tsk-tsk the faithful. He may have been thinking over a muttered intimation by Monsignor Dunn, who lives in the rectory and has some exposure to the young priest's habits. Or perhaps some gossipy observation has reached his ear. *Father and that Kane girl are certainly chummy.* No doubt, what he prefers to think is that his priest is offering Christian kindness to a widow, befriending her sons, providing her daughters with a father figure. Whatever his conjectures, the bishop's miter carries a primary responsibility: to preserve the visible institutional structures of the Roman Catholic Church.

The parishioners of St. Joseph's church in Chelsea rejoice in their good fortune, a priest of their own. 'Father, come to supper tomorrow evening.' 'Father, do you need someone to mow the lawn at the rectory?' 'Father, I made these brownies for you. Florence heard you love chocolate.' No one in a tiny parish in Iowa is prepared to criticize or to chaperone a young, intelligent, well-educated priest who knows more about God than all of them put together.

Driving the hour or so from Chelsea to Dubuque is less convenient for Father, but not prohibitive. He visits 1125 Cleveland Avenue when Marcella is away playing cards with friends and eleven-year-old Carol is upstairs asleep for the night. One evening when Carol lies awake complaining of an ache in her side, Father goes to her bedside to investigate. Her appendix, he theorizes, but her wary eyes curtail an examination.

Other times, he stops in specifically to see Marcella, sometimes with a shirt and a stray button in hand, or a seam to mend, but always primed to join family activities. When Marcella asks him to supper, he stays. When Walt suggests a trip to Chicago together for a Cubs game, he makes eager plans. Whenever he hears talk of a family poker game, he volunteers his presence. *'He's* here,' Benita calls to her family around the dining room table when she sees his car slow in front of their house. Ever since that afternoon in the confessional, she has stopped calling him 'Father.' She doesn't address him with any name. He is *him* or *he* or *you*. *'He* just pulled into the shed,' she tells her mother.

When Father invites Marcella and her daughters to vacation with his parents at their family's cottage at Hartwick, she accepts enthusiastically. When he asks if she'd mind chauffeuring his parents to the cottage in their car, she replies, *Mind? Father, I'd be honored!* His mother is her dear friend. Benita welcomes the chance to fish and swim and acquire a tan, perhaps even to regain a little of her mother's trust. Eleven-year-old Carol prefers a week in the country with cousins her own age.

The two mothers, Marcella Kane and Emma Dunkel, spend their time in lawn chairs, alternately reading and chatting and napping, while Father's dad, Nick Dunkel, sits apart from them with a glass of whiskey in hand. Benita often rows a small boat out on the Maquoketa river and idles there fishing for awhile before continuing across to the beach at Camp O'Delhi to sun-bathe. That's where she is lying sun-drugged one afternoon when a woman's voice calls out, *¡Cuidado, niño! ¡Cuidado, niña!'* At the sound of Spanish, Benita's eyes spring open to see a lovely dark-haired woman cautioning her two young children. Benita is about to say, *'Hola! ¿Cómo está usted?'* when a man shouts from the door of the little beachside store, 'Benita! Benita! Telephone!' She leaps up and sprints toward him. So does the Hispanic woman who takes the telephone handed to her while Benita stands in puzzle-ment. Afterward, when she approaches her to untangle the mys-tery, she discovers that this is the Benita for whom she was named, the pretty, gracious girl Marcella met and admired so long ago. Her marriage to a military man has taken her around the world, but this is the site she chose to return to this summer, a happenstance that delights the two Benitas. When they part, an idea captures Benita Kane's imagination. She holds it throughout the summer and into fall, when, to the delight of Sister Lucilda, the petite, sprightly head of the Spanish department, Benita declares Spanish her major field. Someday she will go to Mexico.

Toward the end of the week, on a muggy Midwestern after-noon, Father arrives at Hartwick, as planned. He has agreed to drive Benita home for a babysitting commitment while Marcella stays on with his parents. Before leaving, he wants to cool off on the river. He strips off his black vest and collar to the white, short-sleeve T-shirt underneath. Benita, in her usual vacation attire, shorts and a shirt pulled over her swimsuit, volunteers to take him out in the boat to fish. 'Like a regular apostle,' says his mother as they walk away. 'Like Peter.'

'If you two catch any souls,' calls his dad as they shove away from shore, 'bring 'em back alive!' He tilts up his glass, takes a swig of whiskey and cackles, 'Or toss 'em back in. Hell, *you're* the priest. *You* decide.'

Nick Dunkel's son, Henry, middle child in a family of eleven, is something of a mystery to him. A smart kid, not much good on the farm, but with a head full of information from books. As a kid, he liked to lie around on the lawn at night and look up at the stars and name everything he saw. Nick wasn't surprised when he decided to become a priest like his uncle and namesake, Reverend Henry J. Dunkel. He was the holy one in Nick's family, too, the one better than the rest of them, the son his mother idolized, the way Emma does their priest-son. Just one year after Nick's brother Henry died, his son Henry entered the seminary. Nick can't figure out why any man, especially a young, healthy one, would give up what women have to offer. About all he has in common with his son now is the pleasure to be found in a glass of whiskey. 'Don't you try to feed that to Benita,' scolded Emma when she saw Nick put a fifth into his suitcase for this vacation. 'I ain't planning to,' said Nick. 'This is for me. She don't like nothin' but beer anyway.' He'd offered Benita whiskey plenty of times, but she always wrinkled up her nose as if he was out to poison her.

Fifty feet out, Father sets his palm on Benita's bare knee, then spreads his fingers and begins moving his hand slowly along her thigh, admiring her suntan, asking how much of her is that same color. With his other hand, he gestures to a wooded site on the opposite shore. 'Let's check it out.' He smiles at her from half-closed eyes. 'The tan, I mean.' After they anchor the boat, he opens a six-pack, hands a can to Benita, puts an arm around her waist, pulls her close and sighs. 'Maybe we could live here. Set up housekeeping right over there.' He points. What they see at the end of his finger is another boat approaching. Benita steps free of Father's hand. The man waves, a red-haired man, a boy, James O'Neill. He pulls into shore and gets out. Benita lowers her beer, and holds it by the top behind her back.

'Hey, Benita! I thought that was you.' His surprised grin sobers on Father. 'Oh, hi, Father. I thought you were somebody else. Uh, so, how are you, Father?' Father declares himself fine, although his crestfallen expression says he felt remarkably better a few moments ago. Nor does James' announcement that his family is staying at Camp O'Delhi cheer him up. He offers James a beer, which he declines. Benita offers him an explanation: she's here with her mother who's here with father's parents and all of them are right over there. James listens politely, turns his head when she points, and leaves. Benita and Father soon follow. The thought of four or five parishioners spying on them is not an aphrodisiac.

They encounter another frustration when they arrive in Dubuque. Walter is making his first swath around the enormous back yard with the lawn mower. 'Hey! Hi, Father! What did you think of the Cubs this week? Want a beer?'

Father smiles. 'Sure.' Benita goes inside and brings out two frosty bottles. She hands them to Father and returns indoors. Father sits down on the step and smokes while he discusses baseball and empties the first bottle. He lifts the second. 'Want this beer, Walt?'

'Nah, I better finish up here. You have it.' Walter backtracks to catch a clump of grass he's missed.

Father opens the bottle, lights another cigarette and watches his hopes dwindle as Walt wanders the lawn. Once, as he mows past, he pauses, gestures toward the house on the adjacent lot and says, 'C'mon over to the house with me when I finish here, Father, Jo and the kids would like to see you.'

Father gets up. 'I'd like to see them, too, but I've got a parish meeting. Give Jo my best.'

When Benita sees him pull away, she feels a surge of irritation at both men, and then an unbearable need. The agony ends later that evening when Father knocks on the door of the home where she's baby-sitting.

Before Marcella returns with Father's parents from Hartwick, Benita throws a party, a reckless gathering I never could have carried off simply because someone was always home at my house. She calls it a high school reunion and invites everyone from the class. We smoke and drink beer and sweet concoctions of gin and strawberry soda. We play poker and bridge and euchre at Marcella's kitchen and dining room tables; we set up an auxiliary card table in the living room beneath a picture of the Sacred Heart. In the middle of everything sits Benita, a cigarette gripped between her lips, her eyes narrowed against the smoke, dealing a hand of poker. I look at her with fascination. That she can be so blasé about breaking rules, about the smoke burrowing into sofas and rugs and curtains, about the dip and chips being spilled on the floor, that she's willing to flaunt her mother's trust for the sake of sponsoring this wild conviviality, that's the side of her that baffles me. I have no way of knowing that this is not Benita, but Benita imitating Father, a way of assuring herself that she is his.

Autumn on the Iowa bluffs along the Mississippi. The many-splendored trees. A sky of intrepid blue. Mellow, sparkling air. Football. As college sophomores, we spend luxuriant September Saturdays flirting in stadiums and crowded together in ice cream parlors afterward. Benita goes through the motions until it's time to slip away and meet Father. After hearing a few tame confessions at his little parish, where occasions for sin are limited and transparent lives discourage confessing them, he drives to Dubuque to pick her up at a chosen site.

One early evening, he suggests that they drive to Dyersville, a small town twenty-five miles west of Dubuque, to check the progress of the house his parents are building there. As it neared completion, they designated a room for him and began moving in a few belongings from the farm where he grew up. His brother, Herb, arrives simultaneously to discover that the usually unlocked doors are locked. 'Hell,' says Herb. 'Outta luck. And I had myself all set for a slug of dad's whiskey.'

Father walks around the house looking for access, spies it and beckons to Benita. 'Here's the place.' To his brother, he says, 'And here's the girl who can help us out.'

'Me? You want me to. . .?'

'You have experience. Remember?' says Father with a wink and a nod toward the unlatched basement window. 'Herb and I will hoist you through. Then you can go up and unlock the front door for us.' In their eagerness, they overdo it and land her shoulder down on the concrete floor, eight feet below. Father pokes his head into the window. 'You okay? Go on up, then, to your right are the stairs. Front door's just down the hall. We'll come around.'

'Good girl, Benita,' says Father when she opens the front door. 'Herb, didn't I tell you that *this* is one very good girl?' He gives his brother a playful jab. They reward Benita with two cigarettes and three swallows of whiskey straight from the bottle, then warn her not to tell the episode to anyone.

Fortunately, the injury that makes her shoulder ache for days is not a break but a very bad bruise. She accounts for the damage to her mother the next day by changing the names and place and purpose into a benign adventure with friends. Marcella listens with skeptical eyes. 'It sounds to me like something a group of twelve-year-old boys would do. Not young women in college.' Unwittingly, she's put her finger on a problem, the psychological immaturity that pertains more to priests than college girls.

CHAPTER EIGHT

When my romantic life is stable, I can more fully appreciate the intellectual aspect of college. I delight particularly in the challenge of a Modern Poetry class taught by Sister Ignatia, a tall, vibrant young nun who strides eagerly into the classroom. Her brimming knowledge and enthusiasm attract me to English as my major field. She introduces us to the surprising, mystical work of Jesuit Gerard Manley Hopkins, whose poetry overflows with joy in creation while simultaneously recognizing a world that is both dark and light. To demonstrate how his packed lines and sprung rhythms achieve that tension, Sister Ignatia reads us a poem from a period of his life when his work focused on desolation and recovery.

> *Not, I'll not, carrion comfort, Despair, not feast on thee;*
> *Not untwist—slack they may be—these last strands of man*
> *In me or, most weary, cry I can no more. I can;*
> *Can something; hope, wish day come; not choose not to be.*

The only way to live honestly in the world, says Sister, interpreting Hopkins, is to confront suffering and death and in spite of it, make a declaration of hope.

Chelsea, Iowa wasn't working out for Father. Or perhaps it was a surge of pure patriotism that inspired him to join the Air Force that October, after only a few months at St. Joseph's parish. Or the inspiration may have belonged to the archbishop who would have been required to endorse him as spiritually, morally, intellectually and emotionally qualified to represent the Archdiocese in the military. In any case, Father is leaving for Fort Slocum, New York to be trained as a chaplain. It's an answer of sorts to Benita's dilemma, but just as she begins to fall into the carefree rhythm of a college girl, he telephones to remind her that she's his. He calls on Marcella's regular card-playing evenings; he calls the homes where Benita baby sits. He writes letters pouring out his loyalty and longing, expressing his ardor in lyrics from popular songs. You're the key to my happiness. Unbelievably warm, wonderful you.

She retrieves his letters from the mailbox before her mother gets home from work, reads them in her room, buries them beneath bras and panties in her dresser drawer. When she confides to him her hiding place, he says he likes thinking of the pages he's touched lying near the clothes that touch her body. She writes him letters describing her day-to-day life, which is lonely and dull without him. She signs her letters with words from a song they call 'theirs,' promising to love him with a true love for all time. Now and then a letter comes from Father to Marcella.

Emma Dunkel is lonely, too. She asks Benita to come to Dyersville and spend the weekend with her and Nick in their new home. Benita makes the hour long trip on the Greyhound bus. The guest room is Father's room; she's been there before, before his parents moved in from the farm, before there was a double bed or lace curtains or that disturbing, poorly executed mural now covering one wall. 'Father painted this,' crows Emma. 'I bet you didn't know he was a artist. Neither did I. But here it is. He's full of surprises, isn't he?'

Benita is surprised at the chaotic, ugly rendition of what appears to be the story of Adam and Eve being cast into hell from a Bosch-like *Garden of Delights* where exotic creatures, sinister monsters, nude men and women writhe in despair, as if doomed by their sensual appetites. She sees a side of Father that unsettles her.

In 1952, on the day after Thanksgiving, a man in the commanding blue uniform of an Army Air Force captain parks a cream-colored Dodge with red wheels in front of the Kane house and walks up the sidewalk to their front door. As Father comes in, Richard is on his way out, to his own home and family. He smiles broadly and shakes Father's hand. 'Hey, Father! Good to see you.' His eyes fall on the silver cross on Father's lapel and then to the bars on his shoulder. 'Do you go by Father or Captain?'

'Depends on the situation.' Father winks and grins. 'What about you? Do you go by Dr. Kane now that you're a full-fledged dentist?'

'Only in my office.'

'How's Ruth and. . .wasn't it another son?'

'Yep. Kevin. Almost four months old now. Doing great. Both of them.'

Halfway down the walk, Richard pauses and turns. 'Stop in while you're in town, Father. Ruth would love to see you. We're just down the block.'

Marcella is at the door, smiling. 'Father! It's so good to see you after all these weeks. You look so dignified in your uniform!' She might have said *handsome*, had it been an appropriate comment from a woman to a priest. 'Are you hungry, Father? Can I fix you something to eat?'

He drops his head and looks expectantly at her from the tops of his eyes.

She bats the air with both hands. 'Oh, Father, you haven't

changed a bit! I'm afraid Friday is one day I have to say no to minced ham sandwiches. Will egg salad do?' Marcella goes to the bottom of the stairs. 'Benita! Guess who's here to see us?'

She's been watching for him, of course, one part of her eager for the reassurance of his arms, another part dreading it, the part that wants to live up to the promise she made in confession last week, to amend her life, never to commit that sin again. But when she sees him standing there, stalwart and strikingly blue-eyed in his blue uniform, holding his military hat by the visor, the way her dad had held his policeman's hat, her whole being cries out with a longing that can only be love.

His ten-day leave provides ample time to disrupt her studies and any developing feelings she has for the attractive Loras College boy she began dating that month. When her classes are over on Monday, Father picks her up at an arranged site near the Clarke campus. No longer the coy school girl, she drops her head onto his lap, confident of their direction. He strokes her possessively, hair, shoulder, breast, working his hand inside her coat to prepare her with his touch.

He drives to a remote motel on the farthest edge of town. It's the first in a week of afternoons they spend at ramshackle, out-of-the-way places. Benita goes in first, feigning calm along with a name, and pays with the bills Father has handed her. As soon as she reaches the room, she goes to the window and signals to him in the parking lot. Soon, he is knocking on the door. When she opens it, he reaches for her. It's the yearning in his eyes that makes her weak, heedless of her resolutions.

On the last day of his leave, Father sits at the kitchen table eating the minced ham sandwich Marcella insisted on making for him and telling her what he told Benita earlier as she lay in his arms. 'You might as well keep my car here and drive it after I leave, Marcella. No point in it sitting unused at my folks' while I'm gone.' The next day he leaves for Texas, where he's been assigned to serve as Catholic chaplain at Webb Air Force Base.

After his departure, Benita feels empty, isolated from everything that matters. Her studies. Her friends. Her family. Her future. She can't live without him. Or with him. What will become of her? Will she ever be able to look honestly into her mother's eyes again?

When she arrives at Clarke behind the wheel of Father's Dodge, I'm not sure how to interpret my surprise. Her explanation makes it sound sensible; my intuition sees it as evidence. But of what? The favoritism shown Benita has always annoyed me. In grade school, the kids preferred her. Ever since eighth grade, Father preferred her. David McCann preferred her. Now in college, Sister Lucilda prefers her, even though I've declared Spanish my second major. Benita's affinity for nuns and priests, her organ-playing and parish-centered activities don't fit with the Benita I know who smokes and drinks beer. There's an edge to her, as if hidden beneath her surface simmers something about to boil over. Teresa is her confidante. I'm her friend, torn between admiration and jealousy. Jealousy, I decide, is behind the flicker I felt at the sight of Father's car. She has wheels; I'm on foot. After our classes, she gives me a ride home. We ride in uneasy silence, both smoking, both under the influence of him. When I get out, calling 'See you tomorrow' as I close the door, I feel released.

Vague symptoms begin to plague her. Fatigue, and a strange butterfly rash on either side of her nose. After the holidays, advises the doctor, she should go to Iowa City for further tests at the University Hospital. There's a possibility of lupus, an autoimmune disorder, her body attacking itself. She hears the suggestion of a serious, possibly life-threatening disease as good news. While her distressed family prays and worries, she privately imagines her death, a notion she confides only to Teresa. Never in our Spanish classes or during our rides home together, or on our double dates, never in any of the multitude of activities we shared, did I recognize Benita as someone wishing *not to be*.

She says nothing of her potential illness to Father. What if he became distraught, rushed back from Texas, took her in his arms and ordered her back to health? *What if he didn't?* That's the impasse clotting her life. But death is offering her a way around it.

Again, her escape plan fails. She does not have lupus. She is sentenced to be. To be bound to a man who can never be hers. To be constantly fearful of losing connection with him. His strategic position in her life makes him as essential as the air she breathes. After Christmas, she writes to him, confesses her illness and describes how worried her family had been. Immediately, he calls from Texas and soundly scolds Marcella when she answers the phone. 'Why did you keep this from me, Marcella? I had no idea Benita was sick. I don't understand this secrecy. In the future, you must keep me informed about these things. Do you understand? Now let me speak with Benita.'

At that moment, Benita is behind the wheel of his car delivering her great Aunt and Uncle Maher back home after an evening visit. She returns to find her mother near tears over the long-distance tongue-lashing she thought she deserved. An hour later, he calls again, this time admonishing Benita. Never, ever again, is she to keep anything from him. Is that clear? Has she forgotten she's his? If she needs proof, she has it. He's taken out some very good stocks in her name. Something called Martin Marietta.

From every long distance call, a few conversational fragments inevitably fall into the ears of the telephone operator, who happens to be a parishioner at St. Columbkille's. A few days after Father's anxious call from Texas, the operator casually asks a friend, *What's the deal with Benita Kane and Father Dunkel? I saw her driving his car.* That friend shrugs and passes the query on to her friend. And so it goes, an offhanded question floating beyond the range of Marcella's ears.

Marcella is well aware of her daughter's anguish. She sees her troubled eyes, the tension in her mouth, the turbulence beneath the taciturn surface. 'Honey, is there anything. . .' she often begins, but Benita responds with an impatient sigh that says, 'Will you leave me alone? Please?' Marcella frets and prays and hopes. She puts money into an envelope and presses it into Monsignor's hand, asking him to offer a Mass for her intention. She offers her daily rosary for Benita's sake. She lies in bed at night murmuring the Memorare. *Remember, O most gracious Virgin Mary, that never was it known that anyone who fled to thy protection, implored thy help and sought thy intercession was left unaided. . .'*

Bea Roscoe, the parish organist who lives across the street from the church, often encounters Marcella after Mass and stands chatting with her on the church steps. The worry Bea sees deepening in Marcella's eyes prompts her to inquire one morning about her health. 'Oh, I'm fine. It's Benita I'm worried about. She hasn't been herself since. . .' Marcella confides the lupus scare.

Bea commiserates, and rejoices in the happy outcome, and somewhere in between, says, 'So *that's* what brought Father Dunkel back.'

Marcella looks at her for a moment without comprehension. 'Oh, no, no, he was on furlough. On his way to Texas to serve as chaplain. The lupus problem came up later.'

'And how *is* Father?' asks Bea with a lift of her brow that suggests she knows the answer but isn't so sure Marcella does.

Marcella smiles. 'He's fine. Just fine. It was good to see him. He's been such a good friend to me, to our family all these years. We miss him.'

'I saw Benita driving his car.'

'He left it for us to use. He's generous to a fault. I hope it doesn't spoil Benita.'

Bea gives her a cautious glance. 'It *is* quite a responsibility.'

Something unsaid in Bea's eyes nags Marcella as she walks home. She drops into the chair inside the front door. Always, in this room, she feels Eldon's presence, his eager gathering of children around the recording machine, his comings and goings through the front door, that last day when he came in so pale and breathless with his hand on his chest. The living room and their bedroom, those are the two places where he still dwells. She sits thinking, praying, asking God and Eldon, too, to guide her. She gets up and rifles through a drawer for a pen and paper, then goes into the dining room and sits down at the table. On a card no bigger than the holy cards slipped between the pages of a missal, she squeezes a poem in her finest teacher's hand, as if by confining her worry, she can pinpoint it.

Words for a daughter, 1953
Though you have shut me out
Your eyes betray some wound
Your speech denies.
That baffled look of pain I
shall not see, for I must
learn to mask my pity and
concern.
And I am proud that you
have shown courage to face
your world alone.
Only remember this; when there
are times when you have need
to share your problems,
I shall always be waiting
for you to come to me—
Eager to help you on your way,
Or blunt the sharp edge of dismay.
Your need of me, if you but knew,
Is nothing to my need of you!
Love and prayers,

Mother

She tapes the message inside the leather cover of Benita's daily missal.

The Korean war ends in armistice on July 27, 1953, a three-year-long battle with three million causalities and no obvious winners, as futile as the fatal row between the gingham dog and the calico cat but dignified with military machinations and rationalizations of just war. As next fall's college juniors, we're glad it's over so we can get on with our plans for a normal future.

Father is still serving as chaplain at Webb Air Force Base in Texas at the end of the Korean war, still writing impassioned letters to Benita, briefs of daily life enhanced with lyrics from popular songs interpreting love as permanent, exclusive, contented ownership.

He continues, too, to telephone her on Marcella's card-playing evenings, or late at night when Marcella is asleep, or at the homes where Benita babysits. Babysitting is one of three jobs she does that summer. In the mornings, she's the receptionist in Richard's dental office. Afternoons, she sells tickets at the Municipal swimming pool. Evenings, more often than not, she cares for children for fifty-cents an hour. All the money she earns goes into a cigar box labeled 'Mexico.'

Chaucer is a semester-long required course for English majors. We read the *Canterbury Tales* in Middle English and outside of class weave its fascinating *eeks* and *whans* and *holts* and *heeths* into our conversations. 'Allas, Allas, that ever love was sinne' we wail in imitation of the bawdy Wife of Bath, whose cry summarizes ages of guilt and anxiety, the very feelings we ourselves are grappling with at the lusty age of twenty.

Benita and I go to movies with Loras College boys from exotic places like Aurora, Illinois and Burlington, Iowa. We date George Stevens sequentially. We double-date for spring prom. She invites her trusty cover-up, James O'Neill, and I ask Bill Sterne, a bookish high school classmate I'd overlooked during those years, but with whom I now forge a romantic alliance. That aspect of my life secured, I can focus on my studies free of the specter of spinsterhood.

Early one evening in mid-October, while Marcella and her daughters are still at the supper table, the telephone rings. Benita scrambles to answer, prepared to call Father 'Teresa' should it prove necessary. He's brief and friendly and asks to speak to Marcella. Before reporting for his next assignment in Greenland, he tells her, he'll be spending a few weeks at home.

'Greenland?' Marcella's smile falters. 'But that's so far away! Your poor mother. Well, you be sure to stop by often before you leave.'

He comes the next day to borrow back his car, which he uses that afternoon to pick up Benita on a side street near the Clarke campus. Through the long Indian summer of his leave, they go wherever impulse and privacy dictate. To the country for a walk in the woods, a respite on a blanket for a beer or two, a few cigarettes, sex. In less fortunate weather, they drive to a motel on the outskirts of town. Their default location is the backseat of his car. And twice, she awakens to Father in her bed.

'He slept here?' asks Richard in early November toward the end of Father's leave. 'Where?' His voice is tight with concern.

'Carol's room,' answers Marcella calmly. 'Carol slept with me. She was happy to give her room to Father.'

Richard sits thinking, tapping his foot, studying the pattern on the linoleum floor. When he was growing up, Carol's room was the girls' room. It's the largest of the three small bedrooms in their house, the sole room with a closet, which is why his mother assigned it to Irene and Benita or the various girl cousins she boarded during the school year. The girls' room adjoins and provides the only access to the boys' room, which he and Walter shared with whatever rural boy cousins were attending St. Columbkille's. The boys knocked to make sure the coast was clear before darting through to their room. *Room*, thinks Richard. A euphemism for that cramped space, not much bigger than the sagging bunk beds pushed under the eaves. God knows how they accommodated boarders. Rearranging sleeping quarters and multiplying beds is his mother's strong suit. Her version of the loaves and fishes. Once, a cousin snoring near his ear sent Richard complaining to her. 'Whatever you do for the least of these, you do for me,' answered Marcella. That boys' room is now Benita's room. She sleeps in the lower bunk bed.

Richard gently asks his mother if she thinks it's a good idea for Father to spend the night. She looks at him with aggrieved surprise, as if about to resurrect the 'whatever you do for the least of these' argument. 'The poor man was exhausted, Richard. It was nearly midnight. And starting to snow. He'd had a beer or two. He was dreading the drive to Dyersville. I told him 'just leave your coat in the closet and go upstairs to bed and you can drive to your parents' house in the morning.'

Father woke a little before seven that morning, just in time to hear Marcella tiptoe down the steps and hurry off to Mass alone, which told him it was a low Mass, without music, which in turn told him the organist was in bed in the next room. When the front door closed, he got up and pulled on his trousers, clutching them unzipped and unbelted in one hand, and stepped into the hall. He paused outside Marcella's room, listened momentarily, then went back through the girls' room to the door of the tiny adjoining room. Slowly, he turned the knob. He had half an hour.

At eight-fifteen, Father was sitting at the kitchen table finishing the toast and coffee Marcella made for him upon her return. He smoked and chatted with her as she tidied up the kitchen. Carol sleepily spooned oatmeal into her mouth. At eight-thirty Marcella took her coat from the closet. Father helped her put it on, then reached for his own. 'What a handsome overcoat, Father,' she said, gesturing to the captain's bars on the shoulder. As they went out the front door together, she waggled a warning finger at Carol. 'Don't you be late for school, now.'

On the front step, Father said, 'Okay if I stop in later this afternoon, Marcella, before I leave for my folks' place?'

'Of course, Father. You don't even need to ask. Stay for supper if you'd like.'

The shadow that passed over Sister's face when Carol bounced into her seventh-grade classroom and announced the good news of Father's visit, kept her from blurting the tale of his overnight stay. Nor did she mention that he slept over the next night, too.

'It would have been wrong to send him out on the road when there was a perfectly good bed upstairs explained Marcella to Walter, who came by the second morning to clear the walk. When he opened the shed to retrieve the shovel, there was Father's car. Just then, the back door opened, closed quickly, opened again and out plunged Father, full of bravado and gratitude for Marcella's generous offer to put up a poor, stranded traveler. Walt constructed a smile and greeted him, but his gut issued a warning.

'The thing is, Mom,' said Walt with a frown. 'Well, you know how people like to talk.'

'What's there to talk about? Father is like a member of our family. You know that.'

Walter dropped it. Father was a good friend; they did owe him a great debt for the kindness and support he'd shown their mother in those grim, early years of widowhood. Walter simply questioned the wisdom of Father's overnight presence in a household of women. Or maybe it was Jo who planted the doubt by pointing out that Benita was no longer a little girl in need of a dad, but an attractive young woman of marriageable age.

Whenever, wherever Benita is alone with Father's admiration, her hope soars; this man who can name the stars has chosen her to be his. But afterward, when she hears her classmates glowing

over fullbacks and romantic goodnight kisses and potential husbands, her star dims. She longs to be like other girls her age, an
ordinary student, able to focus on her studies, free to fall in love
with someone who could be hers, someone she could talk about
to her friends. She yearns to be worthy of her mother's trust.
Some nights, she drops to her knees beside her bed and utters a
plea. *Oh God, help me figure out what to do.* Other nights, her
prayer is a desperate question. *Oh God, how can I go on living like
this?* Sometimes she's glad Father is going far away. But when he
actually leaves, she's tormented by the fear that he will never
return.

Father's distance and prolonged absence motivate her to plan
and execute another cross-town Confession, this time at Sacred
Heart church. It's simpler to do now that she has the Dodge, and
longer-lasting now that its owner is gone. But it's lonelier, too,
returning with her cleansed soul and firm purpose of amendment
in a car that smells of cigarettes and afternoons with *him*, a treacherous scent that makes her yearn for *him* but for something more,
too, something not exactly physical, but on which her life seems
to depend.

The parishioner on duty at the long distance switchboard
hears only the initial fragments of Father's calls from Greenland,
which, like his previous calls, occur on evenings when Marcella
is at her card-playing club, or Benita is baby-sitting. But gradually,
the snippets accumulate into an intrigue. She listens a minute
longer. Then another moment or two. Something is going on
here that she feels obligated to monitor. Something that includes
words like love and longing. Verbal indulgences that make her
blush. Promises no priest can keep. The casual observations the
operator made to friends previously—*I saw Benita driving Father's
car*—become more emphatic. *Benita Kane doesn't seem to care that
Father Dunkel is a priest.*

Delivered to a few key people in the neighborhood, the
telephone operator's gleanings from far-off Thule spread through

an underground tunnel of whispering. Catholics are taught that the tongue is the main vehicle of sin and that its methods are diverse—tale-bearing, backbiting, slander, lying, the telling of secrets, calumny, detraction—but these are venial sins committed impulsively in the kitchen, at the grocery store, over the clothes line, wherever one talkative woman encounters another. *Benita Kane is chasing Father Dunkel. She's after a lot more than his car, believe me. It's disgusting.* Loving neighbors, all good Catholics except for Mrs. Kennedy and the minister, keep the rumors from Marcella's ears.

Ever since the night he was called to the Kane home to administer the last rites of the church to Eldon, Monsignor Dunn has felt great compassion for Marcella's plight. He assures her of his regular prayers; he counsels her, watches for opportunities to help her family and use his influence on their behalf. He finagles a well-paying summer job for Benita at the Dubuque Packing Company, a slaughterhouse and meat packing industry owned by a parishioner and controlled by a strong union. Six weeks there earned more than a whole summer of carhopping at a drive-in or cashiering at a coffee shop. Benita used her influence to wheedle a job for me. We work the night shift surrounded by bloody innards, daunting odors, bawdy language and the resentful eyes of year-round union workers. I spend my days sunbathing and swimming off the Mississippi sandbar; Benita boosts her chances for Mexico with summer school, work in Richard's office and her usual baby-sitting.

Early in that busy summer, along comes Father, on leave from Thule. He vandalizes her study schedule, persuading her to abandon her books and accompany him on summer drives and languid, clandestine afternoons on a blanket in the sun. Picnics, he calls them, with beer and sex the only nourishment. 'C'mon, let's have some fun' he says when he bursts into a critical study session. He hands her a copy of the test he'd snitched from a professor's desk. 'Here, you can learn what you need to know while we go for

This isn't wrong

a drive.' The next day, as she struggles through unfamiliar test questions, her heart sinks. Something has gone awry. The Latin enthusiast who at age sixteen had rejected Father's bid to cheat, finds herself now, five years later, a duped accomplice seduced by the wrong test. She passes by the skin of her teeth or by the grace of a God who, by no stretch of pure justice, would be motivated to save her.

'My comp notes are missing,' she announces to me with shocked eyes after Spanish class one afternoon in mid-December of our senior year. Her notes cover four years of her major field, Spanish. In a few months, shortly before graduation, we will take our Senior Comprehensive Exams. I've accumulated the same notes and offer them to her. 'Whew! You saved me this time,' she says.

Behind her predicament is a tryst with Father, who is home on leave between Greenland and his next assignment, once again in Texas, this time as Chaplain at Reese Air Force Base in Lubbock. He'd picked her up on a side street near Clarke. In the course of their ardent afternoon, she left her notebook in his car. When she inquired about it, he casually replied, 'Nope, didn't see it,' too blithely, it seemed, given the seriousness of the situation. When she asked if he would look again, he grew impatient, as if he heard an affront to his integrity.

Father had arrived from Greenland bearing showy gifts for the Kane women. For Marcella, a glass vase rimmed in 24-carat gold; for thirteen-year-old Carol, a charm bracelet; for Benita, a clock-radio to put her to sleep to their favorite songs and rouse her with a gentle snooze-alarm and the delectable sense of waking in his embrace.

Before leaving for Lubbock, Father presents another surprise to Marcella and Benita: a trip to Chicago. An Air Force buddy has invited him to spend the weekend at the home of his Italian family. Father knows Marcella enjoys going places and meeting new people; he proposes that she and Benita accompany him in his

185

car. In Chicago, he will put them up in a hotel. Benita demurs. She has an important assignment due on Monday, an entire Calderon play, *La Vida Es Sueño,* to read in Spanish and critique. But she hasn't the heart to deprive her mother of an adventure in Chicago.

The hotel is a sleazy place, as it turns out, but luxury has never been Marcella's necessity. The Italian family prepared an elaborate ethnic dinner for their guests. At the table is a remarkably lovely, dark-haired young woman, the sister of Father's friend. Benita notices her immediately, or rather, she notices Father noticing her and finds herself growing edgy and ill-at-ease. Father perceives her preoccupation and offers to take her back to the hotel to do her work. ('No, no, Marcella, you don't need to leave early. I'll come back and get you.') Later, when Marcella returns, she enters the room quietly and turns back the covers on the freshly-made bed. Benita looks up from her chair across the room, exchanges a few comments about the evening, and goes back to her book. Marcella plumps up the pillow where Father's head has so recently been, and slips into bed. Reassured by Father's earnest, albeit hasty lovemaking, Benita spends the remainder of the night with Calderon.

In early February, Father calls Marcella from Lubbock with a proposition no winter-weary alteration lady could resist. His parents want to visit him in Texas. If she would consider being their chauffeur again, he will cover the expenses. 'What a generous offer, Father! You know me. I'm not one to turn down a chance to go somewhere new. And I can't think of anyone I'd rather travel with than your mother and dad.' That's only half true. Nick Dunkel's cigarette smoking and crude ways do not sit well with Marcella.

Emma Dunkel giggles at the prospect of a trip to see her revered son, the priest. 'Texas isn't exactly a hop, skip and a jump, but, well, why not? You only live once.'

They set out in mid-March. Marcella is fifty-two years old, a competent, confident driver. She settles happily behind the wheel of the shiny new green Chevrolet. Emma gets in beside her. 'I'll sit up here with you, Marcella, so we can chat.'

Father's father, Nick Dunkel, retired farmer with a Pinocchio nose, a flask of whiskey usually in his possession and an aura of bib overalls about his person regardless of his actual garb, claims the back seat and the road map and calls to them in his jocular, country style, 'Don't you girls get chewing the fat up there and forget about me. I expect you to take good care of me.' He chuckles over the peculiar towns with their peculiar names, which he slyly mispronounces. When they approach a small town with a bar and a post office, Nick wants to stop. To use the restroom, Marcella assumes, but he walks straight to the bar and orders a double shot of whiskey. The tang assaults her nostrils for the next hundred miles. The concern she brings back from Texas, however, is about Father. 'He seems to need a drink before he can talk in front of people,' she confides to Benita. Immediately, she regrets her uncharitable words. She has no right to speculate irreverently about a priest, especially one who has shown her family nothing but kindness. She—Marcella—is no better than a Pharisee. 'Benita, don't you repeat that.'

A friend sets me up with a blind date for the Clarke spring prom. I'm now engaged to my former high-school classmate who is in the army and stationed in Germany. The arranged date is a practical maneuver designed to provide me, a senior, with a partner for the nostalgic last dance of our college years. Benita invites the popular, good-looking student who in the fall had squired her, one of four young women comprising the queen's court, to the Loras College Homecoming dance. If anyone can trump Father's place in Benita's mind for a few hours, handsome, tall, dark Dick Lechner is a likely candidate. But early in the prom evening, the band plays *Stranger in Paradise*. This is *their* song, hers and Father's, that the vocalist is crooning to the dancing couples.

She tries to listen to whatever Dick is saying, she wants to hear it, but she's caught with Father in the windy paradise of that spring Saturday, lost in the wonderland of their bodies pressed together inside one coat. Kissing. His yearning hands gradually causing her to yearn, too, convincing her that he is the answer to her fervent prayer.

Our song that summer is *Unchained Melody*, but the two people comprising the *our* in my romantic quest are a bit unsettled. I'm engaged to one boy and being swept off my feet and into a corner by another, the prom stand-in. The plaintive longing lyrics earned the song a place among those Benita and Father consider 'theirs,' too.

Oh, the sweet suffering set off by those words. The hungering and loneliness. What all of us have in common is the melodrama of a deceitful alliance. Certainly, the fellow in Germany who bought and paid for the emerald cut diamond ring I'm wearing has a greater claim than anyone to the pathos in the song, the lonely rivers sighing, the forlorn voices crying, 'Wait for me!'

The key players in Benita's future are present in the Clarke auditorium on the early June afternoon of our college graduation: Archbishop Binz, Father Dunkel, and the members of her immediate family. 'And in conclusion. . .' promises the archbishop for the fourth time in forty minutes and immediately sets off on another long-winded detour, swaying back and forth as if he's the captain of the Titanic earnestly exhorting his doomed passengers to trust in God while he himself clings tenaciously to the helm.

The graduates exhibit a skill mastered in the last four years, the fine art of dozing with open eyes. The audience endures— the parents and siblings, grandparents and aunts and uncles who are here to watch their beloved descendants begin that infamous march of uncertainty on the highway of deceit. Finally, with a triumphant nod, the archbishop keeps his word. He concludes. He smiles pleasantly through the polite applause, then strides to the dais at the side of the stage. From there he will present the diplomas to the graduates. The protocol goes like this: the graduate, in black cap and gown, steps forth when her name is called, walks briskly in her high heels across the stage, genuflects in front of the archbishop, kisses the amethyst episcopal ring on the third finger of his extended right hand and receives the diploma he proffers with his left, then smiles at him, says 'Thank you, your Excellency,' and rises, switching the tassel on her mortarboard from the right to the left as she descends from the stage to the audience applause. It's a feat requiring coordination and practice and suspension of critical thinking.

'Benita Kane, *cum laude*.' No, that's not right. She doesn't receive honors. Nor do I, although both of us come respectably close. Only four graduating seniors earn the 3.6 four-year-average required for honors, which may be related to another statistic, the subject of a feature article in the Des Moines Sunday Register magazine section on July 3, 1955: *One Diamond Ring for Every Three Diplomas at Clarke This Year.* However, thanks to the progressive BVM's who have lined us up from tallest to shortest, the opposite of the Presentation way, I do exit the auditorium at the head of the class. And Benita receives a scholarship from the Iowa Women's Clubs for a year of graduate study in a Latin American country.

Before Father returns to Texas, he drops in at the home where Benita is babysitting. 'Come to Lubbock,' he murmurs as he bids her a fervent farewell. They're in the pantry with the lights out and the door locked. 'Take the Santa Fe. I'll pay.'

'Well, we sure had a good time when we went down there, didn't we, Marcella,' says Emma Dunkel when she hears of the plan. 'She will too. Father will be tickled pink.' Her unflagging optimism causes Marcella to examine her conscience: small-mindedness, worrying about the neighbors' opinions, mistrust, there's no virtue in any of it, nor is doubt her natural inclination. Benita will be staying with a couple who are friends of Father's, an Army sergeant and his wife who will oversee her well-being.

The next day, Marcella sets out across the yard to Walt's. Halfway there, she stops and turns back. As much as she needs to talk over her worries, it isn't fair to burden him. He's the father of four young children with more than enough concerns of his own. She would only aggravate his misgivings.

A face hovers over Benita's bed that first night in Lubbock, a woman resembling the sergeant's wife and brandishing a knife as she angrily hisses, 'Remember, he's mine!' Father chuckles at Benita's melodramatic report, but quickly changes her quarters to a barracks. Unnerved, she cuts short her vacation. For the first miles of her return trip, she puzzles over what happened. Was it a dream or a reality? The closer the train gets to Dubuque, the more fantastical it seems.

In mid-July, Benita leaves for La Universidad de las Americas in Mexico City. Wistfully, I watch her depart for her foreign adventure while I stay in Dubuque, living at home, waiting for the right job, the right man, the right moment to break out of my parochial life.

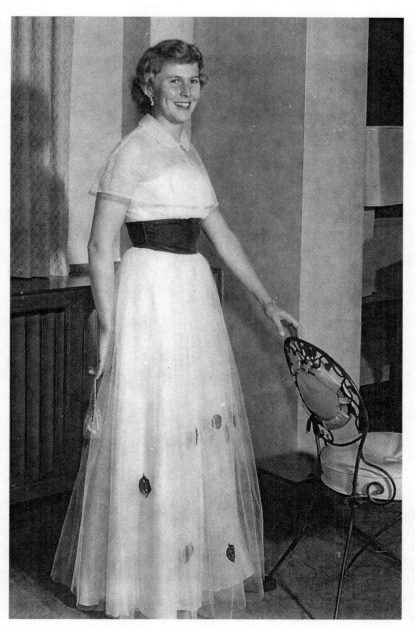

College prom, 1952

Graduation from Clarke college, Dubuque, Iowa, 1955

PART THREE
José and Topper

CHAPTER ONE

As the zephyr streaked east toward Chicago, and the July landscape blurred from past to future, a shiver of excitement went through Benita. She pulled the soft blue wool jacket, a gift from Father, closer around her shoulders. Packed inside her suitcase, among the skirts and blouses and red blazer in which Marcella had sewn a secret, theft-proof pocket, was her dream of becoming a Spanish teacher. At O'Hare, she boarded the plane for Mexico. It was her first commercial flight; she felt a rush of joy as the plane gathered speed and lifted off, then a glorious sense of release.

She had no wish to escape Father or to renounce the astonishing pleasure he gave her. Now that he'd quit bringing up her need to go to Confession, she'd begun to believe what he'd been telling her all along. What they did together wasn't wrong. Freed of that anxiety, she counted the weeks until his promised visit to Mexico in October. 'I can't do without you very long,' he'd said.

She and four other American students would live in the home of a German couple transplanted to Mexico, Señor and Señora Zolly, from whom they had rented three bedrooms, each with its own bathroom. Benita arrived first and chose the largest room for her own, not to accommodate Father—the Zollys made it clear that their home was not a love nest—but because it was the room she'd pined for in the crowded upstairs of her childhood.

Benita was a confident, enterprising student. Male students forgave her for being bright because she was pretty. Female students forgave her for being pretty because she seemed oblivious to it. Evenings when the group gathered in a bar or restaurant, invariably one of the men would position himself next to Benita and suggest going out for a cerveza, or for a walk to Chapultepec Park or to a movie where they might acquire a few Spanish words. These innocent invitations challenged her covenant with Father. Fidelity was the virtue that justified and elevated what otherwise might have been sordid in her life. The infrequent dates she did accept were amiable, noncommittal, a sham.

Father's impassioned letters arrived regularly, reminding her of his love and desire and loneliness, his plan to come to Mexico in late October. As she read his words, she felt his presence, the urgency of his eyes and hands. *You're mine. Don't ever forget that.* She could *never* forget, she replied in her letters. No matter how far away she was, she would always be his.

As July turned into August, her dilemma over him began to burn away like fog in the hot Mexican sun. As she sat with the other students around the dining table eating the international fare of Señora Zolly, as she became more proficient in Spanish, as she biked in Chapultepec park with Cynthia, her new friend, or shopped with her at Papagallo, the mercado near Zolly's, as they traveled together to Acapulco and Revolcadero beach and the mineral springs of Cuautla, she began to glimpse the possibility of another life, one without *him*, the man she long ago ceased to call 'Father.'

He was 'Captain' when he got off the plane in Mexico City in late October. Missing from the lapel of his blue Air Force uniform was the silver cross that designated him 'chaplain.' Benita had arrived at the airport an hour before, too fidgety to endure the dragging hours in her room. The last day had been unbearable, the waiting and anticipation, the neediness thrumming through her body this morning as she eagerly prepared it, showering, shampooing, oiling her entire self with an aromatic lotion that roused her desire. She passed more time rearranging her desk, dusting her room, leafing through the pages of her textbooks where she saw only his face. She took the early bus to the airport. The nearer she got, the more uncertain she became. He wouldn't be on the plane. At the last minute, he had decided not to come. He would be on it, but immediately sorry he was there. He would take one look at the crowds and confusion and dirt and blame her for luring him to such a miserable place.

Then, suddenly, there he was, walking down the ramp, vigorous, blue-eyed, smiling as he opened his arms to claim her, drawing her to him like a thirsty person to water after days of trudging in the sun, unaware how dry and depleted she was. They went to the Compostela Hotel where he rented a room. 'Ah, El Capitán,' said the desk clerk, acknowledging his uniform and the captain's bars on his shoulder, 'Welcome to Mexico. *Y tu, tambien, a-a-h, es Señora o Señorita?*' He spread his lips in a shrewd smile. Father squeezed her hand.

'Si,' said Benita ambiguously. El Capitán advised the clerk that he would be there for a week, then eyed Benita and said 'or possibly several days beyond that.' It was a small room with a double bed and one straight chair, a space suitable for one Spartan person, or two people like them, interested only in the bed. She spent the weekend with him, spent the passion that had built up between them, which left them with not much else to do, so they got up, dressed, (she was wearing the plaid skirt and red blazer containing Marcella's secret pocket) went out to Los Turcos, a night club of Mideastern decor. Later that evening, when he leaned to light her cigarette, something in his eyes, a flash of triumph or meanness, alarmed her. An old mantra began in her mind. 'This is wrong, a sin, you'll be sorry.' But when he reached across the table and took her hand in his, stroking her fingers, one by one, telling her she was his, 'his precious Benita,' she felt absolved, safe again. And giddy with sudden hunger.

'Buenas noches, welcome,' said the waiter at Csardas, a flamboyant restaurant with Bohemian violinists whom Benita was eager for Father to hear. 'You've been here before then,' said Father. She nodded; she'd hurt her date's feelings that evening by telling him she was interested only in friendship. It was impossible for her to be contented with a boy when her heart and soul and body belonged to a man. Where would El Capitán like to sit with his pretty señorita, the waiter wanted to know.

With no outward sign to designate him 'Father,' the Mexican people quickly dubbed him 'El Capitán.' Benita began to call him José. He called her Topper. José and Topper, an ordinary couple caught in the throes of love. Or lust. It didn't matter. Whatever it was, they could surrender to it here in this foreign land, with no fear of being discovered. She could go to class, be with him, and if her conscience flared, which it did from time to time, she could shed the top layer of guilt by going to Confession after he left. The rare times they entered a church together, they went as tourists.

José stayed on through the next week. Late afternoons, after her classes, she went to the hotel and up the worn, gaudily-carpeted stairs to the second floor. When she knocked on his door, he opened it and led her through a labyrinth of pleasure, every turn surprising, but taking them to a predictable place of gratitude, contented sighs, pledges of love and trust. Afterward, they slept for awhile. When they woke, they dressed and went out to whatever restaurant Topper recommended.

Sometimes they strolled along the Paseo de la Reforma, modeled on Paris' Champs-Elysees, with its numerous glorietas, which, Topper told José, was the name for a turn-around in the street with a monument in the center. When they stopped to listen to a mariachi band playing on the street, José bought a song and they followed the people drifting into the cantina for tequila and tortillas wrapped around grilled chorizo and melted cheese. He ordered tequila. She turned it down and told him the story of the evening she and Cynthia had been there with some Mexican guys—good guys, she amended, at his quick, stern look—nice guys simply showing them around the city. They had introduced them to the ritual of tequila, the fuss of lime and salt, the counting, uno, dos, tres, the merry guzzling that made her horribly sick. The way to fix your stomach, said the Mexican guys—nice guys, good guys, she repeated reassuringly—is to stay awake and eat hotly spiced tomato soup.

At this point, José pressed his index finger gently against her lips. 'No more of this. I want you to promise me something. From now on, when you go out, you'll have no more than two drinks of hard liquor, or three beers. Unless we're together.' She abided by his rule. He was El Capitán. She liked being subject to him. On week nights, he returned her to her room at Zolly's. She had classes the next day. She intended to stay on course, to make the most of this opportunity.

One evening, after sating their sexual hunger, they lay in bed, two linguists playfully constructing a secret code from their new names. J (José) + T (Topper) + S (siempre) = *JunToS*. *Juntos*, the Spanish word for 'together' became JunToS, the symbol of their union. On this foundation, they began to construct a life. Someday he would take her to the island of Mauritius in the Indian Ocean off the coast of Africa. In that idyllic place, they would be together forever, José and Topper, living happily ever after.

Before he left Mexico City, before he retrieved the silver cross from his pocket and fastened it to his lapel and slipped from José back into Father again, he and Topper went to a silversmith and had two identical silver bottle openers made. They were shaped like the island of Mauritius and engraved with the word, JunToS, the symbol of their union. Seeing their secret word etched in silver reassured Benita. Someday they *would* be together. They could create a place for themselves. She was sure of it. Some day she would be with the man she loved on the island of Mauritius. With Father, *him*, El Capitán, José. Throughout the many, many love letters they exchanged were allusions to that imagined life.

In November, Marcella, ever the happy wanderer, flew to Mexico City for a two-week visit. She stayed with Benita at the Zolly's, ate dinner with the students, and every evening chose a site she wanted to visit the next day. Benita wrote directions for her in Spanish. In the morning, Marcella handed the paper to the cab driver and went off to explore while Benita went to class. She visited cathedrals and museums and the Basilica de la Diosa de Guadalupe, where she stopped every day to pray. One day, she bought a gold medal for a remembrance.

Marcella felt at home with the Mexican people. They were poor but warm and affectionate. Their spiritual life, like hers, was dominated by Roman Catholicism. Their loyalty, like hers, was to the basic things—family, culture, religion, place. Their roots in the landscape were deep and complex and tumultuous. Marcella was an easy guest. She appreciated the simple things, the genuine smiles of Lupe and Luisa, the maids who served at Zolly's dinner table, laughter, poinsettias in bloom. She spoke often of Eldon. 'He'd be so proud to see you here,' she told Benita. 'And so happy to see me here with you. He always thought you were special, did I ever tell you that? His special little girl, he called you.'

Benita laughed. 'He called Irene and Carol that, too.'

'I know,' said Marcella. 'But it was true. Each of you was special to him in your own way.'

On Sunday, Marcella and Benita went to Mass together at Our Lady of Guadalupe church. As they walked home, a ragged, dark-eyed little boy pursued them, calling, 'Señorita Benita! *Por favor. . .*' He cupped his palm for her coins, grinned, and darted away. 'Mario is a street urchin,' she explained to her mother. 'The students at Zolly's call him their buddy. We're buying him a new outfit for Christmas.' The next evening, when Marcella and Benita attended a lecture together, the speaker talked about the grievous problem plaguing Latin America. Street urchins were proof. The Roman Catholic church was the cause. Its anti-birth control message was ruining the country. Marcella was quiet on the walk home. 'I wonder where Mario is tonight,' she mused.

'He's been banned from this area,' said Benita. 'He was caught stealing silverware in a store here.'

'I'm getting fat,' moaned Benita to her mother a few evenings later as she tugged on the waistband of her skirt, trying to fasten it before going down to dinner in the Zolly's dining room.

Marcella waved her hand dismissively. 'You're just right. You were too thin before. Fretting off everything you ate. You're more contented now. It shows.'

'A contented cow, that's what I am.' Benita rubbed her stomach, swung her hips. 'The Zolly's are fattening us up for the slaughter. A big breakfast, a complete meal for lunch, and then, an hour before we go to bed, an enormous dinner. Plus the bolillos and chihuahua cheese we eat in between. I'll look like Luisa by the end of the year.'

'Luisa is a joy!' said Marcella. 'Those dark flashing eyes. She's so lively and jovial.'

'Lively and jovial and fat. And I'm going to look just like her before long.' The beer that went down in copious amounts whenever the students gathered was a factor Benita left out of her account.

'By the way,' said Marcella, 'while I was waiting for my cab this morning, Luisa told me something about a man called El Capitán. A *militario* man.' Marcella described how, in a mix of Spanish and English, Luisa had asked, 'You like *el capitán*?' When Marcella frowned in an effort to understand, Luisa laughed. 'No? Ah, *comprendo*. Benita *es joven*. Young. El capitán is *mas viejo*. . . old. Es rico?' (Is he rich?) She had rolled her eyes enthusiastically.

Benita went silent, feigning perplexity.

'She seemed to be talking about a man in uniform who was here,' said Marcella.

Benita brightened as if struck by an inspiration. 'Oh, she meant Father! Yes, he *was* here. I haven't had a chance to tell you. I've had a constant stream of visitors this past month. Dick Lechner wrote and asked me to meet his parents when they flew in. I took them to the festivities for Columbus Day. And to a bullfight. Then Father came through on his way to Mazatlan. *(Not exactly a lie. He'd told her he wanted to go there together sometime.)* People hear so much scary stuff about Mexico City. They want someone they know to meet them and show them around. The trouble is, I came here to go to school, not to be a tourist guide.'

'You should have told me.'

Benita turned cautious eyes toward her mother. 'Told you?'

'That you're tired of visitors. I wouldn't have come if I'd known.'

'Oh, Mom! I don't mean you. You haven't disrupted my schedule one bit. I love having you here. In fact, I was thinking we should go to Toluca this weekend. It's the basket-making city. You'll like it, I know.'

They rode to Toluca on the third class bus with chickens and pigs and sundry farm animals as fellow passengers. In spite of the diversions of the weekend, Marcella's uneasiness was not resolved. 'Did Luisa know El Capitán was a priest?' she asked casually.

Benita laughed. 'I doubt it. She was too busy pairing us off to notice the cross on his uniform.' Two lies within one conversation. Neither of them blatant or destructive, told only for her mother's peace-of-mind.

Marcella decided to quit asking questions, which only escalated worry, which, in turn, revealed a lack of trust in God.

'He went to Mexico?' asked Richard, sounding as stunned as

he was the morning he learned that Father had spent the night in Marcella's house. 'When?'

'I don't get it. Why would he barge in on her when she's in another country going to school?' fumed Walt.

'Maybe Benita invited him,' said Irene disgustedly.

As she understood it, Marcella told them, Father was one of a series of visitors, all with the same goals in mind. To see the people, visit the churches, learn a little something about another culture with Benita there to act as guide and translator. 'I think she was getting a little tired of it by the time I came along,' said Marcella. 'Shh-h,' she said and gestured with her head toward the stairway. Carol was on her way down.

As soon as Carol closed the backdoor behind her, Walt said, 'You're her mother. You had a right to be there. Who's he? To Benita, I mean.'

'A friend. He's been a good, loyal friend to all of us for a long time. Especially to me and Benita. He's like a member of our family.'

'But he's not,' said Richard. 'He's not a member of the family. And he's not a kid. He's thirty. . .what. . .five? Six?'

'It was bad judgment for him to go there, if nothing more. It worries me,' said Irene.

'Me, too. I don't get it. What's the guy up to?' said Walt.

Marcella's fair skin flushed. Her eyes widened in disbelief. 'Walter! What are you implying? That Father was deliberately trying to. . .what? Sidetrack Benita?'

Walter lifted his palms in a gesture of frustration.

'It bothers me to hear you speak that way about Father. He's a priest.'

'I know that, Mom. But he's not God. He's a man. '

'He's a man of God.'

Walter tried to put the implications of Father's trip to Mexico out of his mind. Aside from listening to his mother worry, which she did more and more often, crossing the street to Irene and Don's house or the backyard to his to go over and over some troubling thought, there was nothing to be done. What he did do was revive a devotion from his youth. He began dropping into church after work to kneel before the statue of the Blessed Mother. He meant to pray, but his mind meandered from worry to worry, always winding up in the same place, at the bottom of the stairs where the emergency team had set down the stretcher that held his dying father.

The thought of Benita alone in a foreign country over the Christmas holidays motivated her family to chip in and fly her home. Carol eagerly contributed every quarter she'd collected from babysitting nieces and nephews.

'What happened to Benita? She's turning into a blimp,' blurted one young niece to another when Benita arrived.

'Big fat Beets,' said a nephew.

'Shush,' said Irene, their mother.

A high school classmate took Teresa by the arm after Christmas Mass. 'Is Benita. . .do you know if. . .? I mean, she *has* gained a lot of weight. . .' She arched her palm over her midriff. 'Do you think. . .?'

Teresa steadied her wide green, darkly-lashed eyes on the inquisitor and delivered a silent, shriveling rebuke.

Aggravating the conjecture was the fever and queasy stomach that kept Benita in bed for several days. Her limited contacts caused the eyes of the curious to meet in wordless speculation. 'Is it possible?' 'Father's baby.' 'Poor Marcella, she doesn't deserve this.' Some received the gossip skeptically, the way they did weather forecasts and the promises of politicians. No priest would do such things. Nor would any daughter of Marcella Kane's.

The Kane family seemed oblivious to what was happening, yet no one—no trusted, long-time friend or fellow parishioner, not Bea Roscoe, not Hilda Saul—took 'poor Marcella' aside and told her gently and honestly of their concern.

The man most logically concerned about the possibility of pregnancy, wasn't. He returned to Mexico in late January and pronounced Benita 'more womanly and curvaceous,' pleasingly rounded out in all the right places, hips, stomach, breasts, places he caressed as he spoke. She was relieved and grateful. And she was not pregnant. All through the day, as she sat in class or ate lunch at the Zolly's, her thoughts were on him, remembering, anticipating, greedy to share everything with him—herself, Mexico, friends—in the security of unasked questions. In the evenings, they drank cerveza and smoked cigarettes and made love, then went to dinner and planned their next day. It was no good to go to the restaurant first. They had tried it. As they sat side by side in Chalupas, a restaurant near Zolly's, José slid his hand under the tablecloth and found her knee, eased his hand under her skirt and felt along her leg until he found the garter fastening her hose. He began to fiddle with it while he fondled her with his eyes. She glanced around casually and said to him in a matter-of-fact voice, 'Wait. *Por favor.*' But what she meant, and what he heard was, let's go back to the hotel and go ahead with it. They hurried through the meal toward the lovemaking that was their dessert.

Her body stirred now, in class, with memory and anticipation. Her eyes kept straying to her left hand. There, on the third finger was an engagement ring, a stunning sapphire with a diamond on either side. Gazing at it thrilled her. So did the words he'd said last night, when he slid it on her finger. 'This means you're mine. Don't ever take it off.' Later, they walked to Chapultepec Park, past the castle and along a pathway where they stopped to search the sky for constellations. He stood behind her with his arms around her waist while she pointed and named.

Then he gently turned her to him and kissed her. 'You're mine. Eternally.'

The ring made it easier to turn down dates, but more difficult to focus on her studies and the purpose of her year. The future she had glimpsed without him faded before the sparkling promise of the ring. What did she care that her best friend, Cynthia, thought the captain was 'too old for her.' He had chosen her to be his. Anonymity gave them the freedom to be a couple in love. They could walk about the streets together without guilt or fear of being caught. Everything really *would* come out in the wash, just as Father had promised.

In April, jarred by the realization of the dwindling year, she launched a frantic effort to write the papers she'd let slide; she tried to pull her thesis together. Fifty-six credits and her Master's degree—her future as a Spanish teacher—hinged on what she accomplished within the next three months. She would sit down at her desk and organize her books and shuffle through blank note cards and sometimes even write a word or phrase down on one, but her focus and momentum were gone. One day blended into the next. The work seemed irrelevant and useless, like reading an old newspaper when you know everything has been determined. Conscientious student lapsed into day dreamer, drifting through page after page of text with her thoughts on him, anguishing, aching hidden desires and lascivious images that could make her blush if another student happened to catch her eye just then. At dinner, the students laughed and talked with the Zolly's about their day's adventures, and Benita joined in, but some part of her was absent. Her thesis was no further along in mid-May when he returned.

'José,' she called softly and tapped lightly on the door of his hotel room. She was drenched. She'd loaned him her umbrella and been caught without it in the sudden downpour that occurred almost daily in late afternoon; she was too impatient to be with him to wait out the five or six minutes in a doorway. She arrived dripping at his door, a pathetic puppy begging its master to be let in, begging *her* master, the master of lovemaking.

The door opened and then his arms. 'Take off those wet clothes. And come to bed with me.' Afterward, they left for a romantic weekend in Acapulco, with an overnight stay in the flower-draped city of Cuernavaca along the way. Next came Taxco, where they walked the cobble-stoned streets winding past countless silver shops. And then Acapulco and the white sand of Caleta beach. As they lazed there in the afternoon sun, she mulled over her academic woes. It would take a miracle, she told him, for her to write a thesis by July.

'Don't worry about it,' he said. 'Come to Denver when you leave Mexico.' He was stationed there now as chaplain at Lowry Air Force Base, after being transferred in March from Lubbock. 'You can get a job teaching. I'll give you a letter of recommendation.'

'Señorita Benita!' called Señora Zolly hurrying toward the front door when Benita came into the house on Sunday evening. José had dropped her off after their return from Acapulco. 'A phone call has come for you while you were away. I didn't know where to reach you. It is about your brother. You are to call home *imediatamente*.'

Richard, thirty-two years old, the father of four children, the youngest two months old, had had a heart attack. Marcella's optimistic message failed to disguise the tears in her voice. The attack was not as bad as it might have been. He was young and strong. Resting now and doing well. 'He's thrown away his cigarettes,' said Marcella. 'But, oh Benita,' she went on, her voice breaking, 'I can't help but think of your daddy.'

Coming at the end of her wanton weekend, the dreadful news awakened Benita's slumbering guilt. While her frightened family worried and prayed, she had been lying on the beach at Acapulco, drinking beer and basking in the sun, indulging in the pleasures

Father brought her. Her family's generosity and encouragement had brought her here and she was on the brink of returning empty-handed, with nothing but an accumulation of lies to show for the year. She had to finish her work. She would rally, work day and night, as she'd done in college, and return home with some shred of pride.

Her instinct was to pray, but to whom? The *alter Christus* of her childhood, the priest who was God's representative on earth, was now a man with whom she drank beer and went to bed. José had appropriated the role of highest power in her life. She turned to the Virgin of Guadalupe, the patron saint of the country. She lit a candle and asked her, not as a heavenly creature, a concept she'd begun to doubt, but as a friend, to be a source of strength to Richard.

'Remember, you're mine,' said José, as he was leaving Mexico City. 'In Denver, we can be together all the time.' He pinned the cross on his lapel and was gone. This time, she was relieved to see him go. His two-week stays were consuming her life. Just when she would begin to gain momentum as a graduate student, to feel her mind delving wholeheartedly into the language and culture of Mexico, he would blow in like a gust of wild wind scattering her plans and attention every which way. After he left, she would rush about gathering things up, sensing there was something some-where that she had overlooked, would never find. Without him, she could study and travel and learn and enjoy a freedom that vanished when he was in a hotel room a few blocks from Zolly's. Fervent letters continued to fly back and forth between them, but finally, she could settle down and learn something.

Her resolve came too late. His devotion had robbed her of focus and drive. All that love-making had drained her of energy and left her as sluggish as a cat stretched out napping in the sun. She had no hope of completing her thesis by July. She contacted her sponsor, asked for an extension of her scholarship, and began planning to stay on in Mexico City until she accomplished her

Master's Degree. *We regret that because you haven't completed your thesis, there is nothing we can do,* came the reply. Standing at the window in her room, she read the letter again. She could see the snow-capped volcanoes, Popo and Izta, radiant and deceptively peaceful in the setting sun. Her own gut churned; all the lofty aspirations she'd brought here had dissipated. Why hadn't she done what she came to do? She hated herself for being so weak.

CHAPTER TWO

In late July, bereft and humiliated, she returned to Dubuque to face her family's disillusionment and the discouraging news that because she had failed to write the papers required by her classes, she would receive absolutely no credits for her fifty-six graduate hours. Wasted, then. All of it. The entire year had come to naught.

When the news of Benita's return reached Sister Lucilda in the Spanish department at Clarke, she summoned her to come and retrieve the textbooks she needed. 'Get to work finishing those papers.' Benita obeyed, but that mandate was soon overruled by another. 'Come to Denver, Topper,' said Father over the telephone. She went. She followed his orders as if she were a private in an army under his command. As if she were a pup summoned by its master. But before she left, Richard handed her an envelope. 'This is a loan, Benita. If you need it, use it. If you don't, you can send it back. I don't want you to be beholden to anyone.'

The three hundred dollars Richard had given her represented an anxious family meeting provoked by a telephone call to Marcella. Don't worry about Benita going off to Denver, Father had told her. He would be there to watch over her. He planned to meet her train and help her settle in. Marcella could no longer dismiss the reactions of her older children. Walter was suspicious, Irene furious, Richard pragmatic. 'Look,' he said. 'She's twenty-three. We can't stop her. But we can give her an out.' Marcella gave a separate envelope to Monsignor Dunn and asked him to say a novena of Masses for her intention.

Father met Benita's train and set her up in an efficiency motel, a kitchenette and an alcove with a bed. She applied for a position teaching Spanish in Englewood, Colorado; her confidence surged when she was offered a contract. But during the next days, as she gathered her textbooks and prepared her class schedule, she sensed something awry. Twice Father had arrived late for their dates, smelling of cigarettes, as usual, but of whiskey, too. On this particular day, they agreed to dinner at six in her kitchenette. She walked to the grocery store and carried home ingredients for what she, at twenty-three, considered a pleasant meal. Hamburger, baked potatoes with sour cream, salad. When six o'clock came, he wasn't there. At seven, she put away the food. At eight, he rattled the door knob. He was disheveled, slightly drunk and complaining about a cocktail party he'd had to attend. He was sorry, he said, and was there anything to eat? He wasn't used to drinking on an empty stomach. She warmed his dinner and set it on the tiny Formica table. He ate quickly while she sat leafing blindly through her textbooks. When he stood up and approached her, she clenched. 'Aw, c'mon, Topper. Don't be so hard on me.' He knelt down beside her and put his head on her lap. She anguished in silence for a few minutes more, then lifted her hand and gently began to stroke his hair. 'She's always been jealous of you, you know,' mumbled Father.

'Who?'

'That snobbish Grandview Avenue girl. Mary. She was at the party tonight. She and her fancy doctor husband. They live here.'

Was it true, Benita wondered, disarmed. Mary was the girl

whose poise and lovely clothes she had envied all through school.

Father pulled her to her feet and kissed her, then slipped his hands beneath her light blouse, unhooked her bra and began caressing her breasts with a gentle, soothing touch as he urged her to bed. 'See how happy I can make you,' he murmured into her ear later when she cried out. But what he'd heard as a cry of ecstasy was, in fact, one of desperation.

Benita lay awake for a long time trying to rearrange the facts. It was hopeless. The fantasy life of Mexico was over. 'I have a favor to ask,' she said to Father the next morning. 'I want you to take me to school so I can drop off these books. And then you can take me to the train.' At the station, she opened the envelope Richard had given her and bought a ticket home. Father stood by, strangely acquiescent, and watched her go.

Back to Dubuque, then. Back home once again, back to her relieved family, back to the dismal prospect of trying to find work as a teacher in mid-September, two weeks into the school year. Back to the curiosity behind people's averted glances. Back to a continued descent into despair.

Marcella asked Monsignor to say a Mass of thanksgiving. Her prayers had been granted. He waved away her offer of money. 'I'm thankful, too,' he said.

The young woman who'd gone off to Mexico with aspirations to become a high school Spanish teacher found work as a substitute grade school teacher. She alternated mornings and afternoons between two elementary schools. More ashamed and alone than ever before, she resolved to pay off her debt to Richard and get back on her feet. She put her energy into teaching and earned extra money by tutoring Spanish. Among her students was a Presentation postulant who lived in the motherhouse at Mount Loretto. As she entered the reception hall one afternoon, Benita overheard two nuns whispering in the adjacent parlor. 'She's the one, you know. She's been after Father Dunkel for years. I'm surprised Mother Superior lets her come here.'

She drove to and from her various teaching jobs that fall in his cream-colored Dodge, hers to use as long as he was in the service. At the end of her teaching day, she went home to fix supper for fifteen-year-old Carol and their mother arriving later on the bus from her downtown job. Carol's task was to wash the dishes, but she vociferously excluded the ashtrays Benita used. Marcella had given up fighting her daughter's dreadful habit; she took Carol aside and told her to be gentle with Benita. The sister Carol admired was now strangely fragile.

As a grade school child, Carol understood Father's visits as evidence that her family was special. He was a priest, the most significant thing anyone could be; he liked to come to their house, which meant he liked *them*. She proudly announced his comings and goings at school and sometimes toted along the gifts he brought her. Whenever he was home on leave, Father stopped in, but something had changed since Benita's return from Mexico. Now when he came whistling up the sidewalk in his Air Force blues, confident of the usual enthusiastic reception—Marcella opening the door before he could even knock, an invitation to supper in the kitchen, an evening poker game, a picnic in the country—the family exchanged quick glances. Her mother's smile was strained. Walter seemed aloof. Benita was on edge. Yet Father seemed to have no notion that he was on shaky ground. On Marcella's card club evenings, he arrived a few minutes after she left, turning Carol into an unsuspecting chaperone until she went off to bed.

Over the next months, Marcella's worrying in the kitchens of her adult children became more frequent. The grandchildren shooed out of earshot of those hushed conversations were put in Carol's care, who at fifteen was still considered too young to know the truth. The secrecy and whispering told her something had gone wrong; so did the earnest, mumbled conversations between Walt and Irene's husband, Don, an attorney. But asking questions

was futile. She would not receive candid answers. All this shelter-
ing left her unprepared for the events of early May.

'Mom! Why are you reading that?' Carol blurted when she
came upon her mother sitting on Benita's bed absorbed in her
daughter's old diary. No response. Her mother seemed to be in a
trance, unable to see or hear. Carol dismissed it as one more adult
mystery. But there was no dismissing the sight she encountered
the next day when she came home from school. In the living
room, collapsed on the sofa in a seizure of grief, lay Marcella. She
looked at Carol with wild, unseeing eyes and tried to speak. What
came out was sobbing, incoherent babbling, gibberish, a language
of such terrible distress that Carol went racing across the street to
her oldest sister's door. 'Irene!' she screamed, 'Something's happened to Mother!'

'You caused that,' murmured a voice into Benita's ear that
evening as she stood with her family beside Marcella's hospital
bed. Or did Benita imagine the words? Or had she said them herself, after learning of her mother's breakdown? Not aloud, but
over and over and over again in her heart until she began to hear
them in her head. Marcella was worn out, said the doctor. Emotionally and physically exhausted. During the next days, Benita
skipped lunch and spent that hour with her mother in the hospital. *You caused that,* she thought when she saw the fatigue and
profound sorrow in her mother's eyes. *You're responsible.* Whether
anyone else said it or not, Benita knew. What she didn't know
was that the incriminating little book she had dropped into her
dresser drawer five years ago and forgotten was the final blow
bludgeoning her mother with the brutal, undeniable truth.

Marcella had read the pages over and over, then wandered
from room to room in a daze of disbelief. *Father! A priest! Her
trusted friend! And Benita, her own daughter. How could this be?
Why? Why would God allow this to go on? How could she have been
so blind? Eldon!* she cried out, *Eldon! What shall I do?* The heaviness that descended into Marcella's heart with her husband's death

had never altogether lifted. Trust in God and the church had sustained her. Now, her world had come crashing down. She dropped wailing onto the sofa.

After she recovered strength enough to be released from the hospital, she once again walked to morning Mass and received Holy Communion and stayed afterward to light a vigil candle, but she couldn't seem to summon the 'old Marcella' who could pray and work and smile through tribulation. Even on her good days, when she felt a rare surge of hope or glimpsed a ray of light, her eyes displayed an enduring sadness that haunted Benita.

Marcella's quandary was relentless. What should she do, what *could* she do, she asked God unceasingly. At last an answer came. She put Benita's diary into her purse and walked to the rectory. The housekeeper answered the door. 'Molly, is Monsignor Dunn in?' asked Marcella.

Oh, Monsignor, I'm so ashamed. And worried. I don't know what to do. I need your advice. Please, please, can you help me?

*This is a matter of grave concern, Marcella. You were wise to bring the information to me first. We must handle it with the utmost discretion. I'll contact the archbishop about. . .*he held up the diary . . .*this. He has jurisdiction over. . .*he searched for a word. . .*problems of this sort. He will advise us on the best course of action. Meanwhile, say nothing to anyone else.*

The archbishop telephoned Marcella to assure her that with her cooperation and God's help, they could put an end to the wretched situation between her daughter and his priest. Meanwhile, she should say nothing to anyone.

Walt observed his mother's stoical silence. Several times he asked if she needed anything, if she was doing okay. She brushed off his concern. 'You have your own family to take care of. You don't need my troubles on top of everything else. God will give me direction.'

It was true. Walt had a wife and four young children and a job as an insurance agent that required him to work evenings during the week. Richard was in the same situation, a wife, little kids, a dental practice, and the added worry of a weak heart. But both sons felt a responsibility toward the widowed mother they loved. Walter kept up his daily visits to church; Richard counted on a little help from Providence.

A week later, a call came for Benita just as she arrived at Franklin School for her last teaching session of the year. She was to report to the chancery at four that afternoon, the diocesan chancellor informed her. The chancery was a formidable red stone mansion that housed the archdiocesan offices, including that of the archbishop. She stumbled through the afternoon's teaching tasks and transported herself downtown in the cream-colored Dodge. She made her way up the stone steps to the chancery door. She rang the bell.

The door was opened by a priest with a bright red crew cut who introduced himself as Father Roach, the diocesan chancellor. Meekly, she followed him to the waiting room. A few minutes later, he ushered her into a large, carpeted, heavily draped office.

There, behind a polished span of desk stood the archbishop gazing out the window. As he turned, light caught the pectoral cross dangling from his neck. The dim room and his dark attire gave his face a heavy pallor. Sullen, bespectacled eyes gazed at her from beneath a high, broad forehead. His thin lips twitched in an effort to smile as he greeted her. He gestured her to sit down in the chair across the desk from him. He sat down in a massive leather chair, set his elbows on its arms and intertwined his fingers over a genteel paunch. Sparkling on his right hand was the amethyst ring Benita had kissed on her graduation day.

He steepled his index fingers and tapped them together as he studied her, the young woman who had authored the diary now in his desk drawer. He had skimmed it the other afternoon. Foolish, girlish drivel, most of it, except for those shameful passages of lust, her brash assault on the virtue of a young, vulnerable priest growing bolder from page to page. Something had to be done about the problem before she brought scandal to the name of Holy Mother Church.

He cleared his throat and cast a look in her direction. 'You understand why you're here.'

Benita nodded.

'Look up, young woman.'

She lifted her eyes and quickly dropped them again.

'We have been receiving some very disturbing reports for some time now.'

Silence. The secret was out. Someone had been watching her. Who? And what had they said?

'You understand what I'm referring to.'

She sat motionless, eyes directed downward, wishing she had a cigarette.

'You have embarked upon a very dangerous course. You have put yourself and one of our good priests in grave spiritual danger.'

An excruciating pause. She was guilty, she knew that. There was no need to torment her with accusations.

'What you are doing has brought great suffering to your dear mother. She prays for you unceasingly. She lies awake at night with a heavy heart. I, too, am deeply concerned about this dreadful problem.'

Slowly, Benita lifted her eyes until they almost met his which seemed fixed at a point in the middle of her forehead 'You've told her?'

He tilted his head back and looked askance at her. 'We share the same deep concern. This sinful, dangerous path you have chosen can lead only to disgrace and sorrow. Think of the scandal to the people around you. The innocent little children in your classroom. Your fellow parishioners. What are they to think when they hear tales of a woman who. . .who has carelessly dismissed the sacred vows of a priest? Caused him to violate the pledge he has made to God. The threat of scandal here is a very, very serious matter.'

Benita felt the sting of tears. She chewed on her lip.

'You are risking your very salvation. You must abandon this sinful course at once. Do you understand?'

Benita caught her breath, whispered 'Yes.' She was frantic for fresh air.

'You must stay away from this priest. There must be no contact whatsoever between you and Father Henry Dunkel.' The archbishop's gaze was unflinching as he waited for some sign of acquiescence. 'Did you understand what I said? *No contact*. What you have done is very, very serious. A grievous sin against God. A disgrace to your church, your family, your very soul. It is my responsibility as your archbishop to warn you that this shameful behavior must stop. *Now*. Is that clear?'

A nod.

'Well, then.' He leaned back and cleared his throat. 'You may go. Father Roach will see you out.' The red crewcut appeared on cue.

Her legs managed to carry her out of the archbishop's office, out of the mansion, down the steps, into the Dodge. Hands trembling, she started the car, eased it from the parking space and onto Locust Street. She'd gone only a few blocks when a dump truck going in the opposite direction swerved and lurched toward her. She heard the whack, felt the thump, but the truck kept going and so did she, ignoring the pedestrian waving and shouting to her from the sidewalk. When she stopped at the red light on the corner, the man caught up. He pointed toward the rear of the car and yelled through the closed window. 'That guy left a helluva dent in your back fender, Miss. My wife wrote down the number of his license plate.' He signaled to the woman poised mid-block 'If you pull around the corner there, we can give. . .'

'No,' mouthed Benita and shook her head. 'No, I can't stop. I can't talk to you.'

The man cupped his ear. 'Huh? Whadja say?'

She shook her head again. The light changed and she drove off, faster now, down Bluff, up Dodge to Bryant street, onto Cleveland, home. She parked the damaged car in the shed, lest Walter should see it and take up the matter where the man on the street left off. She ran into the house, up the stairs, through Carol's bedroom and into her own. She threw herself onto her bed in a rage of tears. Carol listened for awhile to the sound of her weeping, then went into the room and silently held her.

Walter considered the dented fender a God-given opportunity. Even before Benita's impetuous Lubbock trip and Father's rash visit to Mexico, the sight of his sister driving around town in a priest's car had bothered him. But now, he had his mother's well-being to consider and, well, dammit, thought Walt, I'm a man and so is he, priest or not, and I'm past sticking my head in the sand. Here's a chance to get her out of that car at least. He delivered the Dodge to the farm where Father's brother lived, located a used black Chevy sedan and subsidized his mother who supplemented Benita's contribution. They jointly purchased the car and dubbed it the Black Beetle. Marcella put a scapular in the glove compartment to invoke God's protection. She and Benita went for the country drives Marcella loved; they shopped for groceries together; Marcella picked up Great Aunt Maggie and Great Uncle Larry and took them picnicking with relatives in the country. Sometimes on weekends, Carol came home from an evening with friends to find Benita and her mother contentedly watching a TV movie together.

Obeying the archbishop's directive to stay away from Father was possible for Benita as long as he was on duty as chaplain at

Lowry. Strictly speaking, letters were a form of contact and also forbidden, but when the radio played one of 'their' songs, she wrote to tell him of that hunger, that nagging need for him. Let the archbishop declare divine right over his territory; she was no longer one of his faithful sheep. Her sinfulness had freed her from the flock. Or so she told herself in moments of bravado. The truth was, a cloud of dread that might burst at any time hung over her in Dubuque. Only concern for her mother and guilt over the anguish she had dealt her kept Benita living at home, doing whatever she could to atone for her sins, which included a cleansing confession at St. Mary's.

Sister Catherine, principal at St. Columbkille's, saw Benita's teaching potential, considered it more relevant than the rumored condition of her soul and offered her a position teaching third grade. It was a quasi-promotion, a full-time teaching position in exchange for a sub-standard Catholic-school salary. Ostensibly, her $3000 annual salary—more than any other layperson at the school received—was meant to lure her from the public system, but it was also an efficient solution to the problem her presence in the diocese created for the archbishop. Her daily activities could be kept under the surveillance of the church and her employment dependent upon good behavior.

On the surface, she led an orderly, even nunnish life. Her social life consisted of interacting with the other teachers in the faculty room between classes. One day, as she and a young nun jousted with classroom pointers, a group of novices from Mt. Loretto entered. One of them was a young woman with flaming, as yet unshorn red hair, who had gone through St. Columbkille's a year ahead of Benita. She looked at her with a strange, lingering gaze and seemed on the verge of speaking, then changed her mind and turned away.

Beneath the facade of placid days churned her passion for Father, as untamed as ever. It attacked her at undefended moments: when a melody on the local station caught her off guard; when she lit her last cigarette of the day; when she stood in the backyard and searched out Sirius; when he quoted in a letter a line from a song and said it 'described his feelings exactly.'

During his interim as teacher and coach at St. Columbkille's, Father had relied upon his status as priest to gain random admittance into whatever classroom caught his interest. Now, home on leave from Lowry Air Base, he went straight to the third-grade door. Benita opened it. There stood the José of Mexico, restored to the role of chaplain by the cross pinned to his blue Air Force uniform. 'I've come to see *you*,' he murmured, lowering his eyes in a stealthy glance that roused her body and made her blush as thirty-five eight-year-old children looked on. Father eased past her into the room. 'Hey, kids! I came all the way from Denver to check up on Miss Kane. Has she taught you your prayers? Who can say the Act of Contrition for me?' On his way out, the chaplain whispered to Miss Kane, 'Meet me at seven. Our usual place.'

Hierarchical mandates faded before the thrilling demands of their love. So did the disturbing memories of her days in Denver. Only when she thought of her mother, collapsed in the living room, did she hesitate. But she *needed* him, that was all there was to it. She was on the path to ruin but she could not stop seeing him. The Beetle that Walter hoped would free Benita from Father gave her more freedom to be with him. Instead of arranging a furtive pickup at some remote street corner, they could drive separately and judiciously to the site of their rendezvous. Their preferred place had always been a woodsy hideaway near the tall white water towers west of Dubuque. As soon as they turned off Highway Twenty toward Centralia, a dreamy ruthlessness would overtake her, then a tingling impatience that began in her pelvis and moved through her whole body into the very tips of her fingers.

Now, as she drove to meet him, a sickening memory crept through her. Denver, the efficiency motel room, warmth slowly draining from her body and the food, both waiting, waiting, waiting to be devoured by him. What if he came two hours late now?

What if he didn't come at all? But he had! She saw the red wheels, just a flash in the dwindling daylight. Relieved, she turned and followed him with growing excitement, down the makeshift lane along the edge of a cornfield. She hoped there would be no spongy spots to slurp up a wheel and sink the Beetle. He stuck his arm out the window and waved to her. A signal. Stop. We're here. The cornfield had given way to a paradise for lovers, a grove of Midwestern trees, oak and elm and cedar, the underbrush ripe with early September, growth tall and lush enough to accommodate clandestine vehicles and strenuous lovemaking. He spread out a blanket and opened a beer for each of them.

Afterward, when they had calmed down, they drank another beer while they sat smoking and talking. Father fingered the sapphire ring he'd given her. In spite of his directive at the time—*This means you're mine. Don't ever take it off*—she could not wear it openly in Dubuque. 'We'll get there yet, I promise,' he said and paused until she asked where. 'To the island of Mauritius. I'm going to take you there. You'll see.'

'Not if the archbishop can help it,' she said gloomily. She told him again what she had written to him, the details of the humiliating visit to the chancery. She pointed to the still-unrepaired fender on the Dodge and blamed the dent on the archbishop. If she hadn't been flustered, she would have seen the dump truck in time to swerve.

He laughed and opened a third beer. 'That car's done its time. So have I, as far as the archbishop's concerned.' Again he paused and waited for her curiosity to build. He planned to marry her, he said.

The thought of it! To be with him, far away from threats of disgrace and damnation. If only they could go away now. Anywhere. 'But you can't. How could you?'

He shrugged. 'I'll figure something out. I wouldn't be the first guy to opt out.'

'Mauritius,' she mused. 'Could we really go there? It sounds so far away.'

'It *is* far away. That's the point.'

She bolted upright. 'Did you hear that? Listen! What is it? A car?'

'A tractor. Some farmer who can't quit until it's too dark to see his hand in front of his face.'

The 'farmer' was Richard driving back and forth along the cornfield, watching for some evidence of a car having entered. Bent-down weeds in the borrow pit. A row of flattened cornstalks. When he saw the Beetle pass his house that evening, a premonition seized him. He decided to follow it, to follow Benita, which was easy enough until she turned onto that lonely road. When he hung behind to avoid being seen, he lost her.

'Can you believe the guy?' Walt had said to him the night before. 'Sitting here big as life eating supper at Mom's table, then twenty minutes later, off he goes for a test ride in Benita's 'new' car. Bullshit, I say.'

Richard agreed. What puzzled him, he said, was the amount of leave time Father seemed to have. 'Am I wrong—is he around a lot, or does it just seem that way?'

Whenever he had a moment's leave, Father came to Dubuque. Whenever he was in Dubuque, he stopped in to see Marcella. She tried and for the most part succeeded, to treat him hospitably. Her part, Archbishop Binz had said, was to watch and pray and say nothing about the diary or the revelations it contained. For the sake of her family and the church.

The family had adopted a policy of caution around Benita. They treated her gingerly. They monitored their words and deeds for fear of pushing her further into Father's camp. Her brothers were losing patience with what was either an astonishing naiveté or an extraordinary insolence on Father's part. But short of tying up Benita, or following her around trying to catch her in some act with Father, what could they do? Exercising surveillance over their grown-up sister's life was impossible. And not their primary responsibility, Ruth had reminded Richard tonight before he set out.

Still, that's what it came down to. Standing by idly waiting for evidence to pile up was not their idea of brotherly love. They began to follow up—literally—every inkling of something afoot. When Benita left on some obscure errand and three minutes later Father got up from the table, stretched and yawned and said, 'Well, Marcella, that was another wonderful meal, but it's time for me to hit the road to Dyersville,' one of her brothers followed. Richard trailed them evenings when Walt worked. Walt did week-end duty. What they saw made the information in the diary moot. The Beetle and the Dodge parked in front of an out-of-the-way motel near Centergrove. The Beetle and the Dodge disappearing into a grove of country trees. The Beetle and the Dodge concealed in a limestone quarry carved out of the hills south of Dubuque, off the road to Bellevue. Benita hunted agates there with Irene; that's how she knew about the place. That's where Richard caught them late one crisp October Saturday afternoon—not in the act, not yet, but fifteen minutes later they would have been. The stage was set. They'd parked their cars side by side and scouted out a grassy site and were spreading out their blanket when Benita alerted. 'Sh-hh. Listen! What was that?' A car was approaching.

'Quick,' said Father. 'Over here.' They scrambled into the quarry and crouched down behind a stand of box elder trees sprouting through the rock. The car stopped. A door slammed. Father ground a string of obscenities through his teeth. Benita eased out far enough to see. Richard! Her brother, Richard, was walking with determination toward the quarry. He was a slight man with fair Irish skin and dark curly hair, but in his black cashmere topcoat, (he'd bought it when he became Dr. Kane, the dentist) he looked large, almost ominous. He kept coming, closer and closer to their hiding place. 'Get back,' whispered Father and pulled her by the arm. She saw the pistol then. Father was pointing it at Dick.

'Dick! Look out!' yelled Benita from her hideaway.

Dick stopped, shoved his hands into his coat pockets and looked around.

'Get back in your car!' she shouted. She showed herself now and gestured frantically for him to go. He took a few more steps toward her.

'Get out of here!' she yelled. 'Go!'

He did then. As soon as he was safely inside his car, she dashed from the quarry to her own car and drove away.

He'd heard stories, Father said afterward, and she must have, too, about couples attacked by some pervert who came upon them parked in a lovers' lane, or on a secluded country road. The man beaten, the woman raped. The gun was for her protection. She hadn't asked him to explain it—questioning the man who was her strength and hope did not occur to her—nor did she pass on to Richard Father's explanation. In fact, she refused to talk to her brother at all about the encounter. She'd gone home that afternoon and straight to her room where she remained the rest of the evening. She heard Richard come in, heard him in the kitchen talking to her mother and Walt. She recognized the anxious tone, but she stayed upstairs, cringing like a soldier in a foxhole, hungry and frightened and trapped. A war was going on and she didn't know which side she was on. Cordoned off in her room, she felt like the enemy of everyone, fighting all alone for her survival.

No, Father was with her. They were in the foxhole together. He said so in his letters from Lowry. There would never be anyone else. She would be his true love. Forever. Remember Mexico, he said. Remember how good our love was then when we didn't have to hide. That's how it will be again, when we're married. Be patient, Topper, he said. Be brave. He signed his letter, *Vaya con Dios, my darling, José.*

Teresa was with her, too. She was her friend in need and a hindrance to the successful beleaguerment of Benita. She received a call from the chancery advising her that she was risking her good standing in the church by associating with Benita.

The light, rapid knock on the third-grade door a few weeks after the quarry incident carried an urgency that set Benita's heart pounding. She opened the door to Sister Catherine, the principal. 'A call just came into the office from the chancery. You are to be there this afternoon at four.'

Gathered in Archbishop Binz's office were her mother, Richard, Walter, Irene. Only Carol was missing. The warning shot the archbishop had fired over her head during her first summons had become all-out warfare. But it was a war that had to be waged in secret. The priest's name, the issues involved, the ignominious details must not be mentioned. The battles must be quick and silent and efficient and won. The family must be ever mindful of the damage that could be done to their name as well as to the name of Holy Mother Church if this matter became public.

As for Benita, said the archbishop—all eyes turned on her— she had been warned before. She was being warned again. Not harshly, but out of Christian charity, concern for her true happiness. She must have no more contact with Father Dunkel. None whatsoever. No letters; no telephone calls; no visits. Her family had agreed to help the archbishop enforce this mandate. Out of love for her, and concern for her immortal soul, they would work together to put an end to this disgrace. Her responsibility was to seek God's grace through the sacraments—confession, holy communion—and to amend her life. Only through true contrition and the firm resolve never to commit this sin again could she obtain the grace to quit this path that was endangering her own soul and the soul of a man dedicated to God.

Benita returned from the chancery to the house of the enemy, her mother. She was surrounded by hostile troops: Irene, Walter, Richard. Only Carol was neutral, her unapprised younger sister who once again came into her room to hold her through her tears. Everyone else, Benita avoided. She refused to eat, drink or speak with them, or even to take a lunch from home to school. Sister Catherine suspected a problem when Benita skipped eating and spent the noon hour shooting baskets on the court behind the priest house. Several times, she went out to her with an offering of a candy bar. As a way to avoid her family in the evening, Benita began selling encyclopedias. The glossy, crammed pages of World Books and Childcraft that had excited her as a child, still did. *Where is the Taj Mahal?* she asked her customers. Her enthusiasm brought success; she set aside her extra earnings for the trip to Mexico Father had proposed.

What better way to renew the covenant they made in Mexico than to go back, he said in early March when he returned on leave. He wanted to drive there mid-summer in his new Volkswagen. He called it their honeymoon-in-reverse. Instead of driving *away* after being married, they would drive *back*, back to the place where he had given her the sapphire ring that made her his for life.

Father home on leave meant another round of patrol duty for Walter and Richard. 'I know you were with him in Wisconsin Saturday night, Benita,' said Walter. 'I saw your cars outside the Hazel Green motel.' Benita looked at him as if he were speaking a foreign tongue. Walt wouldn't ease up. 'And the night before that, it was the Centergrove motel.' For the first time in months, Father was home and her brother thought it was his job as assistant-to-the-archbishop to follow them around. Why didn't he mind his own business? Why was it so hard for him to understand? She and Father loved each other, the same way he and Jo did. It was only a matter of time until the church changed its rules about priests marrying. That's what Father said. What was now considered wrong would then be right.

Once, Walter's Irish temper flared and his face reddened and he threw up his hands and said, 'Break it up, Benita. For God's sake—and Mom's, and your own, too—just break it up! It's not going anywhere. It can't.' A few minutes later, he shook his head, sighed with remorse, and said gently, 'I'm sorry I blew my top. I'm worried about you. We all are.'

'Well, you can quit. I'm not a little kid, you know. I know what I'm doing. And it isn't wrong. Why should I give up every-thing I want because of some crazy rule the pope could change tomorrow if he wanted to?'

Richard tried the same approach. By reporting to Benita what he'd discovered on his tour of duty, he hoped to. . .what? Shame her? Scare her? Let her know she wasn't getting away with it? The truth was, it was all he could think to do, the only way he knew to show her she hadn't been abandoned. 'So last night it was Cen-tergrove again. They must be getting to know you two pretty well out there. Aren't you afraid someone will tip off the archbishop?'

She shot an angry look his way.

Marcella cautioned her sons to be gentle or they might do more harm than good. Her greatest fear—one that haunted them, too—was that Benita would run off with Father and they would lose her forever.

Marcella observed many of the comings and goings of the black Beetle and the Volkswagen but what happened in between she could only imagine, worry and pray about. More evidence was not what she needed, but rather consolation, the assurance that something was being done to rescue her daughter. The heart of the matter, as far as the family was concerned, was that youth and naiveté had lured Benita into a forbidden romance. She was not a Jezebel but a young woman in need of deliverance. To accomplish that, they looked to the archbishop, who ruled his diocese in the name of Christ and in union with the pope. By divine right, he was teacher of the faith, legislator, judge 'of first instance' and shepherd of the faithful. He selected, and provided for the education and training of candidates for the priesthood. Those ordained as parish priests were men he declared competent to help guide his flock.

Marcella's routine source of counsel was Monsignor Dunn, her pastor and friend, who listened sympathetically and accepted the envelopes she handed him. 'Please, Father, offer a Mass for my intention.' Sometimes the envelope was thicker and her request was for a novena of Masses.

Walter turned to Monsignor Dunn, too, out of a desperate need to talk to someone about the problem engulfing their entire family, both the family he'd grown up in and the one he was building now with Jo. By imposing silence upon them, Archbishop Binz had locked up the secret inside their houses and intensified their frustration and shame. As painful as it was, said Monsignor Dunn, silence was essential or there would be a terrible price to pay. Their family, the parish, the entire Archdiocese of Dubuque would suffer from the irreparable scandal.

At Sunday Mass during Lent, the words of Saint Paul's letter to the Ephesians struck a chord in Walt that failed to harmonize with what was being required of them.

Brothers and sisters: You were once darkness, but now you are light in the Lord. Live as children of light, for light produces every kind of goodness and righteousness and truth. Try to learn what is pleasing to the Lord. Take no part in the fruitless works of darkness; rather expose them, for it is shameful even to mention the things done by them in secret; but everything exposed by the light becomes visible for everything that becomes visible is light. Therefore, it says: 'Awake O sleeper, and arise from the dead, and Christ will give you light.'

CHAPTER THREE

For Benita, leaving Dubuque mid-summer was like being let out of jail. To drive away from all that prayerful vigilance! To escape the stifling propriety of Dubuque and the vicious headaches she suffered there! To relax with Father, suspended in time as they drove southwest to Mexico, the country of convivial people and mostly happy memories. She had filtered out the anxiety of her final month in Mexico and the graduate degree that might have been. Living a double life had taught her to be selective about what she noticed, questioned and remembered.

Driving through the barren heat of Texas, Father and Benita congratulated themselves for escaping the archbishop's noose. No doubt, that was the rope dangling behind her mother's ridiculous request: *I would like you and Father to separate completely for one year.* Benita put on the diamond; he took off the cross; they were Topper and José again, on a three-week honeymoon to Mexico City by way of the beautiful beaches of Guaymas and Matzatlan.

As the days and the journey wore on, the drama of starting out deteriorated into bouts of boredom. Hunger and thirst plagued her along the way. The cheap hotels and run-down Mexican inns where they stayed—one with only a communal outhouse, no warm water or showers, another with a filthy patio and a roving band of crowing roosters—dulled the glossy promise of the trip. So did the breakfasts of tortillas, refried beans and beer. They spent the beauty of Guaymas in a stifling room with a ceiling fan that succeeded only in rousing a swarm of resident bugs. In Mazatlan, as José lay dozing on the beach beside Benita, she grew restive and decided to go for a swim. She slipped off the gold Bulova she'd won at high school graduation, set it on the blanket near him and skipped over the hot sand into the water. When she returned, José was still asleep and her watch was gone. His sundrugged lassitude made her flare, but she knew the fault was hers. In Mexico anything valuable was vulnerable to the nearest thief. Every glance at her bare wrist chastised her.

José saw an opportunity in the theft. With nothing to gauge time passing, they could sample the endless bliss that would be theirs on the island of Mauritius. They began by returning to their hotel room for sex. Afterward, he again slumbered contentedly while she lay awake, fretting. She was bored lying around like a dormant snake inside this darkened room while all around them beckoned the excitement of Mazatlan. 'José,' she said, nudging his arm, 'Are you awake yet?' He snored on. How dismal, how solitary that snore sounded in the droning silence of midafternoon.

When she got into the Volkswagen, the slam of the door declared a dreary end to their Mexican idyll. She should have felt happy and satisfied, but the stolen watch had been more omen than opportunity. There had been too many bad moments, too many lagging hours, too many bizarre incidents during these weeks for her to feel anything but disappointed and perplexed.

On the drive north, she was harassed by hazy memories of odd episodes. What actually had happened that evening in Mexico City when they stopped for a nostalgic drink at the Arabian nightclub, Los Turcos? She'd awakened six hours later lying on a floor cushion in a small, curtained, circular room in the recesses of the club. Next to her sat José. He would not have allowed evil of any sort to befall her in that interlude. She was his precious Benita whose ears he had shielded from obscenities on another day when two little shoeshine boys approached them in the cantina. 'No, no, no, no shoe shine,' José had said, holding up his hands, frowning and shaking his head vehemently. The rejected boys spewed all the epithets in their English lexicon. 'Fucky you. Fucky cerveza. Fucky zapatos. Fucky Americano.' José's eyes widened in horror. 'Basta,' he said angrily and put his hands over Benita's ears. 'Basta!' The boys scampered off. He turned to her and fumed, 'You are never, ever to use that filthy, disgusting word.' He was still simmering the next day over what he called the assault by those dirty boys. Why, she wondered, was that word worse than the vivid obscenities that poured from him at frustrated moments? But she didn't ask about these things. She couldn't question him. She was still his student, trusting him to lead, needing him to be strong and reliable so that her hopes would be safe with him.

In a box on the back seat of the car was a bowl they'd purchased at a glass blowing factory. It was a wedding gift for Sally, a classmate and friend, who would be married at St. Columbkille's church in September. The gift became an unmerciful passenger taunting her with the questions the Zolly's had asked when they visited them in Mexico City. *Your mother, she is the same happy woman? Your brother's heart is better? And you, you are a Spanish teacher now, yes? Capitán, you marry this girl in Mexico, no?*

No. No, no and no. No to everything. She dreaded the return to her forlorn future. José would pin a silver cross to his lapel and transform himself into Father Dunkel, an Air force chaplain going about his Father's business while she would sink back into third-grade teacher at St. Columbkille's, 'that Kane girl' left to face the inquisition alone. She tugged off the ring and put it into her purse. When they'd stopped at the Mexican National Pawn

Shop, *La Piedad*, to say 'hola' to Luis, he let slip that the sparkling sapphire set off by diamonds had come from there.

News of the bold vacation in Mexico incensed the archbishop; so did Father Dunkel's offhanded request to be discharged from the service. He had nowhere to put the man. No parish was far flung enough to discourage this young woman's obsession. Even Father's stint in Greenland hadn't cooled her burning pursuit. The only solution was a well-planned counteroffensive. The opening gambit was an October meeting in the chancery, summoned in the usual way: Sister Catherine's knock on the door of Benita's third-grade classroom, the intoned order, *You are to report to the chancery at four today.* The door was opened by the same red-haired priest who announced himself with a new title, as if they'd never met. 'Come in, Miss Kane. I'm Monsignor Roach, the new vicar general. His Excellency is waiting for you.' He led her to the archbishop's office and signaled her to sit down.

The archbishop pulled himself upright in his chair, frowned, cleared his throat and said with steely-eyed disgust, 'This trip to Mexico! Have you no shame? No respect for the sacred vow of celibacy? No remorse for ruining one of our priests? No concern for the disgrace you are bringing to the church and to your own family?'

She could have answered 'Yes' to every question the archbishop had asked. She was deeply ashamed, overcome with guilt, and unable to change her ways. What could she possibly say to defend herself? She sat in downcast stillness.

The archbishop nodded to the vicar general who continued the harangue. 'This is a scandal of grave concern. You cannot ignore the effect of your behavior on your church. And your family.' And then, as an afterthought, 'And your own soul.'

Once during the scolding that followed, Benita looked up, as if on the brink of a comment, but dropped her eyes and maintained a pretense of indifference.

At home, she was greeted eagerly by her new friend, Holly, a black Field Spaniel who listened with bright-eyed curiosity as she angrily mimicked the two clerics. *Have you no shame? No concern for the scandal you are causing your church?* Benita scoffed. '*My church?* It's *their* church, Holly, not mine. They don't give a damn what happens to me. And I don't give a damn what happens to *their* church.' Holly's ears perked up. She tilted her head and seemed to be thinking over the matter. Holly had started out as a pet for Irene's three children, who quickly proved too young to be responsible caretakers. When Irene returned her to the pound, Benita sympathized with the dog's plight and rescued her. Walt, ever vigilant for ways to demonstrate his loyalty to his sister, built a dog house in Marcella's backyard. Now, as Benita's fury dissolved into tears, Holly approached her and whimpered sympathetically.

Carol came upon the two of them and once again took her sister in her arms and embraced her as she sobbed, praying that God would make whatever was wrong, right. Carol was a senior in high school now. She was taller than Benita and her curly hair was auburn, but she had the same Irish blue eyes, ivory skin and slender, wholesome good looks. The family's effort to edit trouble from her life had not completely worked. Despite the card games and family dinners, the horseshoes in the backyard and summer picnics in the country, she felt the cloud of pain enveloping them. She knew that serious matters existed between her family, the church, Father Dunkel and Benita, secret matters that no one outside the family was allowed to know. When Father came home on leave before his mid-August transfer to New York City where he would serve as base chaplain, he presented Carol with a string of cultured pearls as a high school graduation gift—*from Greenland, I've been saving them all this time for you.* She put up her palms like stop signs. 'No thanks, Father. I don't want them.' His indulgent smile switched to an angry frown; he snapped the box shut and shoved it into his pocket.

Benita, on the other hand, had a surprise for him. She promised to show it to him at their hideaway in the woods. When she arrived near the white water towers west of Dubuque, his Volkswagen was already there. She pulled up beside it. He opened the door, and in one gesture, swept her from the front seat into his arms. He kissed her greedily, again and again, then stepped back and surveyed her car, a brand new white Chevy Biscayne. 'Wow! Whose is this?'

She set her hand on the fender. 'Mine.'

'Yours? Where'd *you* get that kind of money?'

'Selling World Books.' In a way it was true. Her success in that endeavor was all the evidence Richard needed to declare her credit-worthy and loan her the $2900 purchase price. It was another of his brotherly business deals, intended as a vote of confidence, a nudge toward independence.

Half an hour later, as they lay on a blanket, satiated and exhausted from their frenzied lovemaking, Father said maybe he should start selling World Books. 'Maybe when I get out, that's what I'll do. We could do it together. Save our earnings and go to Mauritius.' He opened two beers and handed one to her.

This mention of Mauritius irritated her. Her drab routine of the past year, days in third grade, evenings at home, the only drama in her life coming in the form of humiliating visits to the chancery, left her impatient with fantasy. She tipped up the beer and took a long drink. She was thirsty. It slid cool and calming down her throat.

Father lit the cigarette she slipped away from the pack. She leaned into him and they sat smoking and drinking and talking about what, in fact, they would do.

'I want out,' he said. 'Out of the Air Force. Out of that collar.' His eyes went to the circle of white tossed on the blanket near his black vest. 'I've asked for a dispensation from the priesthood.'

She caught her breath. 'You did? When? Will they do it? *Can* they?'

'Rome can do whatever they want. But they make it tougher than hell. And they're slower than molasses in January. But they can do it. The archbishop is going to look into it when he goes there this fall.'

'You talked to him?'

Father nodded. More accurately, the archbishop had talked to him. There were concerns about Father's affinity for alcohol, sightings of him in bars and nightclubs featuring strip tease, risky behavior that could bring serious scandal to the church. The part the archbishop left out in that chancery session with Father was that he had written a letter to Archbishop Francis Spellman of New York City. Archbishop Spellman was the military vicar, the head of the ecclesiastical entity charged with the primary authority and responsibility of determining if a priest was spiritually, morally, intellectually and emotionally qualified to represent his church as a chaplain in the Armed Forces. How well that chaplain was exercising his pastoral and priestly duties was determined by subsequent evaluations. The Dubuque archbishop urged in his letter to Spellman that Father Dunkel's authorization to serve as chaplain be removed because of 'no fulfillment of duties and obligations.' In Rome in October, the two archbishops would review Father Dunkel's performance. If he could be kept in the service and out of active ministry, the church could wash their hands of the man. A solution that might be attractive to Father himself, or any priest wanting to loosen the leash of the hierarchy.

'I'd have to quit saying Mass, hearing confessions, administering sacraments, all that,' Father went on. He stroked her leg and let his hand come to rest on the tender inside of her thigh. 'This is what I want. You. We could get married.'

'When? That could take a hundred years.' She sighed. 'Ten, at least.'

'C'mon, Topper. Don't give up on me now. Here, have another beer.' He opened one for himself, too. They smoked another cigarette. 'Mauritius,' mused Father. 'That's where we'll go.'

'It doesn't have to be an island,' she said. 'It could be Colorado. Or Pennsylvania.'

'Nope. It's gonna be Mauritius.' They sat in silence for awhile. He emptied his beer and reached for another. 'Damn.' He tossed the empty carton. 'We're out of supplies.' He chuckled. 'Now that's a problem we can solve without the archbishop. Let's drive that fancy new car of yours to that grand metropolis over there.' He scrambled to his feet and swept his arm toward the straggle of buildings that were the town of Centralia.

It was nearly midnight and several beers later when they left the bar, calling out blurry good-byes to their bar chums. Benita stumbled on a step. Father steadied her, then lurched along beside her as they made their way to the car. He got in behind the wheel, overriding her argument that she could drive, that after all, it was her car. 'I know. I know. Ish your car. Your wun-ner-ful new car. But I'm gonna drive it. Because *I*,' he thumped his chest, then lifted his hand like a wobbly baton directing his words, 'am in better shape than you.' The baton came to rest on her chest.

Before they were out of sight of the bar, he swerved off the gravel and smashed into a bridge abutment, shattering headlights, crumpling the hood. He leapt out, yelling back to her, 'Move over! Get behind the wheel!' as he fled down the road and vanished into the night. Their beer-drinking buddies rushed to the scene to find Benita, baffled and tipsy, sitting behind the wheel of her inoperable new Chevrolet Biscayne.

What explanation she offered to her family, what lies she might have told them, what truths she may have withheld, she didn't know. Nor did she know how she got home that night or who hauled her damaged car to the Chevrolet garage. She woke the next morning knowing only that something was seriously wrong with her. Why, otherwise, would she keep hoping for a future with a man who brought her so much confusion and shame, who claimed love and then disappeared like morning dew from the grass, leaving her to face the consequences alone. Even so, when he called that afternoon, she was relieved to hear his voice. 'We don't have much time left. I leave for the big city in two days. Who knows when I'll be back. Your car working? No? Okay, I'll pick you up. Six o'clock. Bryant and Curtis.'

'I saw you waiting for him on the corner last night,' Richard told Benita after that rendezvous. 'Walt trailed you out Highway 29. Everybody knows, Benita. But to tell the truth, I'm getting tired of playing sleuth. I just can't believe this is what you want.'

'Quit then. Mind your own business. I didn't ask you to save me.' As soon as the words were out, she regretted them. Richard *did* look tired. Pale, too. She knew he cared about her. So did everyone in her family. If only they would stop trying to run her life.

The next summons did not surprise her. Some whiff of Father in the Dubuque air—a hint of his presence or its aftermath brought a predictable response from the hierarchy. The archbishop and his new vicar general, Monsignor William Roach, had once more rounded up the entire family—Marcella, Richard, Walter, Irene. When Benita arrived at the chancery, they were lined up together like a Greek chorus chanting their message. Give up the sinful alliance with Father Dunkel; go back to the sacraments; repent and reform. Unless you wish to bring down disaster upon the church and everyone you love, you have no other choice.

Benita sunk her teeth into her lip and nodded silently for her mother's sake. Marcella's long-suffering eyes were her greatest torment.

'You agree then, Benita?' prompted the vicar general. 'Are you telling us *yes?*'

Another nod.

'A verbal acknowledgement would be appropriate,' said the archbishop.

She was cornered. If she wanted to leave this room, she had to feign cooperation. 'Okay then. Yes. I'll do what you want.' But no matter what she agreed to, no matter how distressed she was by the grief in her mother's eyes, no matter the doubts that nagged relentlessly in her own mind, she was incapable of changing her course.

Carol had decided to become a nun. She loved children and wanted to teach. This, combined with her parochial upbringing and her mother's typical Irish dream—to see a child of hers dedicated to the religious life—made the choice logical. In early September, she would enter the Presentation convent to take a vow of poverty, chastity and obedience. But before she left behind the world in which she had never participated, Benita and Marcella took her on a holiday to Mexico City. They stayed at the Compostela and from there, went out to the sites Benita had visited as a student—Xochimilco, the Floating Gardens, the pyramids, Acapulco, a bullfight, cock fights. When they returned to the hotel at the end of the day, they passed without remark the site that once had been Benita's favorite destination. Behind a certain door on the second floor, was the room and the passionate bed where a thrilling alliance of love had been forged. JunToS: *José and Topper, Siempre.*

On September 3, six weeks after her eighteenth birthday, Carol entered the convent. On that same day in Minneapolis, Marcella's brother-in-law, steadfast Uncle Larry, died. His funeral Mass was held in Dubuque at St. Columbkille's; he was buried near Eldon in Mt. Olivet cemetery. Once again, Carol was excluded from the grief, not because of her family's protectiveness this time, but because as a nun, she had forsaken worldly distractions.

Marcella and Benita were alone now with routine as their consolation. By day, Marcella altered clothing at Stampfer's department store and Benita taught third grade at St. Columbkille's. Evenings they sat together at the dining room table, pencils in hand, and corrected the stack of papers Benita had brought home. Now and then, one would point out something and the other would nod or comment or smile. On balmy Sunday mornings, they went to Mass at six a.m. and then fishing with a neighbor. But congenial activity and small talk could not bridge the gulf of mistrust, disappointment and shame dividing them. At Mass, Benita sat like an infidel through Communion. Periodically, Marcella felt conscience-bound to make an overture. 'Benita, if only you would return to the sacraments. I know that the Eucharist would give you the grace and strength to, to . . . .'

'Mother,' Benita would say emphatically. 'Don't.'

Both of them missed Carol intensely. Marcella found comfort in the belief that God had blessed Carol and through her, their family. The loneliness and anger that beset Benita when she walked through Carol's empty bedroom at night ended in pillow-muted sobbing. The sister she longed for was a five minute walk away, but convent regulations specified four Sunday afternoons each year when the Kane family could spend two hours with Carol in the convent parlor.

Carol's choreographed memories of a perfect family, a happy home, Benita as the older sister she idolized, came to an end during her early months in the convent. The awareness buried inside her during all those years of watching from the sidelines spilled out as troubled mumblings during her sleep. The nun who overheard these revelations dutifully reported them to the directress of novices who went to Sister Edward for advice. Carol was called in, and in the presence of the directress, Sister Edward told her the truth. The disclosure was devastating for her, but clarified a multitude of mysteries: Benita's fragility, her mother's collapse, the whispered worrying, her family's growing wariness toward

Father, the discomfort in her own gut when he dropped in. Sister Edward counseled Carol daily, using the hour allocated to novices for recreation. Once again, Carol was set apart from the group. The first time she visited Carol in the convent, Benita cried bitterly the entire time, sobbing that she had destroyed her childhood. There was nothing Carol could say to convince her that as a child, she felt fortunate to be part of such a happy family. Excluded from their fears, she had navigated happily in her own world of neighborhood, school, and friends.

Richard's lethargic heart had begun to compete with Benita's endangered soul as a subject of family concern. Bound by two distressing family secrets, Marcella worried incessantly to Walter and Irene. Hierarchical mandate hushed up Benita's shameful situation; Richard's heart trouble was kept quiet for fear news of it would harm his dental practice and the security he was trying to establish for Ruth and their five children. Marcella's own heart ached at the couple's predicament, so painfully like her own. With so few places to dispel her anxiety, she began to turn more and more to the archbishop for counsel. Walter often accompanied her when she called at the chancery on Sunday afternoon.

Immediately after their September visit, Marcella sat down to write a humble letter of appreciation.

Sept. 14, 1959

Your Excellency:

Words will never be able to express the gratitude we hold in our hearts for your paternal interest and kindness in our problem. It has been a source of great comfort to know the deep understanding of human nature which you bring to problems such as ours. We shall pray daily that God will use you as the instrument which will bring about the final solution.

Sincerely hope we gave you the needed information. . .so far as we know, only one member of his family, a married brother, knows about the problem. . .You mentioned he had not visited you for some time. He told us he went to you for advice about getting out of the service and he could not see you, but was told by someone there that you wished him to stay in because you had no place for him at that time. . .I feel sorry for him, he could be doing so much good.

This has been and now is a heavy cross. Feel if my husband had lived this would never have taken place. He always said we could not help the children very much financially but there was never a breath of scandal on either side of the family to harm them. . .now the children are worried because of thirteen grandchildren.

He surely needs help, perhaps a miracle of grace will wake her up. Thank you so much, your Excellency, for all your kindness, but most especially for the thoughtful consideration given us Sunday.

Gratefully yours,

Mrs. Eldon Kane

The discrepancies between Father's reports to the family and what the archbishop told them prompted Walt to begin paying his own visits to the chancery. He was weary of driving around on back roads in search of evidence secrecy wouldn't let them use. The thought of Benita disappearing with that man behind some cheap motel room door tormented him. 'It's time to *do* something,' he told the archbishop. Be patient, came the advice. Acting in haste could lead to regret. By working slowly, steadfastly, silently—'as Mary did, containing Christ in the darkness of her womb'—they could solve the problem without bringing scandal to the church or tarnishing his family name. Walter's four children bore that name. He deferred to the archbishop.

Monsignor Dunn passed on to Marcella some news that disturbed her. On his way to Rome, the archbishop had met in New

York with Monsignor (Major General) Finnegan, the chief of military chaplains, who was now reviewing Father's military status. In Rome, Archbishop Binz met with Archbishop Spellman, the military vicar, to discuss the matter of Father Dunkel, who, it seemed, might be discharged soon.

Nov. 4, 1959

Most Rev. Leo Binz, D.D.

Your Excellency:

I want you to know we are most grateful to you for sharing so much of your valuable time with us last Monday. . .I appreciate your thoughtfulness in giving me that beautiful rosary, I will cherish it always and use it in praying for you. Am sure the girls feel the same joy in possessing theirs.

Sorry about my feelings last Monday afternoon. . .a terrible, hopeless feeling came over me when Msgr. Dunn told me about your interview in Rome. . .I can't shake the fear that they will leave for the south after his release from service. I told her about our recent interview because she seems to feel we are all against her and holding information from her. I asked her to send a message to him through you to encourage him to save his soul. . .she will go to you anytime you call her even though he advised her against it.

She blames the church, as he has for some time. I am glad she has a nun to talk to because she may be able to get her to consent to talk to a disinterested priest who would explain to her the relation between Christ and the Church. In that way she may be given the needed grace to go to confession. She does not trust any of us. . .it is hard to live this way but worth it if it helps save their souls. . . surely all those wonderful prayers and Masses you offered for them will be heard. . .I sincerely hope you will get an answer from Msgr. Finnegan. . . we will continue to pray and sacrifice for the salvation of their souls.

I have had at least ten Masses offered each month for the past three years, besides a novena of Masses several times, will with God's help continue to do so.

With deep appreciation, I will close.

Gratefully,

Mrs. Eldon Kane

Marcella had put onto paper the family's greatest fear. Out from under the military thumb, Father and Benita might marry and disappear into the land of lost souls. As long as they remained under the archbishop's governance, their souls were his concern.

The nun Marcella referred to in her letter was Sister Edward, the teacher who salvaged our self-esteem as eighth-graders, who was the source of Benita's hope and sanity since college, the intelligent woman engaged in earning a doctorate from the University of Minnesota, a professional nationally recognized for her expertise in teaching reading, but who, in the end, was a woman. Like Mary, she was destined to be a mediator. She could put Benita in touch with some 'disinterested priest,' the only competent interpreter of the imagery found in the writings of St. Paul—Christ as bridegroom, the church as bride, the priest as alter Christus. Out of that metaphor came the rationale that denied marriage to priests and ordination to women. Father Dunkel would never be available to Benita. The church was his bride.

November 6, 1959

Dear Mrs. Kane:

Please believe me, that I do share deeply the worries which afflict you. They have been with you, of course, much longer than with myself.

I have had no word yet, since I left Rome, neither from Monsignor Finnegan nor from Father Dunkel. . .I have given Father Dunkel the directives which it seemed to me should be

given. How far he will be obedient, I do not know. I am, how-
ever, storming heaven with my prayers. . .The darkest part of
the picture is that there is no evidence they themselves are pray-
ing. . .they are not receiving the sacraments. Neither are they
turning to the Church in any way for guidance and help. . so
far as I know, the Church does not grant the dispensation on
which they have set their hearts. . .they are not the first ones for
whom the answer has been given that a priest is held to the
obligations he has assumed. I shall not fail to call Benita if
there is any development which would make a further visit
advisable. . .

One of the most difficult things for some of us to do is wait.
Waiting, however, does give us time for prayer. Somehow I
have not lost confidence that the good prayers you have offered
in these past years will be heard. Saint Monica prayed so much
longer before her prayers were heard.

With sentiments of esteem and with all good wishes, I
remain,

Sincerely yours in Christ,

(signed)

Archbishop of Dubuque

For the archbishop, the situation had escalated from nuisance
to torment. Father Dunkel had been advised by the military vicar
to resign his commission and leave the service, a generous offer
considering the alternative, dishonorable discharge. But, contrary
to what Father had told Benita, the archbishop had had 'no word
from Father Dunkel,' no request for laicization and no sign that
he was willing to give up his Roman collar, no guarantee that he
would be obedient if the church decided to defrock him, a grave,
laborious process that normally required the priest's own agreement.

The next summons to the chancery was a tactical maneuver

designed to reroute Benita. Monsignor Roach opened the door with a disarming greeting that caught her off guard. The archbishop, too, made an awkward attempt at conviviality. 'Yes, good afternoon, thank you for coming, Miss Kane. Please, please, sit down.' He leaned back in his chair and pondered his amethyst ring.

Prayer and reflection had given him insight, he told Benita. He had reached a greater understanding of her predicament. His kindly glance almost reached her before it fell. She had gotten off course, he said. She simply needed help in finding direction for her life.

The vicar general nodded cautiously. 'Benita, we've arranged for you to take a vocational test.' The diocese would bear the cost, he assured her, not only for the test, but also for any necessary training. He arched his eyebrows and beamed with pious generosity.

The test informed them that Benita could function effectively as a dentist or a veterinarian. 'So! There you are!' said the archbishop at the follow-up meeting, to which he had invited Marcella. He turned to her now. 'Your daughter has two wonderful options, Mrs. Kane. To become a dentist like her brother, or a veterinarian. Both excellent professions.' His eyes skirted Benita as he inquired, 'Which career do you feel inclined to pursue, young lady?' His smile was broad, benevolent. It vanished with her answer.

'Neither one.'

'Oh, Benita, are you sure?' cried Marcella. 'Dental school is expensive. Not something we could afford on our own. . .and you could make a good living.'

Benita shook her head. 'I don't want to be a dentist. Or a vet.'

The archbishop's thin lips writhed in speechless fury. The vicar general slumped in his chair. Marcella sent Benita a sad, disconcerted look. A few days later, Benita's friend, Teresa, received another notice from the chancery advising her to 'stay away from Benita Kane or there would be serious consequences.' The net closing around Benita was now set to snare anyone loyal to her. 'You'd better watch out, Holly,' Benita warned, gathering her pet into her arms. 'Hang around me and you'll get excommunicated.'

Benita and Father continued to exchange letters and phone calls; she dreamed of him at night and thought of him by day. And always, there were the songs that overwhelmed her with longing. They had never danced together, never gone to a movie at the Grand or the Orpheum together, never walked along Cleveland Avenue hand in hand, but they had created a private life, a union that thrived on secrecy, risk and desire. Lyrics that described their circumstance helped them endure when they were apart. They heard these as a call not to resignation, but rather, to hope. Destiny intended them to be together. It was a matter of time and patience, Father told Benita.

CHAPTER FOUR

On February 11, 1960, thirty-nine-year-old Chaplain (Captain) Henry N. Dunkel was separated from the United States Air Force. He returned to Denver where reportedly he was enjoying a respite as retired chaplain and priest-on-sabbatical. He telephoned Benita, who again this year was teaching third grade at St. Columbkille's, to say he would be coming to see her. He was thinking about going into World Book sales and wanted her advice.

Meanwhile, Marcella waited and prayed according to the archbishop's directive.

March 29, 1960

Your Excellency:

Words cannot express my feeling of deep appreciation to you for your kindness and understanding of human nature which you bring to problems such as ours.

Surely with all the prayers and sufferings of so many, God will hear our pleadings and give them the needed grace to save their souls. How I would love to see him back on the altar serving God in the way he should.

Thank you so much, your Excellency and please say a prayer for me.

Gratefully yours,

Mrs. Kane

The archbishop's reply was dated the next day.

Dear Mrs. Kane,

I shall indeed keep you in remembrance before the altar, at Mass and in my poor prayers. Also I assure you of a continued remembrance of the other intentions we have, both of us, so much at heart.

I know how preoccupied your praying is with those other intentions, but I beg a remembrance also for myself and for the Archdiocese which the Good Shepherd has entrusted to so unworthy a shepherd.

With sentiments of esteem and with all good wishes, I remain,

Sincerely yours in Christ,

(signed)

Archbishop of Dubuque

Walter and his brother-in-law, attorney Don Breitbach, decided to pay a visit to Father's parents. By enlightening them on their son's activities, they hoped to enlist their help in dealing with the matter before he showed up in town again.

'We need to lay it on the line to them,' said Don as they drove to the Dunkel home in Dyersville. 'Get them to understand. That guy has violated more than his priestly vows. He's done things that are downright illegal.' At Walter's inquiring look, he said, 'Supplying liquor to a minor. Cigarettes, too. And then there's the matter of rape.'

'Rape?' Walter was stunned.

Don nodded. 'Statutory rape. Think of her age when this began.'

'Fourteen. Fifteen. But how do any of us know. . .I mean how can we pin down exactly what happened when? How could anybody document that?'

'The diary. That would help make a case. Have you seen it?'

'Mom gave it to Monsignor Dunn. He gave it to the archbishop.'

Don smacked his palm against his forehead and groaned.

The Dunkels were suspicious of this somber visit from Walter and his brother-in-law, the lawyer. Furthermore, there was no evidence whatsoever for the appalling things they implied about Father. Emma Dunkel said it had bothered her plenty when Benita cavorted in front of him in those skimpy swim suits. But she knew her son. He was a good, dedicated priest. Nick Dunkel swirled the ice in his glass of whiskey and said sullenly, 'That's damn crazy stuff you fellas are bringing around here. I think you oughta take it on back home and forget about it. I sure don't want to hear it again.' Father's brother, Herb, said his brother was being falsely accused.

'Struck out there,' said Don as they got back into the car. 'What boggles my mind is how they can *not* see. Or at least be willing to take a look.'

'Maybe it's just as well. We're walking a fine line here. If we stir things up too much, I'm afraid we'll lose Benita forever.' In fact, he feared they *had* lost her, that no matter how this turned out, they might never recover the capable, trusting, spirited person that had been Benita.

'Yeah, your mother's reluctant, too. When I brought up a charge of statutory rape to her, she gasped. Then she got this really sad look. *How could I do that,* she said? *After all the archbishop has done for us, how could I do that to the church? And think of Father's poor parents.* She was on the brink of tears.'

'That's Mom. But she has a point. The archbishop seems to be doing what he can. She's counting on him, that's for sure. We all are.'

Don sighed. 'Well, he has the diary.'

They fell into their separate thoughts and drove the half-hour back to Dubuque in silence. Don knew that the Kane family had every right to count on the archbishop. Canon law imposed upon him a grave moral obligation to safeguard the spiritual welfare of all those under his care. But bishops also made a commitment to protect the image of the church in the world. Their primary concern was to maintain control and to shield the church from scandal.

Gradually, Father wound his way back home and resumed his pseudo-clandestine meetings with Benita. Walter, and less often, Richard, resumed their watch, trailing them to their rendezvous sites and reporting their observations to Benita afterward. They presumed that the mere thought of a brother hanging around nearby would be a deterrent; instead, risk enhanced the lovers' thrill. Once again, the family tiptoed nervously around the subject. The worrying picked up where it had never left off, compounded now by Father's mysterious emancipation and the family's sinking energy and hope.

Benita looked forward to the family vacation in June, when for two weeks she would escape, if not her longing, at least the compulsion to act on it and the inevitable guilt that followed. She and her mother, Walt and his family, and her cousin, Larry, who was her age, and Holly, of course, were going to Uncle Larry's cabin on remote Rainy Lake, forty miles by boat from the Canadian-U.S. border. They were gathered on the lot between Walt's home and Marcella's and in the midst of preparations for the next day's departure when Father stopped. He stood around for awhile watching and listening, then took Walter aside.

'Walt, can we talk? There's something I wanted to ask . . .'

Walt nodded. 'Yeah, sure. . .uh. . .' He no longer could bring himself to call him 'Father,' and nothing in his demeanor or dress—a T-shirt and casual slacks—said it applied. Walt glanced around at the chaos of packing and children. 'Let's run downtown.'

They drove to the Canfield Hotel, settled into a corner in the lounge and ordered a beer. Father stroked his chin and darted a glance toward Walt. He cleared his throat, lifted the stein of beer and took a long drink. He swiped his foamy lip with the back of his hand and said, 'I've never been to Rainy Lake.'

Walt sipped his beer and listened.

'You're gonna be up there two weeks, huh?

Walt nodded.

'That oughta be a good time.'

'I hope so.'

'I have a favor to ask.'

Walter raised an eyebrow.

'I just thought, well, since I'm more or less on vacation, too. . .'

Walt looked directly at him, hoping to head off the idea he heard approaching.

'I'd like to come along with you to the lake.'

'Come *along*?'

Father nodded, rubbed his chin, dark with stubble. 'That's what I'd like, yes.' He beckoned to the bartender. 'Two more here.'

Walt shook his head. 'No more for me, thanks. The thing is, it's just a cabin. Not that big. We're pretty stacked up, as is. . .with Mother, the kids. . .' He refused to say 'Benita.'

'I'm easy. I can sleep anywhere. In my car, if I have to.' Father's eyes and smile were pleading now. He emptied his glass and started the second beer. 'It could be my last chance to see all of you for awhile. I'm gonna be taking off before long. Maybe go south.'

Walter felt himself heating up, his Irish complexion betraying him. He picked up his glass slowly, paused it mid-air near his mouth. 'I sympathize. I do. But I just don't see how we can swing it.' He set down the glass. A bit too firmly, perhaps.

Father looked stricken. Incredulity hung in his eyes, on his parted lips. Then he snickered. 'No room in the inn, is that it?' He shrugged and went mute.

'It's just not appropriate.' Walt was struggling to contain the anger coursing through him. How could the guy even dare to ask? He stood and pulled his car keys from his pocket. Dare to ask! 'I need to get back to the house.' Father drained the last beer from the glass and followed him.

When the group arrived at the cabin, the lonely silence of Rainy Lake and the deep black sky wild with stars filled Benita's mind with Father. Immediately, she wrote to tell him how much she missed him, missed them, missed being together. *All alone I gaze at the stars, at the stars, Dreaming of my love far away,* she wrote. She carried the letter in her pocket the next day when she, Walt and Jo took the boat out on Rainy Lake. When they encountered another boat returning to International Falls, she sneaked the letter to a passenger and asked him to mail it. That night, the letter was back in the cabin, set conspicuously upon her pillow. The incident preyed on her mind through the days that followed and spoiled the majesty of that place.

'Hi, Father,' Benita would call out as a three-year-old child whenever Monsignor Foley walked past their house on his way from St. Raphael's cathedral to the Presentation convent. She often clambered to the window to watch for him, simply for the privilege of delivering her cheerful greeting to the black-haired Irish priest her dad respected so highly. Now Monsignor Foley was the vicar general eyeing with consternation the grown-up Benita sitting across from him in a wing-back chair.

'I don't understand it. I simply don't understand it,' he said, wearily wagging his head as he looked at her. 'Your father was such a fine man. Such a devoted Catholic. Always so solicitous about our priests. What would he think of this. . .this disgraceful . . .' His words trailed off in sad bewilderment. He sent a pleading look toward the archbishop, lodged behind his desk in his imposing leather chair.

'I'm sorry, deeply sorry, that it's come to this,' said the archbishop. 'We've tried everything humanly possible to bring you to your senses and here you are, worse off than before, as far as I can tell.' He told her this in a genial voice and smiled, notifying her that what followed might not be pleasant, but it would be final.

She was in the chancery after a mid-morning knock on her fifth-grade door. School had resumed after Christmas vacation; *he* was on his way to somewhere in Missouri where he planned to sell World Books. Making money wasn't the goal, he'd told her. As a captain, he'd built up a little nest egg that would keep him going, but he was restless. He was on leave-of-absence, a priest forever according to the order of Melchisadech with nothing but time on his hands. He instructed her to come down and join him when school was out.

Monsignor took another turn. 'Benita, I knew you as a little girl. Your dear mother and father had such high hopes for you.' He opened his palms beseechingly and shook his head. 'Instead, you have brought your family disappointment and suffering.'

All of this shaming was unnecessary. If she hadn't been thoroughly disgraced before, she was now, ever since that terrible night in December.

Walt had questioned the wisdom of going out that frigid

Friday evening. Drifts were four feet deep, five in open country. The wind was still whipping snow over the two-lane highway as he drove the treacherous roads west out of Dubuque. Maybe he was being too ponderous about his big brother role, but something he'd been noticing in Benita's eyes troubled him. Jo saw it, too, the look of a captured animal with no chance of escape. Walt could barely make out the water towers outlined against the pewter sky; hunched beneath them were the buildings of Centralia. And finally, the motel. He knew what he would find there—the Volkswagen and the Chevy Biscayne parked side by side. What surprised him was the rage boiling up inside him at the sight. He'd seen it plenty of times before. He'd spent countless evenings following those cars around, endless Sunday afternoons with his mother ruminating in the chancery, too many hours away from Jo and the kids. Now, as he pulled into the shadows and parked, he wanted out. He wanted to walk straight to that door, kick it in, grab that guy by the back of his neck and. . .instead, he went into the grocery store and made the phone call he'd promised to make when he next encountered this situation.

'Monsignor Foley? It's Walt Kane. They're here. I'll wait for you and the archbishop in the parking lot at the motel. I'm driving a green and white Olds.'

The archbishop had dispensed with the usual chauffeur 'because of the delicate situation' and asked Monsignor Foley, the vicar general, to drive the limousine. Bundled up in identical black overcoats and black felt hats, the two men melded into the black upholstery. Only the ruddy roundness of their faces was visible when Walt approached the car.

'Get in, Walter,' said the archbishop through an inch of rolled-down window.

'I'm going to that room,' he replied and bolted off.

'Wait, wait, just a moment,' called the vicar general, but it was too late. Walt had reached the door. No sign of light except the blinking of a neon sign. Motel. Motel. Motel. He knocked. No answer. Again. He rattled the knob. No response. He put his ear to the rickety door and listened. He heard, or thought he did, the pad of bare feet on the floor, not far from the door. 'Benita?' he called softly. 'Benita?'

She was crouched, heart-pounding, on the other side of the door. Father was stretched out, covers thrown back, naked and sound asleep. Or pretending to be. Snoring, in any case. A few minutes ago, he was awake and asking for the whiskey bottle on the table. When she got up to get it, she saw the sweep of car lights across their draped window. 'There's someone out there,' she cried.

'Come back to bed,' mumbled Father.

She'd peered into the half-inch of space between the drape and the window frame. 'Somebody in a big car. Two people. Oh my God! I think it's the archbishop.' She watched as the car pulled up and stopped near a car on the far side of the lot. 'That's Walt's car!' said Benita. Father turned over and flopped his arm across her vacant pillow. 'Walt is coming this way!' She hunkered down near the door and held her breath as he knocked.

Walter retreated a few yards to gain momentum. One thump with his shoulder and that door would be wide open.

'Walt!' cawed the vicar general from the now half-opened window. 'His Excellency wants you to come back to the car. Now.'

Walt socked his fist into his hand. 'Damn.'

'What, precisely, do you intend to do?' asked the archbishop, his words emerging in frosty puffs through the open window as Walt returned.

'Get into that room.'

'And then what?' asked the vicar general.

'I'll get my sister out of there. What happens to him. . .well, that's up to you.'

'And what will you do if they resist?' asked the archbishop.

Walt looked at him. 'I'll play that one by ear.'

The archbishop's face unlocked in alarm. 'We need to be prudent here. Get into the car, Walter, while we think this through.' He waved a leather-gloved hand toward the back seat and when Walt relented, went on. 'This is a volatile situation. Think of your family. The welfare of your children. If something happened tonight. . .if you were injured. . .that would be a dreadful state of affairs.'

'Or suppose the police got involved,' added Monsignor Foley. 'Think of the newspapers tomorrow! The disgrace to your family. The damage to your work.'

'We must wait. We have to wait. That's all we can do,' said the archbishop.

'*Wait*? For *what*? We've been waiting and it hasn't done. . .' Walt was on the edge of the seat, gripping the door handle.

'Walt, shh-hh,' cautioned the vicar general with a jittery look toward the taunting sign, Motel. Motel. Motel.

'I know, Walter. I know,' said the archbishop, gently. 'You're concerned about your sister. Justifiably so. But seeing this situation, being here, *on location*'—the way those words oozed out of him rankled Walter—'convinces me, we *must* wait.'

'Why? What are we waiting for? A miracle?'

'For them. We'll wait until they come out.'

Walt stared at him. Stared and thought. *That could be morning, Your Excellency. I'm sorry, but I can't sit out here all night waiting. I have a wife who would be worried sick. And kids. The kids you just mentioned. What would they think happened to me? Besides, it's going to get pretty damn cold and miserable out here about three in the morning.* What he said was, 'We can wait awhile, but I can't sit here all night.'

The archbishop smiled. 'Nor can I. Or Monsignor Foley.'

They waited fifteen minutes, long enough for Benita to nudge Father, then to shake him, suspecting that he was feigning sleep, that he'd heard the commotion and chosen to ignore it. He made no response and when she looked out again, the long black car that had been lurking in the shadows was slithering away, followed by Walt's Oldsmobile. 'Come back, Walt!' she whimpered into the closed drape. 'Come back. I'm here.'

Her main memory of that bitter night was a feeling of disgust. Disgust with Father for being so heedless of her fear. Disgust with an odor that crept through the room, a putrid mix of alcohol and tobacco and sweat and a smear of something on Father's bare buttocks that reeked of human excrement. Greater disgust with herself for being with him.

'Do you agree?' The archbishop was looking at her now, his head cocked, waiting for an answer.

She came to attention. 'What? I'm not sure. . .what did you ask me?'

Monsignor Foley sighed peevishly. 'You heard nothing of what His Excellency said?'

Another peevish sigh, this time from the archbishop. 'Please try to attend to the discussion. I outlined your choices. I described the fine hospital in Minneapolis where we have reserved a place for you. During your six weeks there you will have an. . .uh, well. . .an evaluation. Tests, interviews with people trained to understand your problem. I've contacted a physician in Minneapolis, Dr. Garvey, an excellent man, an exemplary Catholic, who will oversee your program.'

'A hospital? You want me to go to a hospital?'

The vicar general nodded. 'At our expense, of course.'

Benita's head began to pound. Her stomach hurt. 'I'm not sick.'

The archbishop smiled patiently.

'What hospital?'

The archbishop cleared his throat and launched into an enthusiastic description of the physical facility, the staff, the marvelous treatment she would receive there, the wonderful opportunity for rest. It might have been a resort. 'St. Mary's Mental Health Hospital,' he said finally.

Benita caught her breath. 'Why? When? I'm teaching fifth grade at St. Columbkille's. I can't just. . .'

Monsignor Foley nodded pleasantly. 'Yes, Sister Catherine tells us you're a fine teacher.' He tapped his fingertips together. A frown gripped his brow. 'We've arranged for a substitute. To begin immediately.'

Benita chewed on her lip, shook her head. 'I don't want to go to a hospital. I'm not sick.'

The archbishop leaned forward and said in a level tone, 'It's up to you. If you prefer, you can simply leave Dubuque. Find work elsewhere. And hopefully, some happiness, too.'

So that was it. He had decided she was crazy. Obviously, he was right, she thought, two weeks later. Otherwise why was she sitting next to her mother on the zephyr on the way to St. Mary's Mental Health Hospital, doing exactly what he said?

'You're not the one who should be coming here,' said Marcella when the train pulled into the station. Late that afternoon, as a dispirited Marcella left the hospital for her return trip to Dubuque, she saw the discharged captain in his blue Air Force uniform, smiling at her from across the street. She turned away, trembling, pretending she hadn't noticed, eager to get on the bus that pulled up.

Only Dr. Garvey, the Catholic psychiatrist hired by the archbishop knew why Benita had come to St. Mary's hospital. Not even the vigilant nurses who kept twenty-four hour records of her words and deeds knew what was behind the 'anxiety' entered on her admission record. No mention was made of her involvement with a Roman Catholic priest. Therefore, no one had any reason to suspect that the Air Force captain who came to see her regularly during her six week stay was that Roman Catholic priest, nor did anyone have concern when, arm in arm, they exited the hospital and went out on the town.

On one such outing, they dropped in to see Mary Jane, now a nurse, married and living in Minneapolis. Mary Jane knew who he was, of course, and deduced from their hand-holding, exchanged glances and sly allusions that they were en route somewhere together. All those rumors she'd heard and disbelieved since high school were true then: Father and Benita had something going. She took Benita aside to reassure her that whatever that something was, she could count on her friendship. Long after Benita left that day, Mary Jane remembered her tormented reply. 'I'd have to give up my family to be with him. And I can't. But I can't give him up either.' Then she'd assembled a smile and said, 'It's driving me crazy.'

Contrary to the archbishop's promise, no one on the hospital staff talked to Benita about her troubles because only Dr. Garvey knew what those troubles were. She did enjoy a sense of safety there, out of range of the insoluble problems waiting to assault her at home. On March 10th, she was released to another harsh ultimatum. Marcella, desperate to keep her daughter out of Father's mesmerizing hands, had conferred with the archbishop and devised a plan. Either Benita would remain within the confines of her home or she would be required to leave town. 'I'm under house arrest,' she told Teresa when she smuggled in cigarettes.

A few weeks later, Benita and her friend, Holly, were on the highway driving to St Louis, Missouri. 'Holly, where are we?' fretted Benita when they arrived late on the shabby outskirts of St. Louis. 'He told me to meet him at. . .' She glanced at the note taped to the dash. On it were jotted directions to his hotel. 'Oh, no. I think I turned too soon.' Holly pressed her nose against the car window and observed the neighborhood. Run-down buildings with shattered windows, empty lots, restless young men roaming the sidewalks, skinny dogs. Benita locked the car doors. 'I'm afraid we're lost, Holly. Now what do we do?' She made a few more nervous wrong turns before she stopped at a filling station for directions.

The carpeting at the hotel where he was staying was stained, the furniture threadbare, the mattress sagging. The blankets were frayed and the sheen worn from their binding, but so was he, worn and a little frayed, and she was tired and lonely and welcome in his double bed.

The next morning, they drove to his apartment at Warrenton, Missouri. When he went on his World Book calls, she rode along and waited in the car. José, the bright, middle son assigned to fulfill his family's dreams, and Topper, the girl destined to become an astronomer, or certainly a Spanish teacher, were now a dispossessed pair peddling encyclopedias door-to-door. Faraway Mauritius was a speck off the shore of Africa on a glossy map inside Volume I.

She might have stayed on with him and formed an irresistible sales team, combining her conviction with his charm. Instead, a few weeks later she returned to the dreaded town of Dubuque, drawn back not by a triumph of spirit over flesh, or the fealty to family she'd described to Mary Jane, nor even in response to her mother's persistent prayer, all those rosaries and Masses and novenas sent up on her behalf. She simply ran out of patience and hope. If he had proposed a plan instead of a daydream for their future, if instead of taunting her with post-coital promises, he had renounced the priesthood and married her, she would have given up everything for him.

She returned from Missouri in time to celebrate with Richard and Ruth the birth and baptism of their sixth child and fifth son, Christopher John. Over their joy hung the shadow of Richard's failing heart. The shortness of breath and chest pain that had puzzled Eldon now plagued his eldest child.

Father came and went like an apparition, arriving in Dubuque out of nowhere to hold out fantasies that vanished with him. He pursued her in the customary way: a furtive telephone call, a covert meeting, an urgent seduction on a blanket or backseat or motel room bed followed by boozy pledges of love and marriage. For her, these sessions were followed by deepening remorse, guilt at the suffering she saw in her family's eyes, shame. She was twenty-eighty years old, unemployed, living with her mother. Her future was bleak, her past squandered, yet Father was as necessary as air to her.

Archbishop Binz was being transferred to St. Paul to preside over that archdiocese. Before he left Dubuque in December of 1961, he made a final attempt to clear the Benita problem from his record. He assembled both families: the Kanes—Marcella, Richard, Walter and Irene; the Dunkels—Nick and Emma; and the culprits—Father in clerical garb and Benita, in a prim skirt and blouse, looking as virtuous as a first-grade Catholic school teacher was expected to look, especially one entrusted with preparing children for their First Communion.

The group was gathered in a large room in the chancery for what appeared to be a showdown of the Montague-Capulet variety. The archbishop immediately assured them they were not here to go through a litany of sins or to assign blame, but rather to encourage this unfortunate pair to repent and reform and return to the sacraments. Their blatant disregard for the laws of God and the church could not be tolerated. If they persisted in their sinful ways, they would face the consequences. 'A deeply painful situation for all concerned,' he summed up. He looked around the group, ascertaining that they understood what he was describing. Loss of access to the sacraments. The grace of Confession and Holy Communion no longer available. Marcella's eyes filled with tears. Nick Dunkel shifted awkwardly in his chair and maintained his sour expression. Emma looked at her son, trying to catch his eye, to affirm with her flimsy smile her belief in his goodness.

The confrontation seemed to work. 'Benita went back to the sacraments Christmas of 1961,' Marcella wrote to the new vicar of the archdiocese of Dubuque, Archbishop Byrne. However, the Benita problem was not solved. To the dismay of Archbishop Binz, it followed him. In the summer of 1962, at the urging of a friend and her own misery, Benita moved to Minneapolis. When she was hired to teach Spanish at Washburn High school, she was glad that Sister Lucilda had prodded her to finish the work begun in Mexico. She still lacked the clout of a master's degree, but the fifty-six graduate credits enhanced her resume and salary. She lived with her Uncle Larry's widow, Aunt Guy, and their son, Larry. She stowed the regular letters from Father in the big Samsonite suitcase she'd received as a college graduation gift.

When Sister Edward, who was completing her final two years of doctoral studies at the University of Minnesota, learned that her former student was in town, she contacted her and resumed her gentle guidance, never condemning Benita for her liaison with Father, but rather patiently trying to loosen her from its grip. 'Why would you want to be around such an unkempt person?' she asked Benita one day, thrusting before her the increasing dishevelment she was reluctant to see.

The evanescent World Book salesman floated freely and frequently upriver and down, in and out of the hapless territory that claimed him. Early on a chilly, rainy Saturday morning, he called Benita at Aunt Guy's to say he needed another set of World Books. As they loaded them into his trunk, he proposed a weekend fishing trip to Wisconsin and arranged a meeting site. Benita took along the Garcia Bait Casting Reel that her cousin Larry had given her during her incarceration at St. Mary's. Father, a devoted fisherman, admired the reel, even as he grumbled about Larry's intrusive generosity. Giving gifts to Benita was his domain. Their fishing site was a motel across the Wisconsin state line. Meeting there became the couple's weekend routine.

The Minneapolis-St.Paul archbishop learned of these jaunts and conferred with the Dubuque archbishop. Archbishop Byrne confiscated Father's fishing permit. Archbishop Binz made an astounding proposal to Larry: the church would grant him a dispensation to marry his first-cousin, Benita. Insulted by the maneuver, Larry stopped attending Mass. The two archbishops, obligated to lead these wayward sheep to greener pastures, or failing that, off to some alien turf where their scandalous behavior couldn't contaminate the flock, devised another ultimatum and enlisted Walter as their messenger. He arrived on the zephyr one Saturday morning to announce that if there was one more sighting or rumor of Benita in the vicinity of Father Dunkel, she would be evicted from Aunt Guy's house. 'It's not right to take advantage of her kindness and be involved with *him* behind her back,' argued Walt reasonably.

Benita pored over the 'Apartments for Rent' section in the Sunday newspaper. She and Holly spent the day driving around, following leads that ended with the same three words: no pets allowed. 'You're not a pet, Holly, you're my best friend,' said Benita and reached to stroke Holly. The dog wriggled closer until her nose rested on Benita's leg. Faithful canine friend vs. stray priest lover: an impasse Father could end, if only he would keep his promise, leave the priesthood, get a job, make a life with her, the woman he declared was everything he wanted. She would have gone anywhere with him. All he had to do was ask. So why, *why*, didn't he? She was almost thirty years old, weary of bumping along in this arrangement. Except for brief remissions when she was with him, the predicament haunted her relentlessly. The ultimatum faded away. Benita stayed on at her aunt's, teaching Spanish during the week, fishing in Wisconsin on weekends.

Walter's attention had gone to his brother in Dubuque. Richard had made several trips to the University Hospital in Iowa City, the recourse for Iowans with difficult medical conditions. There was nothing to be done. The clogged arteries to his heart could not be repaired.

The changing of the hierarchical guard required Marcella to acquaint the new archbishop with the humiliating details of their family woe and begin anew her pleas for help.

July 23, 1963

Archbishop James J. Byrne

Your Excellency,

Words cannot express my deep appreciation to you for your kindness in helping Father Dunkel. I am the mother of the girl involved. My husband has been dead for twenty years; this problem has been a heartache to my three married children, my daughter in the convent, and myself for a long time.

I was pleased when Father Dunkel phoned me and asked me to help him, it seemed God was answering our many prayers. I encouraged him to go to you. . .I don't know what you know about this problem, however if I can be of help, please call on me. I have forgiven him and want the best for the poor fellow.

I have suffered much mental torture from this, but after all what matters is their souls are saved. Would you please, Your Excellency, when praying for him, pray for my daughter? We all love her very much. At present, she is attending a Spanish Language Institute at the College of St. Teresa, Winona, Minnesota. . .

Please say a prayer for me, too, being alone now, I worry, am so thankful to God now, however and I do so want him to be the good priest I know he could be. She was so young at the time, I feel God will help her to help him.

Archbishop Binz was most kind to all concerned in this problem. I hope to meet you someday and I will continue to pray for you.

Gratefully yours,

Mrs. Eldon Kane

Marcella had reason for concern. Winona was only a few hours' drive from St. John's Abbey in Collegeville, Minnesota, where Father had been sent for an extended 'retreat.' Benita had envisioned her six-week interval at Winona as a bridge to freedom, a chance to break from the past and him. The intensive program required her to speak Spanish exclusively, which she explained to him in June as she was leaving. When Father appeared in Winona, instead of saying 'no,' or translating into action the words she couldn't say, 'Stay away, let me learn something,' she spent every weekend with him in a dingy motel south of town, loathing her own weakness while engaged in the same numbing routine that had sabotaged her studies in Mexico: smoking, drinking, sex. On the occasional week nights when she went out for a beer with friends, he would be lurking at the end of the bar.

August 30, 1963

Most Rev. James J. Byrne

Your Excellency,

Thank you for your kind letter. . .I appreciate very much your kind invitation to visit you. I phoned there that day but did not get through. . .

He (Father Dunkel) blamed Archbishop Binz so, said three years ago they knew it wouldn't work and he wouldn't let them solve it in their own way. . .I sympathize with his good parents . . .I pity him and my heart aches for her. I know she was strong enough June 11 to tell him that she wouldn't see him again, if she could only turn more to God as she did when she went back to the sacraments Christmas 1961. She can be so strong until she meets him, that was such a worry when I learned he went to Collegeville because she was at Winona. . .she is leaving Monday for Minneapolis where she will teach. Naturally it worries me. I know they are both weak. I pray that she accepts the grace and strength to end this by not seeing him and that he returns to the priesthood.

I just had to tell you my fears, it is so hard to know what to do, I am alone and perhaps that makes it worse.

I hope you have a wonderful sojourn in Rome. . .please extend my greetings to Archbishop Binz and thank him for his prayers.

I wish Father every blessing and pray he returns to his rightful place. I urged them both not to visit or contact each other. I have not heard from him since he called me needing help. He told me he would tell me where he was going, he didn't however.

We all love Benita and want their souls saved. She was only fourteen and he twenty-seven when this started, not maliciously on his part, I am sure. She now is thirty and it will be very hard for her. I worry more about her when she is teaching away from home. . .How I pray this terrible problem ends now. Only God knows.

Thank you, Your Excellency, for everything. I'll be praying for you and would love to know how Father is. Please keep this confidential.

Gratefully yours,

Mrs. Eldon Kane

Marcella's plaintive 'I am alone and perhaps that makes it worse. . .' was now the reality burdening her mind. Carol had vanished into the restrictions of the convent; Richard's declining health made him unavailable; Benita had moved to Minneapolis; Walt had moved to Omaha. Accepting the management position with Prudential Insurance required two compromises he and Jo never intended to make—leaving Dubuque and committing to work that required routine travel. They'd deliberately built their home near Marcella in order to provide security for her and at the same time, establish St. Columbkille's parish as their spiritual home. Moving away was the only way out of the problem consuming their own family life. Marcella was grateful for Irene and Don who lived across the street with their family. But it was Eldon she talked to in prayer, Eldon whose reassurance she most missed. Without him, there was no one to remind her daily that she was beautiful, no one to confide in as she lay in bed at night. *If my husband had lived,* she had assured the Archbishop, *this never would have taken place.* If her husband had lived, he may have challenged her assumption that the seduction of fourteen-year-old Benita by the twenty-seven-year-old priest was 'not malicious.'

The devastating news of the assassination of President John F. Kennedy on November 22, 1963 brought Father straight to Benita to claim her as his partner in mourning. They drove north and checked into a motel outside the Twin Cities where they spent the weekend. Propped on pillows in bed, they lamented the chaotic turn the world was taking as they watched TV coverage of the calamity and its aftermath. Although she still winced at the first swallow of whiskey, the ritual of drinking it together consoled her. So did the blurry sense of well-being that spread through her after it was down. They stayed right through the funeral on Monday, drinking and smoking and grieving Kennedy's death, a tragedy that for three days eclipsed the desolation of their own lives.

Jo and Walt's fifth child, a daughter, was born in February of 1964. His business travel became more onerous, but now and then it did take him to Dubuque where he could look in on his mother and see old friends. It was there that he first overheard the talk. The secrets the family had guarded so carefully had been the subject of parish speculation for years. He also learned that Father was back in Iowa.

Coinciding with the close of Father's long, ambiguous retreat at Collegeville and vague retirement from the Air Force reserves in 1964 was his assignment to a parish in tiny Belle Plaine, Iowa. St. Michael's was a few cornfields east of St. Joseph's parish in Chelsea, where he had served as priest in 1952. The plane flight from Minneapolis to Cedar Rapids was easy and the lovers' meetings at the airport discreet. The drive to Belle Plaine was impatient, full of eager touches and longing glances; sometimes they began en route when he lifted his right hand from the wheel and eased it under her sweater or along the inside of her thigh, setting her tingling. If the rectory had been any further away, they might have risked pulling into a cornfield. She spent several weekends there with him; on one, she arrived with a gift for him, a cue stick in a case. Twice he invited another couple into the rectory for a gracious dinner prepared by his cousin visiting from Minneapolis. He proudly showed them the gift he'd given her, a 4-10 shotgun and case. 'So your cousin is a pheasant hunter?' inquired the male guest, glancing with fascination at Benita.

She liked hostessing these occasions as long as she wasn't required to pose as housekeeper, which would have put her in the kitchen eating alone—an odd prelude to the bed of lust they soon would share. Early the next morning, he left that bed to offer the Holy Sacrifice of the Mass, but she stayed on, warm and sated under the rough wool blanket of their illicit sleep. Pretending to be his cousin at dinner on Saturday evening was one thing; receiving Communion at Sunday Mass from hands that had caressed her through the night was another. Turning sideways to look at him in his sleep was still another. That had happened the night before when, for the slightest second, she saw a stranger, neither the priest of her childhood nor the man she loved, but rather someone living in a twilight world of his own concoction, where others existed for his purposes and the lies he told were true.

He went regularly to Minneapolis, too. They met for sex at a motel on the north side of town. Afterward, they went out to a bar where they drank beer, smoked, played drawn-out sessions of half-hearted pool, ate a sandwich. Once, Benita took a sick day from school and they went to see *Tom Jones*; they held hands through the matinee like the ordinary lovers they had been in Mexico. But they exited into bleak reality, another bar, another beer. Their alliance required the ambience of bedrooms and cocktail lounges, the melancholy scent of alcohol and cigarettes, erotic midafternoon darkness, maudlin juke box songs that described lust as love.

Kennedy's death and Richard's unhappy prognosis haunted Benita. She grew despondent over her wasted life, and increasingly desperate to change it. On New Years she made a resolution. The next time Father called, she would tell him she wanted out. But what if he laughed, as he had before, and said, 'No you don't. You're mine.' Or what if he didn't call? What would she do then? She'd made resolutions before, all of them unkept, leaving her feeling weaker, more ashamed than ever. She couldn't trust herself. She would simply watch for an opening, a sliver of light or space that might show her a way out.

The Minneapolis streets were heaped with snow and the temperature was formidably sub-zero in late January of 1965. Even so, a group of Washburn high school teachers, all young and single, was gathering at a local club to celebrate the end of the semester. Benita had given them her regrets, but at the last minute changed her mind and joined them. Curt Kirschbaum, a man whose overtures she had deliberately avoided these past three years, sat down across the table from her. At closing time, the enjoyable experience of being with peers prompted her to invite everyone to Aunt Guy's for a snack. Curt challenged her to a game of ping pong in the rec room. The others formed a cheering section. It was three a.m. when the last stragglers put on their coats, promised another get-together soon, and went out into the hushed, frigid streets. Benita was picking up coffee cups and glasses when the doorbell rang. There stood a chagrined Curt. He hated to ask, he said, it was so late, so cold out, so inconvenient, but. . .well, his car wouldn't start. Would she mind giving him a ride to his apartment?

As he exited her car, he paused, turned, said, 'Benita, do you think. . . I was wondering. . .would you like to go out to dinner with me some evening?' For a moment she was terrified. Hadn't he noticed the sapphire ring on her left hand? Then she turned and looked into his brown eyes and said, 'Yes. Yes. I'd like that.'

With that daring Yes, something seemed to break open inside her while something else took hold. She knew what she needed to do and was sure now that she would do it. Curt's invitation was the opening she'd been watching for.

Over the next several weeks, she told Father repeatedly on the telephone that she could not continue to see him or communicate with him. He refused to accept what she was saying. 'You don't mean that. You can't do that. You're mine. You know that.' In the next call, he refused to listen at all, interrupting her, overriding her words with his insistent ones. 'C'mon, Topper. I'm lonesome for you. Come to Belle Plaine for the weekend. We can have a good time.' In a subsequent call, she told him that she did mean it. She was breaking things off for good. He flew into a tantrum, raging like a pent-up child. 'No! You can't do that. Who put you up to this? What's going on? Did you meet some rich guy? Or some Mexican? Is that it? You're just tossing me aside like a piece of dirt? Well, you can't do that. I won't let you. I gave you a ring. You promised to be mine. I need you. You need me.'

His long-distance histrionics convinced her that she would have to deal with him face-to-face. 'I'll come to Cedar Rapids next week. You can meet my flight.'

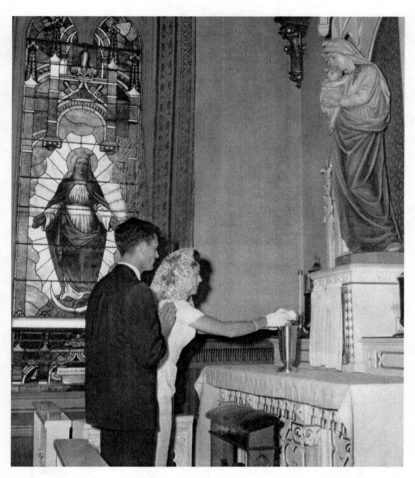

Benita and Curt at Mary's altar, Aug. 14, 1965

Wedding day, August 14, 1965

Benita, her mother, Marcella, and Curt, 1980

PART FOUR

Deliverance

CHAPTER ONE

Resolving to see him gave her courage. She wanted to return the pawn shop engagement ring, but most of all, she wanted to face up to him, to show him that her decision was neither impulsive nor transient and she would not be bullied by his melodrama. She ticketed an early morning flight to Cedar Rapids on February 23 and a return flight that afternoon. She told her mother her plan, then called Walt who said he just happened to have business in Cedar Rapids that day. He gave her the number of the Prudential Office where she could reach him and suggested as a back-up their brother-in-law, Don Breitbach, who stood ready to use legal tools on her behalf. Walt's precautions implied a danger she didn't feel. She was nervous but not afraid.

Curt dropped her off at the Minneapolis airport that morning. Although they hadn't yet had their promised dinner date, they had talked over lunch at school and played ping pong a few times at Aunt Guy's. She wanted to get to know him better; she wanted the freedom to pay attention to her own life, and to her teaching.

Father picked her up in Cedar Rapids. He was dressed in clerical garb, black overcoat, black suit, Roman collar. His genial handshake and expert smile suggested to anyone observing that she was a younger sister, a niece, a woman in some kind of spiritual distress who'd requested his counsel. She asked him to drive to a restaurant where they could talk. As soon as they were alone in the car, he began. 'You're not going to break off with me. You don't mean that. You're mine, don't forget. We're getting married as soon as I can work it out.' He kept it up as they went into the cafe and sat down across from each other in an isolated corner booth, interrupting his rant only beneath the eye of the long-suffering waitress who, at ten a.m. seemed to have spent her day's energy.

'So what are you two hungry for this morning?' she asked wearily as she scooped the fifty-cent piece from the table into her pocket. It was too late for breakfast, too early for lunch. The few people in the room were huddled over newspapers drinking coffee. Benita shrugged one shoulder indifferently. 'Bring a pot of coffee,' said Father. He shook a cigarette from his pack and lit it.

'I do mean it,' she told him as the waitress trudged off. 'I can't—won't—I don't *want* to have any more communication with you. Ever again.' She opened her purse and retrieved a small box. 'I came here to return this.' Cradled in her palm was the ring.

He recoiled, stricken, as if she were offering him a poisonous reptile. 'No! I don't want it. It's yours. I gave it to you in Mexico. I put it on your hand—that night in, where were we? Los Turcos?—and I told you to wear it all the time. You belong to me. You always will.'

She shook her head and thrust her palm forward, urging him to take the ring.

'No!' Louder this time. He shied farther from the venom he saw in her hand. 'It's yours. Put it on. You promised to be mine forever. We have a pact. *JunToS*. Remember? José and Topper. *Siempre*. You can't break that.'

'I am breaking it. Now. Please take your ring.' She quickly withdrew her hand when the waitress thumped down the coffee pot and two white mugs.

'Can I get you anything else, Father? Cream? Sugar?'

He waved her away with his cigarette without looking up. She turned, obviously stung at this slight from a man of the cloth.

Benita extended the ring once more. He hunched forward and said in a low, earnest tone, 'It's not my ring. It's *yours. I don't want it.*' A wild look possessed his eyes. 'Why are you doing this to me? You promised. You. . .you said. . .' His voice broke.

Benita glanced around. 'I do not intend to go on with this. Or with you. It's over.'

'You're ruining my life. How can you say that? I need you. Don't you understand?' He began to cry. 'After all these years, all this time together. . .how could you do this?' He covered his face with his hands and kept talking through his fingers, a muffled, slobbering sound. 'You're the most important person in the world to me. My true love through all these years. How could you. . .' He seemed on the verge of breaking down. A woman a few tables away glanced at them and glanced away, mumbling in puzzlement to her companion.

Benita tried to think of something consoling to say, some words that would calm him down, make him feel a little better. They were making a spectacle of themselves. She took a cigarette from his pack on the table and lit it.

He swallowed hard and gulped back his tears. 'I can't let people see me like this. Let's go some place where we can talk in private.' He nodded toward the window. 'There's a motel across the road. Let's go over there so we can talk this out.'

'I've said everything I need to say.' She smoked as he swiped at his tears with the back of his hand. She hadn't anticipated this weeping, not by a man, certainly not by Father, although there had been a few occasions when they'd shed tears of mutual pleasure. 'I don't have anything else to talk about.' She sighed sympathetically. 'I'm sorry, but I just don't.'

'I do. I have things to discuss. But I can't do it here.' He looked around. His eyes still glistened with tears. 'C'mon. Let's get out of here.' He stood and reached out his hand. Even as she shook her head 'no,' she put out her cigarette, took his hand, and out of habit, fear, pity, followed him.

His snuffling quit as they drove across the road to the motel. He opened the door and ushered her into the room, put his black brief case onto the bed and took out the sole contents, a bottle of bourbon, which he set next to two glasses on a small table in the corner. Then he returned to his crying, mixing into his tears pleas for mercy and statements of disbelief. 'Please don't quit on me. You can't. You're everything to me. You're just telling me this. You can't leave me after. . .after everything we've been through together. Remember Mexico? Remember those afternoons in the Compostela? Remember how we slept in the sun at Mazatlan. Remember all that?' He looked at her and smiled through his tears. He nodded toward the table. 'Hand me those glasses. Let's sit down and have a drink.'

'I don't want a drink.' She walked to the window and fumbled for the cord beneath the drapes, intending to open them. He followed her, reaching out tentatively to touch her arm, then pulled her to him. 'C'mon, at least give me a kiss.'

She twisted in his arms and wrenched free. She moved as far from him and the bed as space allowed. 'Whatever it is you have to say, say it. I need to leave.'

His face contorted in a confusion of hurt and anger. 'You need to leave. Why? Am I some kind of leper all of a sudden? What happened to you? When did you get so high and mighty? Christ! At least take off your coat.' He approached her, arms out. 'I'll help you.'

Hastily, she took it off and draped it over the back of the chair nearest the door. The victory fed his bravado. He lit a cigarette, inhaled, let out the smoke slowly, eyeing her. 'Now put the ring back on your finger.' No response. 'For our sake. José and Topper.' She was like stone. 'Put it on. Now!' Nothing. 'Why are you doing this?' he demanded.

'I made a decision. And it's final. I'm flying out this afternoon. And I don't intend to see you again.'

Any remnant of hurt vanished in a blaze of crimson anger. 'Okay. Then leave! And when you do, your name is coming off the stocks I bought for you. You liked having those, didn't you? Benita Kane, owner of Martin Marietta stocks. Well, they won't be yours anymore!'

Her face, eyes were impassive.

He crushed his cigarette in the ashtray. 'Don't you understand? I can't live without you!' He was shouting now. 'I love you! Haven't I shown you that?' He lunged for her and caught hold of her sleeve. 'C'mere, just c'mere, I'll show you again.' He had her by the arm now. 'I'll prove how much I love you.' He twisted her arm with a force that flung her to the bed. He unzipped his fly and threw himself down beside her, panting, 'I'll show you I love you. I'll prove it to you.' He grabbed her skirt and pushed it up and began tugging at her panty girdle, yanking it down along with garters and nylons.

'No!' she cried. 'No, you won't do that to me.' She could see his penis, a giant, threatening purple thing, looming from his unzipped pants. 'I won't let you.' She twisted in his grip and pounded her fists against his chest; she clawed at his face.

'Bitch! I'll kill you. And that bastard who took you from me, too. Whoever he is. You won't get away with this.'

She fought for her life now, hitting and pushing and kicking until finally she rolled free of him, off the bed and onto the floor, hobbled by the disarray of her clothing. His feet swung over the edge and thudded down beside her. He was sitting on the side of the bed hunched over her, looking down at her with violent eyes. She'd seen him overwrought and ready to lash out before, but never had she seen this viciousness. 'Wait!' she cried in terror. 'Wait. Let's. . .let's have a drink.' She caught her breath, looked up at him, said as calmly as she could, 'Let's sit down, like you said, let's sit down at the table and have a drink and talk.' He eyed her warily as she tried to scramble up. 'You pour the drinks,' she said cajolingly. 'And just go ahead and have one while I. . .' She gestured toward the tangle of clothing. 'While I put myself back together. And then. . .'

He was sullen and suspicious, but he helped her to her feet. She clutched her skirt, retrieved her purse and shuffled into the bathroom. As she straightened and fastened her clothing and combed her hair, she calculated. 'I'll be right there,' she called soothingly at the sound of clinking glasses. When she came out, he was sitting at the table smoking. He was still disheveled and his zipper was still open, but the whiskey had settled him down. She set her purse with her coat on the chair near the door and joined him. He glanced up, poured bourbon into the glass she extended, then lit a second cigarette and handed it to her. She took it, watching him from the corner of her eye as she smoked and sipped and waited.

Suddenly, he brightened. 'Let's run away. Today.' He stubbed out his cigarette and leaned forward, enveloping her with his eyes. 'I'll leave the priesthood and we can just go. Now. Nobody can stop us. We can do whatever we want.'

She was silent.

He reached for her hand. She let him hold it. 'Put the ring back on your finger. That's all you need to do. Then we can be back where we were. Happy again.'

'Okay, I will.' She spoke in an agreeable, light-hearted tone, as if soothing an impetuous child. She set her cigarette in the ashtray and started to get up. 'It's in my purse.'

'No.' His eyes contracted, locking her to him. 'I want to put it on your finger. Like I did in Mexico.'

She was on her feet now. She touched his shoulder and drew her hand back, brushing her fingertips over his cheek. 'Okay. I'll get it for you.'

He kept his eyes on her as she crossed the room to the chair near the door. She picked up her purse, opened it, brought out the tiny box, set it on the chair. Then, with one fluid motion, she scooped up her coat, sprang to the door and turned the knob. It was locked.

He was beside her, in a rage now, his eyes and hands grasping her. 'I'm going to kill you for sure this time,' he yelled as he worked to subdue her flailing arms and fists. 'Bitch! Fuckin' bitch. You're not getting away from me.' He was breathing hard. She shoved and fought against him and kept fumbling for the door knob, trying to unlock it. When it clicked, she twisted violently in his arms and landed a hard kick on his unzipped fly, then yanked open the door and ran. She ran without looking back, ran shaking, stunned, heart drumming, unsure when she stopped at a busy intersection where she was. She ran knowing only that she had to get away from there before he hunted her down with his car.

She didn't remember going into the drug store or getting out the note on which she'd written the telephone number. She did recall Walt's voice asking, 'Where are you? Where? Benita, just tell me where you are.' When he picked her up, she was pale and shaken and frightened to the core. All the way to the airport, Walt told her later, she spoke only twice.

Curt was waiting at the gate in Minneapolis but she was too numb to talk about the horrors of the day and he didn't pry. In the middle of that night, she woke in her bedroom upstairs at Aunt Guy's; outside a streetlight swinging in the wind danced a pool of light along the wall. For a moment she was disoriented. And then the memory of the day flooded her and with it, came one thought: I did it. I did it. I did it. No matter what, I did it. The telephone rang at four a.m.; a voice whispered to Aunt Guy that people were going to hear about Benita Kane.

She dreaded telling Curt the details of her entanglement with Father, which were bound to test the affection and trust developing between them. But if they were to have a future, she would have to reveal her past. She had no idea how to go about explaining to a baptized Lutheran who had abandoned organized religion the appalling mess she had made of her bizarre Catholic life. She was thirty-one years old and unable to make sense of it herself.

She began with the tale of her adolescent fascination for a Latin teacher, how it slowly blossomed into forbidden love and ultimately into a painful dilemma. Curt heard the story as more common than shocking. Catholics had their odd beliefs—pronouncing bread flesh and then eating it, turning to priests for forgiveness from sin—and their strange practices—novenas and incense and magical rosaries—but sexual restraint was not among them. He'd heard that plenty of priests kept a woman in the role of 'housekeeper.'

'We're adults, what happened in our lives up to now is our own business,' Curt responded to her confession. 'Let's think about the present.' Then he took her hand and said, 'And maybe the future.' It was the 'maybe' that drew her to him. Instead of claiming her 'his,' he gave her space to think and choose. But as the bizarre incidents multiplied—the furtive driving lessons, the gun in the quarry, the shame and secrecy, the violence in the motel room, Curt knew that what Benita was describing was no ordinary love affair.

CHAPTER TWO

The spiteful telephone calls that had begun in February extended in range and intensified in anger and frequency throughout the next weeks and months. Benita's fellow teachers and administrators at Washburn High School received middle-of-the-night calls asking if they knew Benita Kane had been kicked out of Dubuque because of her immoral activities. Some of the calls came from a woman who informed them that their sweet-faced Spanish teacher had been fucking a priest since high school. What would her students think of that? As a sixty-three-year-old widow living by herself, Marcella was a prime target, easily upset by three a.m. calls from a man telling her that her daughter was a whore.

A two a.m. call woke Curt in his apartment. The mystery woman said she thought he might want to know that 'that angel face of a teacher has been sleeping with a priest for fifteen years.'

'I don't give a damn about that,' replied Curt and hung up.

'You better give a damn," said the woman when she telephoned the following night. "We're going to get her.'

Benita worried about the effect of these accusations on her teaching, both on her ability to concentrate and on her job security. Her family was anxious for her physical safety. And Curt's. And at times, their own.

Most. Rev. Leo Binz

My good Friend,

Really I don't know how to write this letter, however we need your advice. . .

Enclosing a picture of Dick and family. He has been to Iowa City, cannot be cured and we are grateful he can work half days as that helps him.

I just want you to know, Benita has broken completely with Fr. Dunkel. . .She flew to Cedar Rapids Feb. 23 to tell him. He did not accept it very graciously, since that he has resigned, phoned her and threatened to kill the young man she has been keeping company with, get her job and break her down. She calls Sister Carol, Walter, Don and me for help as to what to do.

He is in Minneapolis now, says he has an apartment and a job. Benita told us he has a woman helping him, she was housekeeper at Belle Plaine. . . I believe she left Belle Plaine before Christmas and lives in Minneapolis. Walter went to offer help to him at Belle Plaine. Don saw him in Dyersville. He promised not to bother her, however, he is. Don doesn't know what to do, however he thought of you in case this woman goes to the school where Benita is doing such a good job.

You have always been such a friend to me and understanding. I called Msgr. Foley, he advised me to write to you. . .the whole thing is, you joined with us in this bond of prayer, through God, she has awakened full of remorse and frightened, very much. . .we all feel she is in grave danger, and what to do? Sister Edward feels the same. Hope you are well. I read that you were in Rome. Words cannot express my deep appreciation for all you have done. I always pray for you.

  Gratefully yours,

  Mrs. Eldon Kane

Marcella's thoughts leapt like wildfire from one worry to another as they raced toward Archbishop Binz for counsel. She had skipped over the drama of Richard's desperate drive through a snowstorm to Iowa City to volunteer himself for a new procedure called angioplasty only to learn that the condition of his arteries ruled him out. He returned home and entered a competition with death, plunging himself into work to accumulate security for Ruth and their children.

Marcella's most immediate fear was of the violence erupting in Father who reportedly had resigned in a pout from Belle Plaine. He was now on the loose in Minneapolis, exacting vengeance with the assistance of a former housekeeper. Monsignor Foley declined involvement in the family's effort to confirm her identity, saying Father 'might come to him for help sometime.' He passed the ball to Archbishop Binz.

The archbishop's reply to Marcella was dated April 9, 1965. He thanked her for the picture of Richard 'and his fine family,' expressed sorrow at the diagnosis and took up the topic of Benita.

I had prayed so much for her . . .it is wonderful to know that our prayers have been answered and that her break with the past is so complete. . .she seems repentant and happy. . .it was an answer to prayer. Benita is worried, of course, about the threats and such things to which she is being subjected. I have written of them to His Excellency, Archbishop Byrne, but there has not yet been time for a reply. I don't really know if there is to be an answer. I am sure, however, that he will study all the facts fully. He will be anxious, of course, that no harm will befall either Benita or Curt. If he finds out anything which would point to any danger, we may be sure of his deep interest.

I am most pleased, of course, with Benita's change of heart. I feel completely sure of it for many reasons. Not the least of these is the fact that the divine and human combine so perfectly in the arranging of it. I feel sure that her change of heart will bring about Father Dunkel's sincere conversion. Both you and I, I am sure, will keep up our prayers for him.

With sentiments of esteem and kindest regards, I remain,

Sincerely yours in Christ,

(signed)

Archbishop of Saint Paul

The archbishop's panglossian letter was a pretense, another soothing, clever avoidance of action. Nor did Benita's repentance bring the happiness he assumed. She was tormented by shame and self-loathing, desperate to rid herself of the vile memories, which is why one Saturday morning, she opened her Samonsite suitcase over the trash barrel behind Aunt Guy's garage and shook out the letters from Father. She lit a cigarette, dropped the match into the barrel and smoked as she watched the pages flare and disintegrate.

Curt and Benita were falling in love, plain, old-fashioned, heart palpitating, I-want-my-friends-to-meet-you kind of love. They used spring break as an opportunity to take the train to nearby Midwestern towns to meet one another's relatives. At week's end, they returned to Minneapolis to discover Benita's Chevy Biscayne missing. The police found it. The car was intact, but her treasured Garcia Bait Casting Reel and all of her fishing tackle were gone. Left were two golf clubs and the shotgun given to her the previous fall by Father, who loved to fish, didn't play golf, and still had a key to the car.

'Get your hair done, Benita. Put it up on top of your head.

Wear my mink stole. And my diamonds,' said Aunt Guy when Benita and Curt were chosen as chaperones for the Washburn high school spring prom to be held in the ballroom of the Sheraton-Ritz hotel. 'Do you remember how you used to tell Uncle Larry you were going to be a star? Well, stars let their light shine. So don't hide yours under a bushel.' She paused, tilted her head, smiled. 'You're going dancing at the Ritz!"

On prom afternoon, Benita was seated before a mirror in the beauty salon following Aunt Guy's advice, when the telephone rang. The receptionist smiled coyly at Benita. 'For you. It's a man.' Father delivered an hour by hour account of her whereabouts and activities for the past week, as well as his knowledge of tonight's plan for the prom. 'I'll be watching you,' he said. 'And you two better be watching over your shoulders. Because one day I'm going to kill both of you.'

Early on a May morning, Benita parked her car in the Washburn lot and began walking toward the high school, her thoughts on the demanding day ahead. Suddenly, from behind a nearby car, Father shot up. 'Just remember!' he yelled. 'Someday I'll kill both of you.' She reported this unnerving experience to Curt when they passed in the hall. Curt was concerned about Benita's safety and Father's unsettling effect on her but he refused to be bullied out of the life they were planning together. A few nights later, when the woman heckler called again, he made a calculated guess. 'Alvina Couchman, if one more call comes from you to me, I will come over to your place and you will wish that you had never made it.' Father's former Belle Plaine housekeeper was dumbfounded into several years of silence. Father, however, had not quit his claim on Benita.

The archbishop dealt with Father's criminal behavior by offering him his first pastorate, a triangle of small parishes sequestered deep in Iowa's beneficent landscape—St. Patrick's in Petersburg, Immaculate Conception at Allison and St. Joseph's in New Hartford. From that remote, unsupervised base, he continued to

launch his malicious phone calls, while according to the Archbishop's wishful Augustinian thinking, Benita's repentance and
conversion worked in his heart.

CHAPTER THREE

This column, accompanied by a photograph, appeared in the Dubuque *Telegraph Herald* on an August Sunday in 1965.

Benita A. Kane and Curtis J. Kirschbaum, both of Minneapolis, Minn., were married at 11:30 a.m. Saturday (August 14) at St. Columbkille's Catholic Church...Given in marriage by her brother, Dr. Richard J. Kane, the bride wore a floor-length sheath gown of sheer organza over taffeta styled with short sleeves, round neckline and bodice accented with lace motifs...She wore a mantilla of Spanish lace and carried a single long-stemmed white rose.

The article described the mint green linen gown worn by the matron of honor, Mrs. Donald Breitbach (Irene), the bride's sister. Among the ushers was Walter J. Kane. A niece served as flower girl; a nephew as ring bearer.

Mrs. Kirschbaum is a graduate of Clarke College and her graduate study was at Mexico City College. She is presently a teacher in Minneapolis Public School System. Her husband, a graduate of University of Minnesota, also is a teacher in Minneapolis Public School System.

All so traditional. So joyously ordinary. No mention made of the policeman strolling the sidewalk outside the church, or of the church doors kept locked throughout the ceremony. Those precautions had been taken by Monsignor Dunn, pastor and celebrant for the ceremony, because of Father Dunkel's ongoing, angry threats against the bride and groom.

No mention, either, of the poignant moment before Benita left her brother's arm and turned to Curt. 'We love you,' Richard had murmured and kissed her. His constant prayer as his health declined had been to live to see his sister happy and settled.

Curt had given Benita an engagement ring in early June. Soon after that, she checked into Mercy Hospital in Dubuque for a scheduled foot surgery—a bunionectomy on both feet—a prosaic-sounding procedure but in context, a declaration that her body was no longer Father's, but hers, and worthy of care. During her two-week hospital stay, she was under round-the-clock vigilance of family and friends lest Father should lash out in revenge. She spent another four weeks recuperating in bed at home. Marcella, whose slender physique approximated Benita's, was assigned the task of shopping for a wedding gown. She spent lunch hour after lunch hour going from store to store trying on dresses, amused by the bride in the mirror, delighted when she finally found the perfect gown.

Daily, during Benita's convalescence, Irene crossed the street to see her and discuss wedding details. As they addressed invitations one afternoon, Irene advised Benita that if she and Curt planned on using the pill, she should not have her premarital medical exam done in Dubuque. 'No doctor here will prescribe them.' No priest could condone them either, at least not from the pulpit. The pope had made that clear, against the recommendation of the Vatican II advisory commission on that issue. The commission had argued that this decision belonged to the couple involved, not to confessors or counselors, whose task was simply to assist people in arriving at a responsible decision. Progressive, educated Catholics, including the Kane sisters, seized this opportunity to exercise their conscience. Benita went to Minneapolis for her premarital physical and hid all evidence of the pill from her mother.

An insured package arrived from Rome, a wedding gift from Archbishop Binz. Inside were the pieces of an obviously expensive statue of the Blessed Virgin. Benita threw it into the trash barrel. Marcella retrieved it, protesting that it was insured, that she should inform the archbishop so that he could have the statue replaced.

'Mom,' said Benita, irritably. 'I don't want it.'

'You don't want a statue of Mary?'

'Not from him.'

'Benita! The archbishop is a kind man. A good man. Think of all he's done for us.'

Because Curt was not Catholic, no Nuptial Mass was said. But other Catholic elements forbidden to a 'mixed marriage' before Vatican II, were now allowed, including the nuptial blessing and the privilege of saying their vows inside the sanctuary. Father Raftis, the teacher we had hectored in sophomore religion class, knelt at a nearby praedium, just as Father Dunkel had done during Irene and Don's wedding. The coveted bridesmaid was now the cherished bride. Her hair had been styled at a salon. She wore the exquisite filigree bracelet Curt had given her as a wedding gift. Bea Roscoe played Benita's chosen music on the organ. After the exchange of vows, Curt accompanied Benita to Mary's altar where she placed flowers. As they stood there hand-in-hand, Ann Marie Kieler, the parish's premier soprano, sang Gounod's *Ave Maria*. A happiness rushed through Benita that she hadn't known since childhood. 'Thank you, Curt, for bringing my daughter back to me,' said Marcella to her new son-in-law later that day.

Only Carol's absence marred the occasion. Her Presentation

community insisted she give priority to her teaching schedule, which meant that the day before Benita's wedding, a very upset Sister Mary Carol left for Oaklawn, Illinois and St.Germaine's Catholic school. But the three nuns Benita considered instruments of her salvation—Sisters Edward, Lucilda and Catherine—were there to share this joyous, extraordinary day.

Summer skies were deepening into the crystalline blue of autumn when Benita and Curt returned from their two-week honeymoon in southwestern Colorado. They moved into a fully furnished house rented from a professor on sabbatical, obtained an unlisted telephone number and settled into 'the happy ever after' of Benita's dreams, an ordinary life.

A week later, on September 3, Richard died. He was forty-one years old, the father of six children between four and fourteen years of age. Marcella could find few words of consolation for his widow, Ruth. Her whole being cried out to the six children watching as their father was lowered into the earth near his own father, buried twenty-two years ago on a similarly glorious September day. At the center of Benita's sadness was remorse. After all those prodigal years, she'd been reunited with her brother only to lose him for good.

Cut off from Benita, Father vented his ire on the woman who had opened her home and heart to him, who had repaired his buttons, made the minced ham sandwiches he loved, entrusted her daughter to him. He disrupted her sleep and peace of mind with random, middle-of-the night telephone calls spewing angry threats and lewd rambling. She kept this treachery from Benita who as Mrs. Curt Kirschbaum, was a happy bride, reconciled with her family and enthusiastically planning her upcoming year as a Spanish teacher at Roosevelt High School.

The newlyweds spent their first Christmas with Marcella in Dubuque. When they entered the overflowing church for midnight Mass, they were sent up the winding narrow steps to the choir loft where Benita had practiced the organ on those darkening evenings when *he*. . . a violin interrupted this thought with the celestial sound of *Jesu, Joy of Man's Desiring*. Later, when Anne Marie Kieler sang Schubert's *Ave Maria*, tears sprang to Benita's eyes with the opening measures. But at Communion time, as she walked up the aisle behind her mother, she kept strict guard over memory and feeling. She tightened the security as she approached the priest with his chalice of hosts. She tried to ignore the choking sensation in her throat, the tension in her stomach.

In June, when the owner of their rented house returned, Curt and Benita moved into their own newly-purchased home and immersed themselves in the pleasure of settling down. They arranged furniture in the rooms, put dishes into cupboards, clothes into closets. Curt spaded up a corner of the yard for a garden. They planted vegetables and flowers. Evenings, they went for long walks, holding hands and chatting about their day. But whenever their conversations strayed toward differences of opinion, Benita went silent. Disagreement felt dangerous. She was ill-at-ease in a relationship based on honesty and respect.

In late fall, the telephone rang at three a.m. Father had tracked them down. He revived his vendetta with strategic calls in the middle of school nights, often calling several times within a few hours. Sometimes he simply hung up; other times, he breathed heavily into the telephone and said her name, sensually elongating the syllables. *Ben-neee-tah.* The briefest connection to him plummeted her into the degradation beneath the surface of her life, the debauchery she had mistaken for love. *You are guilty* was the relentless message thrumming in her mind. *Shame on you.*

Her terrible secret was a deep wound that had not healed but simply scabbed over and now silently festered. Beneath a façade of quiet routine lived the tormented Benita who had been overtaken body and soul by a priest. The double life she had begun as a twelve-year-old child—on the outside, a school girl able to learn, play, work and grow; on the inside, a lonely child trapped in a world of terror and helplessness—had not ended with her marriage.

She and Curt opened their new home to the family gatherings that had always been Marcella's greatest joy. Cousins and uncles and aunts assembled there for picnics, horseshoes, ping pong, cards. Various configurations of the family met for vacations on the beach near Delhi. During those carefree hours of swimming and boating and volleyball, Benita's sordid past receded into a dim distance, only to be propelled to the foreground by a remark, a laugh, a scent that thrust her into a scene as disturbing as the mural *he* had executed on the bedroom wall. Then, suddenly, she would be caught in a terrible, unbidden anger that she could not understand or release.

She tried to quell the inner turbulence with work. As a teacher, there was always something to be done, papers to correct, lessons to plan and prepare, activities to attend and oversee, students to counsel. On weekends, they joined Irene and Don for bridge and evenings of talk over pretzels and beer. By day, Benita and Irene often hunted for agates, a sisterly tradition that inspired Benita to design a ceremony for her students.

At the end of the school year, she set out on a desk an assortment of polished and unpolished agates and invited the students to take one of each, as well as the accompanying sheet containing a message she titled 'Agatas.' An agate, she had written, is an ordinary rock, stepped on, kicked around, tossed aside, insignificant until someone notices it, picks it up, and patiently polishes it until its unique, essential beauty is revealed. Her wish for her students was that in difficult times, the agates would remind them to persist, to maintain faith in their singular beauty and worth. The ceremony became an annual event.

In the midst of these happy experiences, a phone ringing in the night would spill the ugliness of the past into the present. Every call was a skirmish with guilt that left her feeling unworthy of Curt, her family, her vocation as a teacher. She lived in fear that her awful deeds would be revealed and she would be declared unfit to teach in the public schools. Her constant burden was knowing that she had disrupted the lives of her loved ones, that she could never compensate for the anguish she had caused them.

Nor could she be the wife Curt deserved. *His* ghost haunted their marital bed, sometimes in a distressing dream or a waking nightmare. She had known sexually only two men in her life; the first had been a priest, a man of God who held the key to her earthly pleasure and her eternal salvation. The physical power he wielded over her was laden with the irrational power of the spiritual. He was the mediator of grace, yet her unholy passion had blocked the path to that grace. His visage sometimes overpowered Curt's, turning her husband's brown eyes into an icy, accusing blue that contaminated marital intimacy, at times causing a complete shutdown that made the most tender physical contact excruciating. This was not a subject she brought up on their evening walks. There was no one with whom to unburden her conscience, nothing she could do to ease the guilt, no words that would undo her sinful acts. There was nothing to be done but carry on.

Benita's stealthy premarital trip to Minneapolis to acquire birth control pills had been unnecessary. When she and Curt decided to start a family, she learned that the endometriosis responsible for her painful periods meant abandoning hope that she would conceive. During those careless years with Father, this was undoubtedly a blessing in disguise. Now it was more proof that she harbored some terrible flaw.

Young and without children, they became popular chaperones for school functions and student travel. They accompanied the Washburn choir on a six-week tour of Norwegian countries. Benita went with language students to Peru and to Spain a dozen times. She and Curt took Marcella there, too, and to Ireland where, to her joy, they stayed in farm homes. Every Christmas, they went to Dubuque to spend the holidays with Marcella and accompany her to midnight Mass at St. Columbkille's. As they opened the church door, entered the vestibule and walked past the auxiliary confessional, Benita's body stirred with memories for which her mind had lost the words.

Teaching was her panacea and family gatherings the glue that held together her year. On Saturdays, she got up early and cleaned the house. In the summer, there were screens to put up, spider webs to brush away, flowers and vegetables to tend, screens to take down again. Keeping busy was a requirement. But mid-afternoon, she would run into an empty silence that refused to be filled up. Reading made her uneasy. Relaxing was impossible. When it was quiet, when she was quiet, the accusations began. *There's something wrong with you. Look what you've done. You sought Father's attention. Lied in order to learn to drive. Felt a thrill when he put his arm around you and named the stars. Wanted the cigarette he offered you. Followed him into the confessional. You shouldn't have worn that red skirt when you went to the church to dust that day. If you had worn jeans, like any decent girl, it wouldn't have happened.*

'Cómo está, Topper,' Father greeted her in a one a.m. call and immediately went off on a tangent of lewd talk. He repeated the pornographic performance the next night, adding heavy breathing and groaning suggestive of intercourse. Walt's wife, Jo, had received a similar call earlier that day. Father was now living in tiny Elma, Iowa, near the two small country parishes he'd been assigned to in 1973—Our Lady of Lourdes in Lourdes, Iowa and St. Stephen's in Chester.

A siege of post-midnight calls began in November of 1979, alternately coming from Father and a woman who sounded very much like the Alvina Couchman Curt had frightened away fourteen years ago. Whenever the telephone rang after ten p.m. Benita's thoughts leapt to her seventy-seven-year-old mother, now completely alone in Dubuque. Irene, mother of five children, had died of an aneurysm and was buried on her fiftieth birthday. Even Marcella's friend, Archbishop Binz, was dead.

The edginess Father provoked in the family was obvious the day Benita and Carol went rock hunting in a quarry north of St. Paul. As they meandered along, chatting and watching for agates, a jackrabbit darted out. They startled simultaneously, then froze, hearts pounding, as if their lives were on the line. The incident prompted Carol to write to Archbishop Byrne. She brought him up to date on Father's activities and threats, and expressed serious concern for the safety of her family, particularly Benita. After assuring the archbishop that the family was willing to involve the police, she ended with a request:

We just need the reassurance that someone knows and will act if any more fear is caused. I do not want to jeopardize my sister's safety by angering him more. . .I place it in your hands for discretion and thank you for having room for our concern.

He could understand their worry, replied Archbishop Byrne in a letter written a few days later. He urged the family to contact the police if they wished to. *If you and your family are willing that I should approach Father Dunkel on this matter, I shall not hesitate to do so. But I really could not tell you what the outcome of it might be. When this matter came up a few years ago, I did talk to Father Dunkel and it seemed to help matters at that time. But I could not be sure that it might not anger him even more if I were to do the same thing again. However, I do assure you and your family that I will talk to him, if you wish me to do that.*

In the meantime, we can place the entire matter before God in prayer, confident of His love for everybody concerned.

Sincerely yours in Christ,

Most Rev. James J. Byrne

Archbishop of Dubuque

What should they do, the family asked one another. Go to the police and risk reprisal? Wait for some feeble hierarchical gesture that the archbishop implied would backfire? Or pray, the all-purpose solution that handed the problem back to them and let the archbishop off the hook?

Meanwhile, the telephone calls continued, sometimes a flurry coming in one night or within a few days of each other, other times after an interval of calm, even a prolonged silence when she could forget about him, almost believe it hadn't happened, until another round of harassment would jar her back to reality. The intensity of her experiences with Father, the constant teetering between hope and fear, had left her volatile. Inner sadness could switch suddenly to rage. One moment she was friendly and vivacious, the next trapped in frantic isolation, unable to connect, to escape the prison of shame. She spent more and more nights between waking and sleeping, trying not to think or know or remember, panicky at her sense of powerlessness and guilt. She smoked a pack of cigarettes a day and tried to ignore the vulnerable Kane heart. She continued to go to Mass and Father continued to be Father, pastor of a tiny parish hidden away in the cornfields of Iowa, a priest forever elevating the host before the eyes of the devout, pronouncing it the body of Christ, confirming with his unchallenged privilege that she was to blame. That damning belief was planted deep in her being and reached into every domain of her life, growing slowly, stubbornly, pushing upward against the surface of every day. Her only tranquility came during long walks with Curt. Her body began to reveal what her mind denied. In 1980, she had a hysterectomy and oopherectomy. A lethargy and queasiness assailed her when they were in Dubuque for the holidays.

In 1982, powdered cement was dumped into the gas tank of their Volkswagen parked in the Roosevelt High School lot. The distressing telephone calls came more frequently. Sometimes music played in the background and Father mumbled obscenities; other times the message consisted of heavy breathing and groaning; several times he described himself in the act of masturbating. Walt, who had retired to Bloomington, Minnesota with Jo, began to document them: date, time, family member called.

April 10, 1982: a late evening call to eighty-year-old Marcella in Dubuque. Three more calls to her between midnight and two a.m. on Easter Sunday.

April 27: an obscene call to Benita and Curt at 11:15 p.m., another at 1:45 a.m. 'Hola,' the caller began and then launched into sexy, slurping sounds, with a hastily inserted, 'I will see you,' as she was hanging up.

Walt reported his findings to authorities in Dubuque—the police and the archbishop. Yes, they agreed, telephone harassment did, indeed, violate the law. The archbishop advised Walt to make that clear to the priest. Dutifully, Walter telephoned Father and put him on notice: 'The phone calls must stop.'

'I know nothing about phone calls,' said Father. 'Where are you living, Walt?'

'Yes, you do. Calls to Dubuque and Bloomington.'

'If I'm making them, I'll stop. Are you still with insurance?'

'Another call and I turn to the law and the church.'

The next night at one-forty a.m. Father called Benita and told her he was masturbating. Walt notified the Dubuque police chief who wrote to the archbishop who reprimanded Father and asked to see his phone bill which showed no evidence of long distance calls. And so it went. Walt was shuffled back and forth between the chancery and the police department with no one either willing or able to do more than chastise the perpetrator and extract a firm purpose of amendment which he promptly violated.

The archbishop's failure to stop this harassment fed Benita's growing sense that she had been wronged within the walls of the Catholic church. Habit kept her honoring the Sabbath by attending Mass, but tears would spring to her eyes in the middle of the ceremony, and once the swish of a black cassock sent her down the aisle, fleeing the sound that seemed to hold Father in its center, Father holding up something in his hands, something bright and full of promise. *This is my Body. This is my Blood. You're mine. Do this in remembrance of me.* Breathless, she had rushed outside.

In 1988, she experienced numbness in her face and left hand. After a week of hospitalization and countless tests, her doctor concluded that 'in spite of all that smoking' there was nothing wrong. The numbness kept recurring and returning her to the doctor. At the end of the school term, he diagnosed the problem as 'anxiety' and prescribed a round of ativan, which she translated to mean, *You're crazy.* In the spring of 1989, she held one last agate ceremony for her senior students and retired from teaching.

Severe internal pain in 1990 sent her back to her doctor who referred her to a urologist. The diagnosis: cancer of the bladder. The surgery to remove it was a success, but the confrontation with mortality made her long for a faith to hold onto, something to replace the Catholicism that for her, at age fifty-seven, had become a conglomeration of disturbing memories, shame, suffering and confusion.

Marcella was eighty-eight the Christmas eve of 1990 when Benita and Curt walked with her the few blocks to St. Columbkille's for midnight Mass. When they entered the church and passed the confessional door, an odor poured from it, reeking of stale tobacco, alcohol and sweat. He was there, inside the room, sitting on the chair, hunched toward her with his purple stole around his neck. *In the name of the Father and of the Son and of the Holy Ghost.* Even in the dark, she could see the steel blue eyes. Her heart quickened. *Bless me Father for I have sinned.* He looked at her, held her eyes. *What a pretty girl.* He laughed, head flung back, then turned, lit a cigarette, fastened it between his lips, smoking it without touching it, as he reached out for her. *Oh, Benita, no!* If her mother hadn't been relying on her arm, Benita would have fled the church.

'O Little Town of Bethlehem, how still we see thee lie,' drifted a clear, sweet soprano voice over the congregation. 'Above thy deep and dreamless sleep, the silent stars go by.' From her stance in the rear of the church, Benita could have pointed to the pews by number and named the people sitting in them in 1950 when she was the budding organist struggling with her conscience. Now she was here trying to numb her memory while her aging mother strove to rescue hers. 'Benita, what is the name of that girl who's singing. . . Ann Marie, Ann Marie. . .' She paused and closed her eyes, half-saying and half-singing 'the silent stars go by.' She frowned. 'She sang at your wedding, remember?. . .Ann Marie. . .oh, what is it?' She meant the parish soloist of twenty-five years ago. The merge of beauty and loss overwhelmed Benita. Was there no way to avoid losing all that she cherished? No way to avoid despair?

After Mass, Marcella clung to Curt's arm as they stood in the aisle, waylaid by a former high school classmate of Benita's, a gossipy woman who remembered the scarlet letter on her chest and had moved in for a closer look. When they finally went out into the pre-dawn cold, another school mate called out, 'Benita! You *just* missed David. He's been waiting to see you.'

'David?'

'David McCann. He saw you in church. He wanted to talk with you.'

A feeling of disappointed relief slithered through her. She did wish she might have introduced Curt to him. Meeting her husband would have shown David that no matter what he had believed about her and no matter how much of it was true, she had made it. She was here now with a man she loved and was proud of. Later, she telephoned David at his childhood home on South Grandview and caught up on the intervening years. He was a dentist in Des Moines and yes, he *had* married the Visitation girl and they were the parents of four daughters. Or did he say five? Long after they hung up, a question lingered in Benita's mind. 'What if?' Just beneath the surface of their buoyant chat lay the unhappy truth: Father had turned her life upside down. *Stay away from those Grandview Avenue kids. They think they're better than you. Watch out for David McCann. He'll go off and forget you. I'm putting your name on some stocks. You're mine. You're mine. You're mine.* But he was wrong about David. He'd waited for her in the wintry dawn outside of church.

Fall is to the Midwestern landscape what Mardi Gras is to New Orleans—a festival of indulgence designed to alleviate the austerity ahead. Along the Mississippi, the tree-covered bluffs were a sumptuous glow of oaks, maples and elms. Soon enough, they would be reduced to charcoal scribbles against the snow. Early in October of 1991, the Kane family arranged one last Sunday gathering, hosted by Irene's son at his home in Minnetonka, Minnesota. Everyone came, eager to enjoy autumn and one another. Nieces and nephews, grandnieces and grandnephews, in-laws, aunts, uncles, cousins. Eighty-nine-year-old Marcella came from Hopkins, Minnesota where she had moved in August. She lived in a senior housing facility with Carol, her caretaker, who was now teaching at an inner city Minneapolis school. She had taken a leave of absence from her convent, the religious version of a marital separation that so often is a prelude to divorce.

Earlier that summer, Benita had spent several weekends in Dubuque helping her mother clear out the family home on Cleveland Avenue. When they came across the gold-rimmed vase Father Dunkel had brought to Marcella from Greenland, Benita tossed it into the wastebasket. The shatter brought a flinch and a fleeting protest from her mother. 'But the rim was 24-carat-gold.'

'Or so he told you,' said Benita.

Marcella gazed mournfully at the shards. Although her illusions about Father had been thoroughly destroyed, she considered him an isolated case in a priesthood of chaste men whose celibacy

Paul VI described in a 1967 encyclical as the church's 'brilliant jewel.'

On this exquisite October afternoon, Benita stood in the midst of the group and looked around at her family—her mother, Carol, Walt and Jo—and at the man who had salvaged her future, her husband, Curt. The young people who had been shielded from her scandalous behavior were all adults now with children of their own. She thought of the missing people, too— Irene, Richard, her dad.

'Couldn't ask for a better day, huh?' said Walt, squinting upward at the arc of glorious blue. He handed her a beer.

'Thanks, Walt. ' She smiled at him and opened it; the scent of beer fizzed up; she took a sip. Suddenly, the beauty of the day, the steadfastness of her family, the simple fact of being here in their good grace, collided with the enormity of her loss and guilt. Without warning, she burst into tears. The nieces and nephews who had been hustled out of earshot as children now moved off with their own children; others averted their eyes and conversed earnestly about the weather; her immediate family was alarmed. What on earth had caused Benita to come apart in the middle of a family picnic on a radiant autumn Sunday?

The weeping went on and on. Curt took her home, but the tears continued. When Marcella, Carol, Walter and Jo stopped in later, she was still crying, unable to articulate or to contain her woe. A dam had ruptured and over it poured the anguish of all those wasted years. What had begun as a pleasant Sunday afternoon had turned into a storm of memories, trapping her in a chaotic inner world, suffocating her with an unspeakable rage and grief. Exhausted, she finally fell asleep. She woke the next morning to a deep loneliness; she wanted to give up, to run away. And then, as she had done before, she began to imagine an escape. She was scheduled for a biopsy of kidney cysts in November. If luck was with her, death would be her out.

A few days before the surgery, Carol stopped to see her. Before leaving, she set a slip of paper on the table. 'Please, Benita, call that number.' Catching her sister's eye, she added, 'It's the number for a support group. The members are women who have been sexually abused by priests. The group gives them a chance to. . .'

'No. No, you don't understand.' Benita turned away. There was no hope of explaining to Carol, who so desperately wanted to exonerate her, the revolting reality. Somewhere along the way, she had fallen in love with Father, had been his for the taking, hoped to marry him, had taken pleasure in their sexual encounters, had relied upon the soft-focus of alcohol to muffle her conscience and muddle her perception. Only death could release her from the appalling burden of shame.

Once again, death failed her. After the surgery, she returned home to an internal gloom matched only by the gridlock of gray that is winter in the Midwest. Every flake of snow that landed in November stayed, slowly coating the fields in the same dreary shade as the leaden sky. Her spirit labored beneath a similarly dismal accumulation. Night after night, she lay agitated and desperate, unsure if she was asleep or awake. By day, she thought about Carol's advice; a couple of times she picked up the note and began to dial the number written there. But what was the point of resurrecting her despicable past? It was too late to amend her life. There was no fixing the harm she had done.

Carol persisted. 'Benita, please, *please*, just call that number.'

Several more weeks passed. Benita's inner foment became unbearable. Finally, she dialed the number. An assessment interview was scheduled. To qualify for the group, she would have to confess her sins to a stranger and be deemed truthful. The idea struck her as ludicrous. She had indulged in a sinful, deceptive love affair with a priest, a man she now thought of with revulsion. She had no one to blame but herself. For twenty-five years, her family had suffered because of what she had done. She deserved to lie awake night after night, clenching her hands and staring into the dark. Turning to a church-sponsored group for help was absurd. For twenty-five years, one archbishop after another had feigned intervention, but failed to stop the harassment. While Father lived with the dignity and rights of the priesthood, she was humiliated and blamed. She didn't trust the group or the woman facilitating it. Why would she care? Why did she care enough to call Benita and say, 'You're coming, aren't you?'

'I haven't decided.'

'The vicar general assured me that the Minneapolis-St.Paul diocese would pick up the cost. Until Dubuque antes up.'

In mid-December, Benita was still unconvinced. Taking on the truth was too formidable. The numbness in her face struck again, this time extending into her left side. Her doctor prescribed another round of anti-anxiety medication.

Finally, in early January of 1992, she walked trembling and wary into her first meeting of the women's group. When the facilitator, Phyllis Willerscheidt, nodded to her that it was her turn to introduce herself and explain her presence, she felt nauseous and short of breath. 'My name is Benita. I have nothing to say.'

CHAPTER FOUR

As other women in the group retrieved secrets buried for years, Benita listened. The torrent of memories and feelings they released set off her own remembering. Certain images nagged her mind. Her mother's woeful glance; strips of freshly bloodied rags stretched out like snakes in the sun; a blanket spread out on the grass; white water towers in the distance; a cream-colored Dodge rounding the corner, a long, black car sliding through the snowy dark. Certain phrases haunted her. *She is a pretty girl. It will all come out in the wash. Bring Father an ashtray. Oh, Benita, no! Your precious Daddy is dead. David McCann doesn't want to go with you.* Walt calling from the other side of the door, *Benita? Benita?*

As she saw others break through the painful secrecy, she slowly began to gather courage. In February, she put down on paper what had happened between Father Dunkel and herself and gave it to Phyllis who gave it to the vicar general of the St.Paul-Minneapolis diocese, Kevin McDonough. There it was in black and white, her disgraced life for all to see.

'Hello? Hello?' said Father clearly, pathetically, into the telephone on March 13, 1992, at 3:07 a. m, when Benita answered. He had been retired from active ministry for two years and was living as a priest in Elma, Iowa. This final call, documented by Walter, was added to Benita's submitted statement and presented to Vicar General McDonough. He then wrote to Archbishop Kucera to advise him that Benita was exploring criminal action against Father Dunkel to stop his harassment. He asked if there were 'incarceration' resources available within the Catholic Church as there had been in the past, and if so, might they be appropriate in dealing with Father Dunkel? And would the Dubuque Archdiocese be willing to help defray costs of Benita's therapy, which she was just getting started on?

The Dubuque vicar general replied that Father Dunkel recently had suffered a slight heart attack. A month later, he reported that Archbishop Kucera had met with Father regarding the phone calls. Father denied making any since 1965. The futile round of letters and calls dwindled into the usual silence.

'Some of you here feel guilty about not going to church—or not wanting to go," said the Episcopalian priest—a woman—who visited the women's group one evening. She looked around the circle. 'But you oughtn't to. You were ravaged by your church.' Fear and obligation began to loose its hold on Benita. She stopped going to Sunday Mass. She felt like a bird whose cage door had been flung open, free, no longer constricted by the myth of God as male and priests as symbols of Christ on earth. She began to explore Native American spirituality and to find solace in the Goddess of Guadalupe.

And finally, she summoned the strength to tell the group the story of the liaison that had begun so auspiciously in 1945 when she was an innocent twelve-year-old and ended in ruins twenty years later. She described the ensuing decades of torment that in 1992 had brought her to this room, mired in guilt at age fifty-eight.

But she was not guilty, the women insisted. One after another, they repeated it—*Not guilty, not guilty, not guilty*—until she began to hear. The obsession she considered a sinful love affair with a priest and that had brought so much suffering to her family, was the result of a process called 'grooming.' She was not an adulteress sleeping with a bridegroom of the church, but a woman deceived as a gullible girl into imagining herself his chosen partner. He had absolved himself of wrong-doing by calling this exploitation 'love.' It was an abuse of power in which she had no voice or control.

She would have preferred the dignity of guilt to the horrific realization that crept through her. She had been *groomed*, trained like a dog to obey and perform and scurry with excitement at the sound of his approaching footsteps. He had taught her to leap into his car and drop her head into his lap. He had patted her and stroked her hair and instructed her to be his eager, pitiful pup. All of it—the dad-daughter date nights, the driving lessons, the oozing assurances that she was 'special,' the cigarettes and bourbon, the first, tender, innocent touches, the camaraderie with her mother and brothers, even those cherished lessons on the stars—all of it, had been part of a malevolent seduction.

She had looked to him for encouragement and safe guidance into a patriarchal world, a task her mother could not do, even if she'd had the energy and time. Being alone with him awakened hope that he would notice her unique talents and teach her how to use them. When she talked to him, her loneliness lifted. When he listened to her—Father, a priest, a man who showed interest in the faltering words of an adolescent—the sense of connection was indescribably wonderful, like looking at the stars and losing all sense of the difference between heaven and earth, touched to the core with a passion for life that made soul and body, priest and girl, one.

What he had called love that spring day in the confessional was rape. The sexual trauma he had dealt her was their secret and their secret was their bond. When Father said, 'Remember, keep this quiet or that will be the end of it,' she obeyed. *God, what had she done? God, oh God, how could she endure it?* But what God was she praying to? The God who counted the hairs on your head? Who saw everyone as special? She was not special at all. She was a fool, reeling between anger and despair. A fool without a God. A fool who mistook Father's interest as genuine and his gifts as a token of his caring. He had never been interested in her but only in what he could get from her. He had lured her into a whirlpool of feelings—need, longing, respect, trust, a sense of connection and significance—an emotional entwinement that made her so frightened of losing his affection that she readily complied with his sexual demands. He had imprisoned her without a lock or key, without even a door. Without him she felt helpless and hopeless and unable to survive. In exchange for his attention, she had been alienated from her family, her peers, her self. He had used his power to dominate her physically, psychologically and spiritually. He had shattered her innocence and with it, the trust and hope at the root of a child's desire to learn, to feel joy, to have faith in others, to believe in the power of love.

It was a tale common to the group, so common, in fact, that in 1990, the Commission on Women of the Roman Catholic Archdiocese of St. Paul-Minneapolis had promoted the establishment of the support group, Women Sexually Exploited by Clergy. It was facilitated by an independent agency and provided women who had been isolated as sexual victims a community in which they might recover.

Now that Benita had told, the soul searing pain of recovery was before her. She would have to find her way out of the prison where she had cowered so long in maximum insecurity, clinging to what she wanted to be true. As the weeks went on and the layers of memory fell away, she lurched from one devastating realization to another. Father had stolen her childhood, her adolescence, the Benita who could have been. There was no going back, no chance ever to be just a kid. A free-spirited teenager. An industrious graduate student in Mexico. Her life had been taken from her. Her whole being cried out in silent agony. *This is too much. I can't bear it. I won't.* Terror and tears would switch to suspicion and deep anger. Where were the people who supposedly cared for her and could have protected her? Her childhood had been wrenched from her right before their eyes and they had done nothing to stop it. Even Sister Edward had forsaken her, skirting the problem with gentle suggestions instead of going to the archbishop or confronting Father. Why had she simply watched Benita's life disintegrate piece by piece, year by year, while doing nothing? And her mother! Blind, deaf, mute to any possibility of evil in a man who wore a Roman collar.

The incidents of facial numbness recurred. Phyllis recommended that Benita augment weekly group meetings with individual therapy. More cost. More resentment toward the church whose stalling and covering-up had facilitated her downfall. Humiliated by the need, and frightened of the process, she nevertheless began weekly therapy sessions. In June of 1992, upon her therapist's recommendation, Benita saw a psychiatrist who prescribed Prozac. Anti-depressants would become a necessary and at times complicating support throughout her life.

She contacted Sister Lucilda to reveal the truth of what had happened to her. Sister Lucilda described her own frustration at watching from the outside. 'I didn't know the details or the turmoil and suffering they were causing you. . .' Nor did she feel authorized as a teacher to intervene in the life of a twenty-year-old young woman. It was a stance common among those who loved Benita, sensed something awry, but whose deeply-rooted beliefs that priests are superior, incapable of wrong-doing, deserving of unquestioning trust, functioned as a powerful impediment to action. By early summer, Benita's chaotic emotions began to congeal into anger and her anger into a burning need to be heard, listened to and understood. In spite of all those years lived in silence, she *had* lived.

In mid-summer, Carol wrote a letter from her home in Hopkins to her Presentation community in Dubuque, to inform them that Benita had 'broken silence,' which meant that she had disclosed the details of her involvement with Father Dunkel and named it as abuse. Here in this convent where information was gleaned by watching and whispering, this was not exactly news. Nuns knew how the system worked, especially those who spent their lives cooking in bishop's kitchens or serving in clergy dining rooms. They saw the well-stocked liquor cabinets; they watched the clergymen helping themselves to before, during and after-dinner drinks; they may even have excused clerical immorality as whiskey acting up. The radical word in Benita's case was 'abuse.' While her vulnerability as a child may have warranted compassion, her behavior as a grown woman subjected her to harsh judgment. After all, she hadn't been a helpless child when she was brashly driving Father's Dodge back and forth to Clarke.

When a former nun—the red-haired postulant who had gazed at Benita with such brimming eyes that day in 1958—expressed a wish to talk with her, Benita suffered a spate of raging migraines. Yes, said Sheila, from her home in Chicago when they spoke on the phone a few days later, yes, Father Dunkel had abused her, too. And did Benita remember Jane, Sheila's classmate at St. Columbkille's? Yes, Jane, too. Still reeling from the brutal realization that she had been a mere tool for Father's use, Benita was hit full force by another, more staggering blow: she had been betrayed. Not only was she *not special* to Father, she was not even the special object of his abuse. She was a fool disgusted with her own stupidity.

Sheila expressed the hope that Benita would come to the national conference scheduled for Chicago in October, the first gathering of victims of clergy sexual abuse. She and Jane looked forward to talking with her there.

CHAPTER FIVE

'I wanted to tell you that day. I was so close to blurting it all out. But I was afraid,' Sheila said in the Chicago hotel room where the three women gathered between meetings of the first annual conference of VOCAL, Victims of Clergy Abuse Linkup. Before entering the convent as an eighteen-year-old girl, said Sheila, she had made a general confession and in it confessed 'ruining a young priest and as a result, another girl's life.' She paused to look at Benita. 'Yours. All this time, I thought what happened to you was because of me.'

As the three women talked, they uncovered the common tactics Father had employed with them, as well as the common themes that rendered them good candidates for his seduction. All three had grown up in families deprived of a father's presence. Sheila's dad was a traveling salesman, more often away than home. Jane's father was killed in a work accident when she was four. Eldon Kane died suddenly when Benita was ten. All three were from devout Catholic families who lived close to the church, looked to the parish for their spiritual security, were loyal to its tenets and respected priests as mediators of salvation.

As objects of Father's interest, all three enjoyed a sense of specialness and security that they lacked and longed for. They were good Catholic girls, students at St. Columbkille's, involved in the parish, utterly vulnerable to his mystical masculine powers, subjected to the same ploys: evening driving lessons, her head in his lap until they were safely out of sight. As they rode, he would stroke her hair, comment on its beauty—Jane's was long and dark, Sheila's a silky burnished red, Benita's curly and blonde—and tell her how pretty and special she was. Later, he dropped her off on an isolated street with a warning—uttered confidentially if she had been cooperative, 'Don't tell anyone, they'll never believe you and you'll be in trouble'—spit out in anger if she had questioned or protested, 'You tell anyone about this, and there will be serious consequences for you and your family.'

As time went on, other victims of Father's came forward. Some telephoned Benita long distance to share remarkably similar stories of their encounters with him. Others surfaced, unbidden, from her memory. The scent of incense, the sight of a door, a hallway, the stairwell in the church basement, could recall a dreamlike image buried long ago. A recurrent one was of a young nun scurrying red-faced from a sequestered room.

Benita realized then, to her horror, that in a wretched way she *was* special. Father had scarred the others with his predatory ways but she alone had been fool enough to imagine herself in love with him. She alone had squandered two decades of her youth and energy and dreams on what she believed to be a love affair. She alone had been his betrothed Topper.

The anger, disgust, shame! With each new revelation, a sense of worthlessness and violation overwhelmed her. But now she was no longer alone. Now she had someone to talk to who could understand and share the pain.

The three women pooled their anger and resolved to pursue justice, the only path that promised to lead toward truth. They consulted Jeff Anderson, an attorney with a formidable reputation for using the law to hold the hierarchy accountable in the sex abuse scandal. Bolstered by his counsel, Benita wrote to the arch-bishop and demanded Father's discipline, payment for her therapy and psychiatric costs and financial remuneration for the damage she had sustained. Her patience had run out, she said, and if her demands were ignored, she would seek legal recourse.

The archbishop responded promptly, explaining that Father Dunkel had had a heart attack, that he had requisitioned and examined Father's phone bills and saw no evidence of calls to the Minneapolis-Bloomington area. He did not address any of her monetary demands beyond a wan concession 'to do what we can to help you with your therapy bills.' In closing, he said, 'I want to cooperate with you, and I am sorry for any misunderstanding. My prayers are with you for the heavy burden you carry.'

Phyllis Willerscheidt, by now skilled at grasping straws, called the archbishop and arranged a meeting between him and Benita, Curt, Carol and Walt when they took Marcella, now ninety, to Dubuque during the Christmas holidays. The meeting was fol-lowed by a round of letters. 'I am sure you are growing weary of this, as I am' wrote the archbishop in early May. At some point, he said, they would need to agree to a legal document relieving both Father and the Archdiocese of future liability. That docu-ment, *Agreement and Release of All Claims,* was prepared and pre-sented under the auspices of the church. Benita and Curt signed it on June 4, 1993.

It was a gag order. Hush money paid in exchange for her agreement to 'forever discharge Rev. Henry Dunkel, his supervi-sors and superiors, St. Columbkille's church, the Archdiocese of Dubuque, all other churches and schools within the Archdiocese of Dubuque, and the Roman Catholic Church, and their officers, representatives, directors, employees, agents, insurers and any other person, firm or corporation alleged or aimed to be liable, of and from any and all actions, causes of action, claims, demands, damages, costs, loss of services, loss of consortium and support, expenses and compensation, from the beginning of time up to the day of execution of this Agreement and Release of All Claims, on account of or in any way growing out of, any and all known and unknown personal injuries and property damage resulting or to result from the alleged sexual abuse to the undersigned by Rev. Henry Dunkel.'

This proviso included all incidents of abuse which occurred and had not been recalled, or may have been suppressed and unrecalled at the time of signing. It was 'further understood and agreed that this payment is not to be construed as an admission of liability on the part of the parties herein released, acquitted, discharged.' The undersigned 'promise, agree and warrant to treat all the terms and conditions of the agreement as strictly confidential. Neither the allegations, the fact of settlement nor the amount thereof are to be disclosed. . .'

If only this imaginative, remarkably exhaustive troubleshooting had been brought to bear on clerical misadventures! From Ernie, the yellow-toothed janitor who had unearthed Father and Benita in the boiler room, to Pope John Paul II, clinging to lofty ideals of clerical celibacy, the Catholic system was populated by untouchables. In 1993, Benita was a typical victim, intimidated, exhausted by the demeaning process, demoralized, extremely vulnerable, desperate to be heard and believed, willing to settle for crumbs. She was paid off, muzzled and dismissed.

1994. Howling wind. Swirling snow. February cold. In the center aisle in the rear of St. Columbkille's church resided a casket holding the body of an old woman, her fingers entwined in the rosary beads she said nightly, its crucifix tucked into the crook of her left thumb. The dexterous hands that had supported her as a seamstress were twisted with arthritis. Marcella would have been surprised and humbled by the crowd gathering on this bitter morning to pay their last respects to her and the family surrounding her casket. The hour-long viewing prior to the funeral Mass was an accommodation for elderly neighbors and friends who were unable to go to the funeral home for the previous evening's vigil, the first of three liturgical rites of Christian burial, each meant to offer worship, praise and thanksgiving to God for the gift of life which has been returned to Him, author of life and hope of the just.

When a niece in the group asked if there was a nearby rest-room, Carol pointed to the left vestibule. 'Over there.' Then, matter-of-factly, 'That's where Benita was raped.' Benita's eyes rushed to her mother's face. That word! That deed, resurrected so close to her mother's ear, pulling Benita into that suffocating space, assaulting her this morning with the brutality of that after-noon. A cluster of great-grandchildren pointed with wide-eyed whispering at the restroom door. Benita reached for Curt's hand. He had thanked Marcella the day before she died for giving him such a wonderful daughter to be his wife. She replied with the same words she'd said to him in 1965. 'Thank *you*, Curt, for bringing my daughter back to me.'

The full church, a tribute for anyone living to be ninety-one, was even more remarkable in the hostile weather. But Marcella had been a faithful, lifelong member of the parish, a daily com-municant, the mother of a former Presentation nun (Carol had quit the convent the previous year), a good and well-loved woman. Soon she would be lying next to Eldon again, near Richard and Irene in Mt. Olivet cemetery.

'Your daddy appeared to me in a dream,' she had told Benita recently. 'He said he was waiting for me.' She was ready to meet him. She'd almost made her escape last summer, but her children pulled her back with nitroglycerin and prayer. The family subse-quently contacted Archbishop Kucera and asked him to be the celebrant for their mother's funeral, which seemed likely to occur in the not-too-distant future. It was their way of asking him to recognize that, in spite of everything, Marcella Kane had remained steadfast and loyal to the church she loved.

The archbishop declined. In a letter written November 8,

1993, he explained that diocesan policy prevented him from presiding at funeral Masses, even for 'parents of our priests,' even for 'people in the city who have had a very close attachment to the church.' There was another reason. 'I am afraid to do so would probably provoke talk and speculation which would be something that you or I would not want.' He assured them that the vicar general of the Dubuque Archdiocese, Monsignor Ferring, would be happy to preside at the funeral for their mother. 'I don't think that would cause any eyebrows to be raised and would at the same time give you the comfort that you need during that time.' The archbishop did honor them with his presence at the vigil service the evening before the funeral; he was there when her three remaining children expressed their memories of their mother.

Now Monsignor Ferring, and the three assisting priests, their white vestments a manifestation of Vatican II's emphasis on hope, proceeded down the center aisle toward Marcella's casket. 'The grace and peace of God our Father, who raised Jesus from the dead, be always with you,' Monsignor greeted the family surrounding it. He lifted the holy water vessel and sprinkled the lid. 'In the waters of baptism, Marcella died with Christ and rose with him to new life. May she now share with him eternal glory.'

The procession up the aisle began: vicar general, priests, Marcella's casket slowly gliding at the hands of the pall bearers, the mourning family following as the parish choir sang the triumphant hymn, *How Great Thou Art,* announcing that Marcella had been taken to her heavenly home.

As Benita listened to the ancient lyrics tell of stars and rolling thunder, of souls bowed in awesome wonder before a powerful God at work in the universe, she braced herself for the onslaught of memories. Her downcast eyes were looking back, regretting, and regretting the regretting, tired of it, wishing it was over, all of it, that she could put the remorse weighing on her into a casket, close the lid and bury it forever. Carol's eyes, on the contrary, were vigilant, scanning the crowd for him. Should he have the audacity to come, she would ask him to leave.

When the procession reached the front of the church, the pall bearers positioned the casket beneath the waiting Easter candle, symbol of Marcella's baptism into the life of Christ. It would reside there throughout the second liturgical rite, the Mass. 'In the name of the Father and of the Son and of the Holy Spirit' said Monsignor Ferring and the Mass of Resurrection began. 'God of endless ages, from one generation to the next you have been our refuge and strength.'

Benita gripped the pew, steadying herself. Her dust cloth slid along the smooth oak, as she worked alone in the Saturday morning dark, fearing, hoping. . . *Before the mountains were born or the earth came to be, you are God.* . . watching and waiting for him to come along and tell her that she was his special girl. 'Bury it and move on' people advised Benita, but they didn't know that 'it' was buried alive inside her. . . *Have mercy now on your servant Marcella whose long life was spent in your service.* . .if only she *could* get on with her life with the ease others seemed to expect of her. Released, acquitted, discharged. From the beginning of time.

If only she could be present, here, now, listening to the homily which surely acknowledged her mother's valiant life. Instead, she was drifting in a dark, inner world, skirting the vortex tugging her into the dim kitchen corner where her weary mother sits sewing. Where Father sits smoking at the table. Waiting. Wanting something. Supper. A minced ham sandwich. An alteration. Her life.

Marcella Kane was an easy subject to incorporate into a homily. She was the quintessential good Catholic woman whose religious devotion could be held up as an example to her children and her children's children. Inside Benita's purse was the gold medal from Mexico. Marcella had given it to her a few days ago. Benita's turn from the church, the hostility she bore toward clergymen troubled her mother. A few months ago, when they were together on an elevator, a priest got on. Marcella's face lit up as if she'd seen the Messiah. 'Good afternoon, Monsignor,' she smiled, nodding respectfully. Benita muttered a frugal 'Hi.' The moment they exited on their floor, Marcella turned to her daughter with a frown and asked why she hadn't addressed him properly. 'Because he's not my monsignor. Or my father.' Her mother's mystified sigh had irritated Benita that day. Now, the memory saddened her.

'You're not going to Communion?' whispered Curt to Benita, not quite covering up his surprise, as a line of relatives and friends shuffled past their pew.

'No.' She shook her head without looking up. She hadn't received communion for years.

Curt set a solicitous hand on her arm. 'Are you okay?' During the previous summer, the familiar family symptoms, nausea and shortness of breath, had begun to nag her. She nodded. For awhile, unworthiness had kept her away from Communion; and for another while, anger; now, it was simple disbelief. The whole thing was hocus pocus, an enthralling and dangerous pretense.

During last week's meeting of the women's group, Phyllis had suggested that she begin to think about holding a face-to-face meeting with Father Dunkel. Benita's aghast eyes declared an unconditional 'No.' Phyllis had seen that response before. Some women needed years between their entry into a support group and the catharsis of a confrontation: addressing the man who had abused her, presenting a chronological account of what had happened and how it had affected her physically, spiritually and emotionally. The mere thought of it was distressing. The hope was that by doing so, a woman would regain some of the power stripped from her by the trauma of abuse and begin the transition from victim to survivor. Theoretically, confrontation brought closure. Theoretically, her life could move on.

Monsignor Ferring was standing near the coffin and gently swinging the censer over it, releasing the incense that signified respect for Marcella's body as a temple of the Holy Spirit. The choir had begun a song of farewell:

And He will raise you up on eagle's wings,
Bear you on the breath of dawn,
Make you to shine like the sun,
And hold you in the palm of His Hand.

The mourners accompanied Marcella's body to Mt. Olivet cemetery for the last funeral ritual, the rite of committal. Because of February's wrath, an interim service was held inside the cemetery chapel. When the wind calmed and the ground was more receptive, Marcella's body would be committed to the earth 'from which it came.'

After the others had gone, Benita stayed on in the chapel, standing near the casket, her hand resting on the lid as she talked aloud to her mother, expressing her love, her regret, asking her mother for help and guidance. Tears burned along the rims of her eyes. 'Please watch over me. Over all of us.' For the first time since her mother's death, she cried. With a last touch to the coffin, she whispered, 'Bye, Mom.' When she turned to go, she saw that she was not alone. In the corner near the door, stood the vicar general, looking at her with tear-glistened eyes. 'Don't *ever* apologize for what was done to you,' he'd told her in 1992 after their family meeting with the archbishop. What she'd sensed in him then—a rare cleric who believed her and seemed to care—now seemed confirmed.

In group the following week, Phyllis told Benita that speaking out, reaching out, sharing their experience can be a significant step forward for victims of abuse. They could help themselves by preventing others from falling into the same trap. Benita began writing letters to the editor in response to news articles on clergy sexual abuse. She agreed to be on a panel at the Linkup conference in Chicago in 1995. She would use that experience as a rehearsal for the next healing step, the confrontation with Father that, with Phyllis' encouragement, she hoped to accomplish the following year.

CHAPTER SIX

June 7, 1996 in Bloomington, Minnesota, was a morning vibrant with the scent of summer, alive with the hum of getting and spending. There in America's heartland, where the glaciers left behind the richest, blackest soil, the rich and the not-so-rich were leaving behind their money in the Mall of America.

In a one-story, brown brick building on East Bloomington Freeway, Benita was pacing. She stopped, shot a threatening look toward the people gathered in the room with her and said to no one in particular, 'If he's dressed in clerical garb. . .'

'He isn't,' said Phyllis Willerscheidt, coming in. 'None of them are.' The ploy galled Phyllis, who had passed on to the archbishop Benita's request—that Father Dunkel not come to this meeting in clerical dress. 'That's his right!' cried the indignant archbishop, then contrived what Phyllis saw as a clever rebuttal. He'd shed the symbols of his episcopal office, too—clerical suit, collar, pectoral cross—all but the amethyst ring. Now here they were in sportshirts and poplin slacks flaunting solidarity in the guise of golfers—the archbishop of Dubuque, his vicar general and the priest.

She'd seen their taxi pull to the curb, had watched them

emerge. The archbishop's pleasant countenance and assured demeanor suggested to her a cardinal in the making. The vicar general, a strapping, balding man with an Irish complexion, paused and leaned forward solicitously toward the rumpled old man stooped between them fumbling in the pocket of his jacket. He extracted a cigarette, jammed it between his lips, flicked a lighter, took a series of quick, hard draws, coughed out a billow of smoke, cast the butt to the pavement and ground it out with his heel. Behind dark-rimmed glasses, his eyes stared at nothing. His face was taut, closed, like a man on the way to his own hanging. His gray crewcut was stippled with white.

The archbishop and vicar general exchanged a cryptic side-long glance. Archbishop Hanus was new to the Dubuque diocese and heir to this misfortune, a humiliating problem that three previous prelates failed to solve. What was to be done about this aging priest, who had suffered a heart attack a month ago? He was too frail to be subjected to this degradation, a point the archbishop had tried to impress upon the tenacious woman, Phyllis, in Bloomington.

The vicar general opened the door. Phyllis greeted them and led them to a small waiting room. 'We'll start in a few minutes. I'll call you.'

Twenty minutes earlier, Benita, Curt, Carol, and Walter had filed silently, solemnly through a back door into the Family and Children's Services building, past the extra guard on duty, and on to the conference room. It was a course designed to avoid any chance encounters. Phyllis met them, embraced Benita, stepped back to study her face. 'Are you doing okay? Is there anything you need?'

Benita grasped her forehead with both hands and groaned. 'To get this over with. I need to get this over with.'

"In a couple of hours, it will be. It won't be easy, but you'll do it. You've proved your courage. But first, we have to deal with this. . .' Phyllis motioned to a document on her desk, the *Confidentiality Agreement* prepared by the Archdiocese of Dubuque. It referred to today's encounter as 'a therapy session intended to benefit Benita Kirschbaum by providing her an opportunity to express herself in the presence of Henry N. Dunkel for therapeutic purposes.' By signing it, 'parties mutually agree that no communication, suggestion, action, or anything else of any kind which occurs solely during the therapy session shall ever be disclosed to anyone not a party to this agreement or disclosed, except as is necessary for therapeutic purposes, or offered or used in any way for any purpose in any way related to investigation, litigation or threat of prosecution of, or defense against, any claim or possible claim of any party against any other party, and that every such communication will not be discoverable according to Iowa statues of confidentiality. The party holds harmless the Archbishop and Vicar General from any and all claims of any kind or nature arising from any of the foregoing.'

'I swore I'd never do this again,' Benita said wearily as she wrote her name. Three names were already entered on it. Jerome Hanus, Archbishop. David A. Wheeler, Vicar General. Henry N. Dunkel. A flurry of family signatures followed Benita's.

Next, Phyllis reviewed the configuration of people to be seated around the circular coffee table throughout the encounter. On one side of Benita, Phyllis and Gerry, Benita's therapist. On her other side, Curt, Carol and Walt. *He* would sit across from her, between the archbishop and vicar general. After the last chair was put into place, Benita set a sage plant on the table, a plant used in Native American culture to guard against evil.

Phyllis took a step toward the door of the adjoining waiting room, paused, turned. 'Benita, would you like Carol to open with a prayer?'

'No!' flared Benita. 'No! No prayers!' She shook her head emphatically. 'Carol, if you mention Jesus, you're dead.'

Carol lifted her palms in a shrug, bewildered by this unearned scolding.

Curt put a husbandly arm around Benita's waist. 'Don't be impatient with Carol. She's here for you.'

'All of us are,' Walter said, gently. As the big brother, he reproached himself for lacking the words to console Benita. For failing to see what was happening to her all along. He should have taken action in the beginning. Stopped it before it spun out of control. But when did it begin? He couldn't put his finger on a time.

Benita's hand rushed to her mouth. 'I know,' she mumbled through her fingers. 'I know.' She looked from face to face. 'I know,' she said again. 'I couldn't do this without you.' Her eyes stopped on Curt. There were others, too, people around the country who had pledged to be with her in spirit today.

'Is everyone ready?' asked Phyllis. 'Shall I call them in?'

Benita felt her stomach clamp. She chewed on her lower lip, checked her pocket for her reading glasses. Suddenly, she blanched. 'The packet! What have I done with my packet?" She had labored for months over the contents, a ten-page statement printed by hand chronicling two decades of enslavement to this priest. A laborious process, loathsome one day, tedious the next. Today the sordid saga would be exorcised.

'It's right here.' Gerry picked up a sheaf of papers from the table and handed it to her. She fingered the papers, looked at Phyllis, pulled herself erect, nodded.

Phyllis knocked lightly on the door, then opened it. The three clergymen rose as one and approached. The archbishop and vicar general shook hands with Benita and her family. *He* went straight to his chair and fixed his eyes on the floor. His faded red jacket, dingy black pants and shirt might have been pulled out of a laundry bag an hour ago; he hadn't bothered to shave.

After introductions, Phyllis reviewed the format for the meeting. Benita would present her statement, an account of the circumstances and consequences, actual and emotional, of her involvement with this Roman Catholic priest. She could take whatever time she needed for the procedure. No one would be allowed to interrupt. When she finished, she could invite the others to respond, including Father Dunkel.

Phyllis turned to Benita. So did the others, all but the man in the red jacket across from her, who remained barricaded behind downcast eyes and an impassive expression. Benita looked at Carol and asked her to lead them in prayer. Surprise leapt into Phyllis' eyes. Unabashed, Carol prudently addressed her prayer to the Goddess of Guadalupe. The archbishop set his elbows on the arms of his chair, intertwined his fingers and directed a civil smile her way. Leading prayer was customarily his right.

Benita leaned forward over the plant on the coffee table, inhaled deeply, then straightened back into her chair and scanned the faces across from her. Her eyes paused on the seventy-five-year-old priest. He brushed his hand over his crew cut. His eyelids flickered and dropped lower. This was the first time she'd seen him since the May morning in 1965 when she was walking through the high school parking lot and he suddenly rose up from behind a car and yelled, 'Just remember, some day I will kill both of you.'

Her heart began to pound as it had that morning thirty-one years ago. Blood beat in her ears. Strength drained from her. How could it have been? How could she have sacrificed her life, her potential, her self to this unkempt old man slouching in his chair with crossed arms, lowered head, lowered eyes? To think there was a time when she wore a diamond on her left hand and thought of herself as 'his' filled her with disgust. She took a deep breath, afraid she might be sick. Another. She leaned forward again and this time touched the sage plant, then drew herself upright. She would not fall apart in front of him.

She picked up the sheaf of papers from her lap and put on her reading glasses. Her body felt flimsy, too light; her hands were trembling. She took another deep, steadying breath and began. She was relieved when her voice made sound.

'This is not going to be an easy meeting for any of us. My purpose for requesting it is to give me an opportunity to speak my truth. . .and to transfer over to you, Henry Dunkel, all the feelings of shame, guilt, pain and grief that you have caused me to carry for half a century. All the suffering, confusion and sadness you have caused my husband, my family, my friends. And your family, too.'

She wondered if she should look up, try to engage his eyes. Curt set a soothing hand on her arm. 'Maintain a posture of authority,' Gerry had advised. But she couldn't bear to look at him again. Not now. Not yet. She stayed with the words printed by her own hand. 'I was twelve years old when you came to our parish in 1945. A very innocent, naive, vulnerable, fatherless little girl. . .'

He angled his right leg over his left knee and traced his finger along the orange stripe at the top of his white athletic socks. The vicar general sat quietly, hands folded in his lap, eyes on Benita. The archbishop steepled his hands and rested his chin on his fingertips. Light caught the amethyst stone in his ring.

'You began to groom me. You noticed the adolescent changes in my body and continually made comments about them. Sexual remarks that I didn't even understand. You said things about my swinging hips. You called what I thought of as zits, 'hickies,' hinting at something I'd never heard of. You made me feel special, but at the same time ignorant and uneasy. You began your evil control over me then.'

She paused. Her throat was dry. For the first time since Carol sat down, she took her eyes off the priest and looked at her sister. Never before had she seen this courageous resolve.

Benita swallowed and continued. 'Remember how you manipulated and schemed to get yourself invited to our family picnics on Sunday afternoons? And to family card games? How you used your charisma and power as a priest to charm my mother?'

Her tone grew bolder as the session went on, her eyes on him more intense. 'I spent most of my life wishing I could die in order to escape the trap of despair I was in. I resent you for turning my life upside down for nearly half a century. I still feel baffled that you were capable of gaining control over me, a spirited, trusting child. You taught me to lie, something that was never part of me, something that left me confused, guilty and very ashamed. I was torn between my family and you.'

He groped toward his jacket pocket, fished out a candy wrapper and rolled it against his palm until he'd formed a cellophane cigarette. He pinched it between his fingers and lowered his eyes and absorbed himself in the design of the floor.

It was more than an hour later when she finished. 'I didn't realize that the power you had over me was evil, that it was destroying me. But my shame has turned to anger. I know now that I'm not a bad person.'

He kept his eyes down, shifted lower in his chair and put the cellophane cigarette to his nose, twisted it into one nostril and then into the other. A grimace of annoyance passed over the archbishop's face. He raised his right hand to his forehead and massaged his temple with his thumb. The vicar general stretched his neck and ran his index finger along the collar of his golf shirt.

Benita steadied her gaze on *him*. 'Can you look me in the eye?'

His eyes flickered but fell, as if the effort were too much.

She kept her eyes on him. 'Henry N. Dunkel, do you have anything to say?' Her voice did not waver.

His lips clenched. Without looking up, he shrugged and muttered 'So much for. . .' His last word died in a mumble.

'Pardon me, I didn't hear you,' said Benita.

'So much for. . .' Once again, he swallowed the word. The archbishop shifted nervously in his chair.

'Would you please speak up?'

Now he looked up, looked at her with his steel blue eyes, and said clearly, 'So much for consensuality.'

'Consensuality!' she cried. 'I was twelve years old!'

'I didn't do all that to you.'

'You did that and more.'

He lifted his hand, touched his forehead, his chest, his left shoulder, his right, silently blessing himself. 'In the name of the Father and of the Son and of the Holy Spirit. Amen.' He set aloof eyes on her and said, 'When my time comes, I want to go to heaven.'

Five months later, in November, Archbishop Hanus followed up on what he referred to as 'the Bloomington session,' by writing to inform Benita that 'Stewardship over the resources of the Archdiocese indicate to me that payment of therapy expenses should be brought to an end.' In fact, he had ended them retroactively at the end of September. Walt interceded with a calm, reasonable letter asking that reimbursement be continued through December to give Benita time to make other arrangements for payment. Benita's letter of protest to the archbishop sparked a reply.

I appreciate your sharing of your feelings in response to my earlier letter. . .I also have feelings, and these include the feeling that I have tried very hard to respond to your particular situation. Even though the agreement stated that there were to be no more demands, I agreed to several of your additional requests, including visits and the lengthy confrontation session with Father Dunkel present. I feel that I and Father Dunkel have done more than what is required by the agreement.

I have tried hard to respect your privacy, to believe you, and to respond generously. I feel that many (certainly not all) outside observers would agree that we have been generous. . .Again, I thank you for the help you have given me in better understanding the nature of sexual abuse.

In April, after a prod from Jeff Anderson, the archbishop recanted. 'I am willing to respond positively to your request.' He would extend therapy payments through April and requested a legal document signed to that effect.

Father's 'time' came two years later on October 28, 1998. Archbishop Hanus was the principal celebrant of the funeral Mass said on Halloween at Our Lady of Lourdes parish, Lourdes, Iowa. Whatever words Father Bodensteiner, the pastor, chose for his homily, the occasion begged to be seasoned with the gracious voice described by Bassanio in Shakespeare's *Merchant of Venice*.

The world is still deceived with ornament.
In law, what plea so tainted and corrupt
But, being seasoned with a gracious voice,
Obscures the show of evil? In religion,
What damned error but some sober brow
Will bless it, and approve it with a text,
Hiding the grossness with fair ornament?

'He deserves the same as you and I,' the archbishop replied to Karen, a niece of Father Dunkel's, who also had been sexually abused by him as a child. She had protested over what she considered an outrageous charade, his burial with all the honors of a faithful Roman Catholic priest: a platoon of priests commanding the front pews of the church; a bevy of aging Knights of Columbus flaunting the robes and swords of their hierarchical, secretive fraternity; an open casket displaying Father's body, clothed in the customary cassock, surplice and purple stole, the latter the badge of priesthood always put on with the vesting prayer, 'Restore to me, O Lord, the state of immortality which was lost to me by my first parents, and although unworthy to approach Thy sacred mysteries, grant me nevertheless eternal joy.'

An imposing 4x6 foot granite tombstone marks his grave in the parish cemetery at Lourdes, Iowa. *Father H.N. Dunkel Born 31 January 1921 Ordained 28 July 1945 Died 28 October 1998* Four words are engraved in small letters at the lower edge of the tombstone: 'Lourdes, I love you.'

CHAPTER SEVEN

*S*hame   *Schame   Shame on you—sure hope you got your nasty report across to all our good Catholic people in Dubuque. Seems awful funny that you would wait till the death of this so call clergy to bring this nasty scandal out. Mabe the reason is he isn't here to defend himself. Why did this go on so long. Weren't you old enough to help yourself? Mabe you brought a lot of it on yourself like I know of a lot of these so called sexual abuse cases.*

I think you are going to pay for this after you leave this earth and I am no member of any clergy or religious life, just a common lay person that has respect for my church and staff.

Sure hope you're enjoying the money you got out of the lawsuit, that should of been enough to keep your big nasty mouth shut.

This letter, disguised with misspellings and sent to Benita anonymously in 2002, no doubt represented accurately the feelings of many Dubuque residents. After Father's death, as part of her effort to heal, she began to speak out publicly, faithfully following the legal agreement she'd signed, always referring to the town, the parish, the priest with pseudonyms. In Dubuque, gossip made those pseudonyms transparent. Her talks and letters to the newspaper on issues of clergy sexual abuse often drew a venomous response.

Mrs. Kirschbaum—Your letter published in the Monday, Sept. 23rd Telegraph Herald is about the 3rd or 4th time you've hashed over the same thing. Everybody at St. Columbkille's knows that you chased that priest (Father Dunkel)—he didn't chase you. You were the laughing stock of the school and everyone who went to school at the time knew it—that you were the pursuer! Now shut up!

The irate author of this missive nobly signed her name, whereas another letter-writer identified herself as 'one of the thousands who are tired of hearing about your so called abuse from Father Dunkel.'

I remember you as the pursuer—in high school you were among the 'popular' with little notice of most of your class and running after Father Dunkel's attention all the time.

If things were so bad, where was your mother, your brothers and sisters? Most of us think you are much more to blame than Father Dunkel. You got your money and attention, now why not let it rest in peace.

You have two audiences—those who know the truth and your vindictiveness and those that love to hear more bashing of the clergy. Look into your own heart!

Many of us would like to respond in the Telegraph Herald but feel a public forum is no way to go as those of you who relish this crap will never give up and face the truth of your actions.

All we can do is offer our prayers for you and your kind and also for us who fail to understand your continued hatred.

A letter of understanding came from an unexpected source. The sister of red-haired James O'Neill, the boy who had aspired to be Benita's college boyfriend, wrote from her home in Winnipeg, Canada.

A friend sent me two letters that were in the Dubuque paper that really shook my complacency about St. Columbkille's. . .I would smugly think that I was raised in a cocoon of care. Well, I was, but that cocoon was in my home and mind and unfortunately, you, Jane and others were caught in a spider's web. . .now, I have so many emotions to share or shout out. What grief you have endured. . .please accept my apologies and prayers. To go public and allow strangers to know your personal feelings is an act that is very courageous.

EPILOGUE

It's mid-October, 2005, when Benita and I finally come together face-to-face; we're in Dubuque, the landscape of our childhood where this story began. Fifty years have passed since we genuflected before the archbishop and took from his hand our college diplomas, then rose and walked off the stage and into the world.

'I don't *do* Dubuque,' Benita had wisecracked to me over the telephone when I suggested that the Clarke reunion honoring the class of '55 would be an opportunity not only for us to meet again, but also for our classmates to hear her significant, and in view of current events, very relevant life story. Returning to Dubuque revived too many hurtful memories, too much regret and pain, she said. The thought of speaking out to her peers in that setting struck panic in her heart. There was some question, too, of the propriety of imposing this disconcerting subject on a Homecoming celebration. We were gathering for camaraderie, not religious rancor. Hearing another dreary tale of clerical sexual abuse might cast a pall on the group. Most of us were cradle Catholics, many of whom were not quite ready to believe that what we were seeing was real. High-ranking church men lying, covering up, proclaiming through their actions that power and control matter more than virtue. To confront this here, now, might disturb our spiritual comfort as well as our weekend. But hadn't the fifty year interval since college toughened us? Hadn't every single one of us grappled with sorrow and great loss: the death of a child, a spouse; divorce, disillusionment, disease; the harsh reality of our own decline? Hadn't we learned by now to take the bad news with the good? Finally, the hesitant, including Benita, were persuaded. A slot for her was set aside on the agenda.

As our classmates and their spouses assemble for lunch on the patio of the classy new hotel on the river's edge, the bees buzzing over our sandwiches function as a reminder that this is not heaven on earth. Otherwise, we bask in the lustrous perfection of a Midwestern autumn: a glorious sun, bright azure skies, dry, glittery days, the bold beauty of the Mississippi's autumn bluffs. We search one another's faces for hints of the girl we knew. A telling smile, a gesture, a tone of voice. Benita and I watch for and quickly find one another, although in another situation, I may have passed her by unrecognized. I had imagined her aging into a version of her mother, pale, wistful, enduring Marcella. But Benita looks hardy; there's something of the resolute Midwest in her friendly smile, short, golden brown curly hair, an aura of having settled down. But there's an uneasiness about her, too. Behind her blue eyes is a bereft child who has not forgotten.

Beside her is Curt, the quiet, unassuming brown-eyed man who was her catalyst to change and her anchor through the turbulence that followed. She informs me that without his encouragement, my nagging and her commitment, she would not be here.

Later, when it's time to speak to the group, she's visibly nervous. Her hands tremble as she walks to the podium; her face is taut. As she stands before her peers and opens her life to their judgment, I glimpse the tremendous risk she's taking. Here is the vulnerable young Benita, returning home from Mexico, alone and disgraced. Today she has returned to Dubuque with only her words, her trust in the group, that they will have ears to hear. Many are tired of the topic, fed up with the newspaper articles, skeptical of people who after ten, twenty, or thirty years, identify themselves as 'victims' and tell tales of abuse at the hands of a priest. Undoubtedly, there are cynics among us whose eyes will meet and sneer, 'C'mon, gimme a break. At twenty-five she was too helpless to get out of it? I bet she wouldn't be here if he'd married her. Or if he was still around to tell his side of the story.' Others are cautious, admittedly baffled by the dynamics of abuse, the idea that trauma binds a victim to her perpetrator, that damage is compounded when the abuser is a priest, that hopelessness paralyzes a victim into silence.

For Benita to subject herself to the possible misunderstanding of her college classmates, to risk their censure by enfleshing a problem in a church most of them still pledge allegiance to, is an astonishing act of courage. For her to do so with none of the trappings of power, no Roman collar, no staff or miter or amethyst ring, no silver cross to pin to her lapel, no title to buttress her credibility and status, is a remarkable act of faith.

Listening to her story, it occurs to me that it could be offered from the pulpit as a homily on redemption, not in the usual terms of one grand, noble act, but rather as an example of the day-to-day struggle of ordinary people to free themselves from whatever binds them. A priest, a man akin to God, had beamed his light upon her as a twelve-year-old girl and blinded her with its brilliance. He had crippled her ability to function apart from him and constricted her freedom to choose. Escaping his power required a long, agonizing effort by her and her family. When she finally succeeded, she spoke out, boldly describing where she had been. By interrupting the cycle of secrecy in her life, she has encouraged others to do so. Thus, she has become a channel of truth, which is to say of grace, that amazing freedom to pursue what one truly desires.

Some survivors of clergy sexual abuse can continue to believe

in and practice their religion, Benita tells the group; others can't. Being betrayed by a man they saw as an *alter Christus* acting in *nomine Patris* had been too devastating. She herself subscribes to the proposition that religion is for those afraid of going to hell, while spirituality—the awareness of something sacred woven throughout nature and the universe—is for those who have already been there. She will never be finished with her recovery, she says, because she will never be finished growing. She pauses, looks around, asks, 'Am I talking too much?' 'No!' calls out a woman nearby. 'You haven't talked enough.'

Benita's concluding words suggest resignation. 'Both my abuse and healing are part of who I am.' But her tone reveals a residue of anger, something she may never completely let go, something she may need to fend off a harsher reality: two decades of her life were spent enslaved to a Roman Catholic priest and nearly three more in inner chaos, besieged by shame and regret. For another twelve years, she honored the church's gag order. Not until the 2004 article in the *Telegraph Herald,* did she name the parish publicly and even then, she did not identify the priest, although confidentiality agreements were by then a dead issue. In 1984, knowledge of clerical sexual abuse and hierarchical cover-up escaped the secret system and battered the wall of silence until it crumbled in 2002.

For Benita, one tragic fact remains: she will never know what she might have become if Father Dunkel had not usurped her youth. What she has become is apparent to her listeners: a restive woman who has discovered that things are not what they seem, that trusted people aren't always trustworthy, that some roads come to a dead end, some wounds don't fully heal and some beliefs are wrong; a resilient woman who has learned that inside an ordinary rock can be hidden a beautiful agate and out of decades of shame and guilt can come the treasure of a life. Her classmates now applaud that life with a standing ovation.

Afterward, people approach her informally with concerns

pried from their souls by her candor. Others linger to talk with one another about their plight as Catholics. For many of us, Catholicism is a culture as well as a religion. The narrative we were raised on—love is stronger than hate, light overpowers dark, life comes from death—is a source of security and inspiration. We expect difficult times and count on faith to see us through. The trouble comes when that faith is premised on a deceitful hierarchy. We take up the topic of what went wrong.

Some point to mandatory celibacy as the root of the perfidy. "Celibacy might work,' says a sagacious husband, 'but it's never been tried.' As septuagenarians, we're wise to the motivation, if not the history, behind the mandated celibacy that evolved out of the Council of Nicea. By shifting from the horizontal power of the gospel to male dominance over property and women, by requiring celibacy of its bishops and priests, the church consolidated authority and property within the institution, prevented its dispersal to family and community, and warded off female bids to power.

Others are philosophical, saying that this is the human condition, the reality of sin in the world; that the corruption of ecclesiastical culture is part of a larger climate of corruption. Bishops are likened to corporate executives who do whatever they have to do to hold onto power and control. Even Plato is called to account because much of Catholic politics reflects his endorsement of the 'royal lie,' the idea that to keep order in the world, virtuous leaders must filter the messages given to the unwise masses.

The conservatives in the group trace the trouble to Vatican II. The theological dissent set off in the sixties sent the entire church off course. Priests and nuns defected; the laity got hold of an age-old church teaching, *sensus fidelium,* the sense of the faithful, which asserts that nothing can be considered a church teaching if it is not received by the Catholic people; suddenly, ordinary people wanted a say in teachings on celibacy, the denial of priesthood to women, birth control, divorce. Discussing this gives us hope. Perhaps it's us, the people in the pews, who will save the church from the hierarchy. 'If the church is worth saving,' mumbles a skeptic. Someone suggests another possibility. Maybe the survivors of clergy sexual abuse are redeemers in disguise. Their stories have penetrated the wall of secrecy surrounding the celibate/sexual system, exposed the flaws festering there and clarified the hierarchical addiction to power. One thing seems sure: if we want to salvage our belief system, we will have to disconnect it from the hierarchy.

'I don't give a damn if the Church is saved or not,' says Benita when I conjecture about all of this to her. She has given up on the Church because, like Magellan, she has seen the shadow on the moon and knows the world is not flat, but round; but she can't give up on church because she has faith in the shadow, the *real* church of hurting, scarred people. Which is why she is alert for opportunities to denounce abusive power. When a cartoon ridiculing the papal stand on gays was published recently in the Minneapolis Star Tribune, she wrote a letter-to-the-editor commending the cartoonist and decrying the past and present crimes of sexual abuse committed by the Church. A few days later, she came home to an angry message on her answering machine: 'If you are Mrs. Kirschbaum and if you are a Catholic, shame on you. If you are not a Catholic, leave my Church alone.'

'The beauty in this story is that our family was steadfast,' Benita's sister, Carol, told me a few weeks earlier. 'Because the church and society were not.' When she thinks of herself as a grade school girl rushing to school in the morning to tell Sister the exciting news that Father Dunkel was visiting their home, she is disgusted. 'They knew. The nuns *knew*. They could have disclosed it and they didn't.'

'I felt free to say what I thought to the archbishop,' said Benita's brother, Walter. 'And I tried to work with him. But I listened more than I should have. And I realize now that was foolish. The hierarchy cared more about protecting the church than helping Benita.' Walt worries about her ongoing struggle with depression that sometimes lasts for weeks. 'I can hear it in her voice when we talk on the phone.' The effects on her health continue. In 1995, she underwent angioplasty, a second in 2002, and still another in the spring of 2005. Walt has accepted the fact that her effort to reconcile her life may go on until her death. 'We've had lots of good times together through it all,' he said. 'And lots of good laughs. But *that's* always back there. The most painful part of this whole thing is what it's done to Benita. She was a very capable, athletic, beautiful girl. What he did to her was awful.'

Many of our classmates attend the Sunday morning Mass closing the reunion weekend. Benita and I sit and talk in the lazy sun, cherishing the remaining hour together in Dubuque. As we reminisce over thrilling grade school trips through the tunnel of strange underwear and high school efforts to smoke without reeking of it, when she thanks me again for rescuing her in college with my Spanish comp notes, I'm aware, like Walt, of *that* always back there. Suddenly, she interrupts herself in the middle of a sentence, sticks out a leg, says, 'Look! No nylons!' We laugh at the instant flashback: the single-file march of students from St. Columbkille's at day's end; Sister Gabriel stationed on the sidewalk eyeing female legs to determine if they're clad in the nylons mandated as part of our uniform.

I begin to hear something else 'back there.' Sister Ignatia's voice in Modern Poetry class as she introduced us to Hopkins and the period in his life when he encountered great desolation and in spite of it, asserted hope. *Not, I'll not, carrion comfort, Despair, not feast on thee.* We would have to do the same, said Sister Ignatia, if we wished to live honestly in the world.

Benita has made a long journey through unfathomable darkness and found her way. She has yearned for death and gone on living. In spite of the awful events that changed forever the course of her life, she will not feast on despair, not untwist the last strands of her humanity, or most weary, cry, *I can no more.* She can: *Can something; hope, wish day come; not choose not to be.*

Benita's bare legs are my mother's flung cards: a defiant act of hope.

ADDENDUM

On March 6, 2006, the Dubuque *Telegraph Herald* launched an eight-part series: *Sins & Silence: Sexual Abuse by the Clergy*. The first article opened with this: 'It wasn't supposed to happen here. It couldn't happen in the Archdiocese of Dubuque. But it did.' Fourteen accused diocesan priests were pictured in the paper. Among them were Father Patrick McElliott, the fiery retreat master who terrorized us with tales of damned teenage lovers; Father/Monsignor/Vicar General William Roach, the red-haired door-opener who ushered Benita into the chancery; and Father Henry Dunkel.

LaVergne, TN USA
22 July 2010
190473LV00002B/78/P